Sources of
Adult Education

JAMES E. WITTE
MARIA MARTINEZ WITTE
Editors

Auburn University

KENDALL/HUNT PUBLISHING COMPANY
4050 Westmark Drive   Dubuque, Iowa 52002

Copyright © 2009 by James E. Witte and Maria Martinez Witte

ISBN 978-0-7575-5929-7

Printed in the United States of America
10 9 8 7 6 5 4 3 2

Contents

Preface   viii

Acknowledgements   ix

The Editors   x

The Contributors   xi

Chapters

1. **Introduction to Sources of Adult Education**   1
   Mauna S. Duggan
   - Introduction   1
   - Background   1
   - Sources of Adult Education   2
   - Learning Method or Activity Type   5
   - Future Implications   8
   - Conclusion   8
   - References   9

2. **Community Education**   11
   Arlene H. Morris
   - Introduction   11
   - Historical Perspective   12
   - Definitions   13
   - Community-Focused Versus Community-Based Paradigm   15
   - Contemporary Approaches   16
   - Lessons to be Learned from Other Countries   16
   - Current and Future Trends in Community Education   18
   - Conclusion   18
   - References   19

3. **Colleges and Universities**   23
   Tami McCray Olds
   - Introduction   23
   - Definitions   23
   - Clientele   24
   - Historical Overview   25
   - Programs   27
   - Formats   29
   - Resources   30
   - Conclusion   32
   - References   34

4. **Community Colleges**   39
    Tuboise D. Floyd and Jane B. Teel
           Introduction   39
           Historical Overview of Community Colleges   40
           General Education   43
           Transfer Function   44
           Vocational/Technical/Workforce Training   45
           Remedial/Developmental Education   46
           Community Education   47
           Adult and Continuing Education   48
           Emerging Issues   48
           Conclusion   49
           References   50

5. **Correctional Education**   53
    Melissa Askew
           Introduction   53
           History   54
           Recidivism   57
           Learning Disabilities   58
           Technology   59
           Programs   60
           Women's Prison and County Jails   62
           Professional Development/Enhancement   63
           Conclusion   64
           References   64

6. **U.S. Public Libraries and Museums**   67
    Monita G. Hara and Gia Johnson
           Introduction   67
           Libraries: Memory Palaces for All   67
           Roots of Literacy Education in Library Adult Education   68
           U.S. Public Libraries   70
           Events Shaping Adult Education in Public Libraries   70
           National Partners for Libraries and Literacy   72
           Outreach Efforts to Serve Special Populations   74
           Libraries Move into 21st Century Cyberspace   75
           Museums   77
           U.S. Museums: Working in the Public Interest to Educate All 77
           Types of People Who Attend Museums   78
           Museum Programs   78
           Prominent Museums   80
           Museums and Formal Education Planning   85
           Conclusion   86
           References   86

7. **Religious Institutions**   89
    Robert J. Griffith
        Introduction   89
        History   89
        Framework   93
        Current Programs and Content   95
        Counseling   95
        Financial Planning   95
        English as a Second Language (ESL)   96
        Social Groups   96
        Formal Education   97
        Religious Training   97
        Men's and Women's Retreats   98
        Conclusion   98
        References   99

8. **Proprietary Schools**   101
    Nora Gerdes Stevens
        Introduction   101
        The History of Proprietary Schools   101
        Types of Proprietary Schools   103
        Proprietary Schools and Adult Education   104
        Are They Here to Stay?   107
        Conclusion   109
        References   109

9. **Business and Industry**   113
    Shannon Hogg and Debbie E. Stone
        Introduction   113
        Trends in Industry Related Education and Training   113
        Types of Training and Education within Business and Industry 114
        Internal Sources   114
        External Training Sources   120
        Professional Organizations and Standardization   121
        Private Training Companies and Consultants   122
        Partnerships with Educational Institutions   123
        Governmental Agencies   123
        Growing Emphasis on Self-Directed Learning   124
        Conclusion   125
        References   125

10. **Cooperative Extension**   129
    Holly Holman
         Introduction   129
         Demonstration Work   130
         The Boll Weevil   132
         Development of the U.S. Department of Agriculture (USDA)   134
         The Smith-Lever Act of 1914   135
         Cooperative Initiative   136
         Impact of World War I   137
         The 1920s and the Great Depression   138
         Impact of World War II   139
         The Cooperative Extension in the 21st Century   140
         County and Local Extension   141
         Conclusion   144
         References   145

11. **Distance Education**   149
    Cynthia D. Borel
         Introduction   149
         A Historical Perspective   152
         Types of Distance Learning   159
         Categories of Technological Options   159
         Key Players in Distance Learning   160
         The Distance Learning Interaction   162
         Barriers to the Adoption of Distance Education   162
         Organizational Barriers in Distance Education   164
         Faculty Barriers in Distance Learning   164
         Student Barriers in Distance Learning   165
         Elements of a High-Quality Online Course or Program   165
         Characteristics of the Adult Distance Learner   166
         Conclusion   167
         References   169

12. **Military and Armed Forces**   175
    Eli M. Perez Rivera
         Introduction   175
         Background   175
         Educational Programs   178
         Tuition Assistance Program   184
         Military Education Academies   184
         Earned College Credit   186
         Conclusion   187
         References   188

13. **Labor and Workforce Education: A Union Training Perspective**   193
Kristi D. Mathews
    Introduction   193
    The Call of Labor to Adult Education   194
    Labor Training through the Apprenticeship System   195
    Union Apprenticeship Selection   196
    Union Training   197
    National Joint Apprenticeship and Training Committee   198
    Union Wage Schedule   201
    Union Benefits   201
    Evaluations and Reviews   202
    Return on Investment   204
    Conclusion   206
    References   206

Preface

Sources of Adult Education evolved from a challenge to a small group of graduate students into a wonderful adventure in research and writing. It began during a conversation with a group of Adult Education graduate students about some classroom text materials that were dated and in need of revision. The immediate student response was a resounding "yes, updates were needed!" When they were asked if they would like to do a little writing, they soon followed-up with a chapter and author assignment list and a request for authorship guidelines from us.

That small beginning launched a learning activity for all of us. The purpose of this book is to support an investigation of the various sources of adult education and dispel the notion that adult learning only takes place in a classroom. The initial chapter overviews the field of adult education, various providers and sources of adult education, and different learning methods used in the adult education learning settings. The remaining chapters cover the topics of Community Education, Colleges and Universities, Community Colleges, Correctional Education, U.S. Public Libraries and Museums, Religious Institutions, Proprietary Schools, Business and Industry, Cooperative Extension, Distance Education, Military and Armed Forces, and Labor and Workforce Education. The content is organized using introductions, historical overviews, types of programs and formats, and conclusions.

This book can be used to develop a deeper understanding of adult education and a variety of teaching and learning environments that encompass the field of adult education. This information can also be used to supplement class content and course activities. We hope that it will be of value and to serve as a resource for those involved in the most engaging and rewarding work — working with adult learners.

JIM AND MARIA WITTE

Acknowledgements

We are indebted to each of the contributors. Not only does this work represent a long term collaborative effort but the final product represents information and knowledge suitable for passing along to others studying within the field of adult education. Our appreciation also goes to Walden Lechner who assisted with this project through his thorough editing and APA format checks.

We would like to recognize the influence of Drs. Waynne B. James and Michael W. Galbraith. We hope this work is a reflection of the academic rigor and love of learning that they have instilled in us. Above all else, a special thanks to the students who started with a blank sheet of paper and did not stop until this book was created. You have touched us all.

The Editors

James E. Witte is an Associate Professor of Adult Education at Auburn University in Auburn, Alabama. He received a Ph.D. Adult Education from the University of South Florida, Master's in Education – Education Administration from the College of William and Mary, and Bachelor's in General Studies – Business from the University of Nebraska. His academic areas of interest include training program development and evaluation, individual learning styles and how learning is assessed in both conventional and distance learning settings. He has published articles and chapters in publications such as *Adult Learning Methods: A Guide for Effective Instruction; Adult Learning Journal; Entrepreneurship Policy Journal; Innovative Higher Education; Journal of Adult Development; Psychological Reports; Encyclopedia of Educational Psychology; Contemporary Issues in Educational Research; Journal of Educational Research and Policy Studies;* and *Academic Exchange Quarterly.* He has received the Emily and Gerald Leischuck Outstanding Undergraduate Teaching Award (2001), Professor of the Year – College of Education Student Government Association (2001); and the Emily and Gerald Leischuck Outstanding Graduate Teaching Award (2006).

Maria Martinez Witte is an Associate Professor of Adult Education at Auburn University in Auburn, Alabama. She received her Ed.D. in Adult Education from the University of South Florida, MPA Public Administration from the University of Oklahoma, and Bachelor's in Business Management from the University of Maryland. Academic areas of interest include analyzing effective content, context, and processes that enhance the teaching-learning environment, learning styles, and the assessment of learning. She has published articles and chapters in publications such as the *Adult Learning Journal; Adult Learning Methods: A Guide for Effective Instruction; Mentoring and Tutoring – Special Issue: Mentoring and Technology; Innovative Higher Education Journal;* and *Creating Successful Telementoring Programs: A Volume in Perspectives in Mentoring.* She has received the Emily and Gerald Leischuck Outstanding Undergraduate Teaching Award (2003), Outstanding Professor Award from the Auburn Panhellenic Council (2003), Outstanding Graduate Program Officer (2003) award, and the Auburn University Graduate Mentoring Award (2008).

The Contributors

At the time of writing the following were

Graduate Students • Auburn University, Auburn, Alabama

Major Eli M. Perez Rivera

Holly Holman

The remaining were/are advanced graduate students and

those who have graduated are shown with title.

Advanced Graduate Students • Auburn University, Auburn, Alabama

Melissa Askew

Dr. Cynthia D. Borel

Mauna S. Duggan

Tuboise Floyd

Dr. Robert J. Griffith

Dr. Monita G. Hara

Dr. Kenneth Shannon Hogg

Dr. Gia D. Johnson

Dr. Arlene H. Morris

Dr. Tami McCray Olds

Dr. Nora Gerdes Stevens

Dr. Debbie E. Stone

Jane Teel

Advanced Graduate Student • University of Tennessee, Knoxville, Tennessee

Kristi D. Mathews

Chapter 1

Introduction to Sources of Adult Education

Mauna S. Duggan

Introduction

Education has become a continuous process for adults whether work related, goal oriented, or just for fun. "Not only is adult education a great enterprise, but it has also become an essential part of American society" (Hallenbeck, 1964, p. 16). Hallenbeck (1964) reported that an increasing number of the adult population is taking advantage of educational opportunities. Businesses and industry, higher educational institutions, cooperative extensions, proprietary schools, religious institutions, correctional facilities, and the military are providing adult learning opportunities. Since adult education is primarily voluntary and the will to acquire knowledge as well as the reason for learning come from the student, it is up to the provider to change and adapt to the myriad of adult learner interests.

Background

According to Stubblefield and Keane (1994), adult education played a vital role in America since the time of European colonization. Native American Indians taught the Europeans about maize or Indian corn, maple sugar, and other native fruits and vegetables and how to grow them. As the colonists progressed in their learning, newspapers, the almanac, pamphlets, manuals, textbooks of political theory and economic innovations, home medical guides, farming journals, cookbooks, and collections of poetry and prose provided the knowledge and opportunities for self-education. Vocational training began with apprenticeships, which focused on the transfer of skill and knowledge under the supervision of a master teacher. Private schools emerged with the purpose of vocational and secondary education (Knowles, 1960, p. 7).

Self-improvement became the focus for Benjamin Franklin as he founded the Junto in the year 1727. The Junto was an established club for mutual improvement and the purpose was to debate and discuss ideology surrounding politics, morality, philosophy and business affairs. This concept of self-education progressed into continuing education even though adult education was basically unorganized and unstructured during the Colonial period and did not become formalized until the twentieth century.

In 1911, Andrew Carnegie organized The Carnegie Foundation to advocate knowledge for all people. Anticipating the future leisure time of adults and the possible seeking of further education, The Carnegie Foundation helped to create The American Association for Adult Education (AAAE) in March of 1926 for the purpose of organizing the different enterprises of adult education (Beals, 1936). The education of adults has been going on for years, but the concept of adult education as a profession is fairly new starting with the development of the AAAE. Support, guidance, resources, and research are all areas that the AAAE participated in the providers of adult education and their clients. In 1951, The Adult Education Association of the United States of America (AEA/USA) was formed with the executive boards of the AAAE and the National Education Association (NEA) Department of Adult Education simultaneously dissolving and restructuring their organizations.

Between the years of 1981-1982, the AEA/USA merged with the National Association for Public Continuing and Adult Education (NAPCAE), and evolved into The American Association for Adult and Continuing Education (AAACE). The AAACE is a leading source of information and support in the discipline of adult education and learning (J. A. Henschke, personal communication, August 30, 2005). The AAACE is a national association concerned with the entire field of adult education including research and theory, publications, and education. Adult educational opportunities are available through the multitude of options offered nationwide by members of the AAACE. As the years progress, adult education providers are expanding to accommodate the advancement of adult learners and their needs.

Sources of Adult Education

Sources of Adult Education represent varied groups that are often independent of each other. They are difficult to group or categorize due to the diverse nature of the providers. The following categories provide a structure to examine the loosely associated field of adult education. The categories are (1) content purpose, (2) learner provider, (3) learning method or activity type, (4) learner motivation, and (5) institutional type.

Content Purpose

Bryson (1936) described the content purpose providers in four major categories: Lyceums, Chautauquas, women's clubs, and correspondence schools. Lyceums were associations providing a series of community-based public lectures offered in a variety of places beginning in the early 1800's. Josiah Holbrook in Millbury, Massachusetts, initiated the first town lyceum in 1826. Holbrook appropriated the term lyceum in the October 1826 issue of *American Journal of Education* (Stubblefield & Keane, 1994). Lyceums provided both social and educational benefits. The members themselves decided what content they were interested in learning and provided the speakers either from amongst themselves or from an outside source. Lyceums were available in many different settings such as ladies' lyceums, Negro lyceums, seaman's lyceums, teachers' lyceums, college lyceums, army lyceums, and naval lyceums (Stubblefield & Keane, 1994). According to Bryson (1936), lyceums developed into lecture bureaus and continued to flourish until the early 1900s. Lecturing bridged the gap between the social classes and informed all citizens on public issues. Many people supported the concept that lecturing for the benefit of both adults and children supported the public school system.

In the 1870's, the Chautauqua Institution was formed at Fair Point on Lake Chautauqua, western New York. It was originally created by Bishop J. H. Vincent and Lewis Miller as a two-week summer institute for Sunday school teachers and developed into a four-year program of home reading called the Chautauqua Literary and Scientific Circle (CLSC). This book club and study circle's focus was on history and literature. The readings were organized by year to include an English year, an American year, a European year, and a classical year. Diplomas were offered at the completion of the four years. Simultaneously with the four-year home reading CLSC development, the Chautauqua Institution formulated courses into its summer school program and became known as an adult education provider of music, art, theater, religion, and secular thought. Chautauqua was also known to be a vacation spot for the middle class where adults could take informal classes as well as formal ones. Many adults came for the discussions, classes, and conferences on the political, contemporary, theological, social, and international issues of that time (Knowles, 1977).

According to Bryson (1936) women's clubs began after the Civil War when women wanted to engage in self-improvement societies. This movement began in New York in 1868 by Jane Cunningham Croly for the purpose of self-learning and making women useful in society (Knowles, 1977). Forms of these clubs included the League of Women Voters, the Service Leagues, the American Association of University Women, Business and Professional Women's Clubs, and a variety of other clubs stemming from the need to band together. The founding of the Association for the Advancement of Women in 1873 and the General Federation of Women's Clubs in 1890 allowed cohesion among the clubs across the country. These clubs have changed over the years, have flourished, and continue to evolve into more service-oriented organizations.

An organization called The Society to Encourage Studies at Home instituted correspondence education beginning in 1873. It struggled to address the needs of its students and eventually was suspended. In 1878, John Vincent of the Chautauqua movement established a home reading circle to act on his belief that education should be available to everyone (Garrison, 1989). A correspondence course at Chautauqua was begun in 1879 by William Rainey Harper and became so popular that in 1883 a variety of courses were offered for a fee of ten dollars (Knowles, 1977). This home-study program was the catalyst for correspondence schools sprouting up all over the country.

William Rainey Harper ran the College of Liberal Arts, a correspondence school within Chautauqua University, and because of his efforts Harper has been referred to as the father of correspondence education (Garrison, 1989).

Also in 1883, for a short period of time a Correspondence University in Ithaca, New York, comprised of instructors from various colleges and universities sought to address the needs of students who could not physically attend classes in a traditional classroom setting. Correspondence classes were learner oriented and independently operated by universities and commercial institutions. The first commercial institution to offer correspondence study was a course in coal mining by Thomas J. Foster, editor of the *Mining Herald* of Shenandoah, Pennsylvania. This course became so popular that other courses were added and by 1891, this program developed into the International Correspondence Schools of Scranton, Pennsylvania.

With the success of this venture, other private individuals, partnerships, and stock companies followed suit and offered additional correspondence schools (Knowles, 1977). This was the beginning of and the catalyst for distance education, as we know it today. The development of lyceums, women's clubs, correspondence schools, and Chautauquas and the fact that these categories still exist today demonstrates their historical importance and contribution to adult education.

Learner Provider

Self-help. As the learners attempt to better themselves through the pursuit of knowledge, acquiring skills, learning information, and becoming involved in recreational learning outside of the work environment, they are engaging in a myriad of self-help learning activities (Rachal, 1988). The self-help learner seeks knowledge for situational, ephemeral, or personal enrichment purposes. This type of learner knows they can acquire knowledge or refine a skill on their own. They are usually self-motivated and are able to locate the resources needed to acquire the desired information.

Group. According to Knowles (1951), America is a nation of joiners. Almost every person is a member of at least one group. Differences among groups can range from informal arrangements to highly organized associations. Groups are formed to meet a variety of needs such as anonymity, resources, motivation and enthusiasm from others, companionship, and even prestige and their assembly is based on fellowship, instruction, and discussion. Some groups own their own rooms or buildings, but most groups meet in a location that is either rented or borrowed for the length of time of each meeting. Groups can be short-lived or can operate for long periods of time. Some die out, and some dissolve for a period of time and then revive. Some learners prefer group learning. They feed off the energy and knowledge of others and this sustains them in continual learning.

4

One-on-one. Some learners prefer a one-on-one scenario. The provider is typically more skilled or knowledgeable than the learner and therefore serves as a tutor. Examples of this include golf professionals offering private lessons, driving instructors seated next to their students, personal trainers in any sport or physical activity, and providers who teach music lessons. Tough (1979) asserts that within some forms of apprenticeships or internships, the learner will be assigned to one person who may be operating a business, classroom, shop, profession, or other entity and eventually be expected to put into practice the knowledge they acquire from that provider. One-on-one teaching is concerned with the focused learning of a skill or activity and allows the learner to acquire intensely concentrated knowledge within a short or extended period of time.

Instructional Tools. There are a variety of instructional teaching tools and materials to support learners and these include books, audio-books, computers, web-based instruction, podcasts, CDs, and DVDs. As technology progresses, a variety of other mediums will become available to support instruction in the teaching and learning environment (Jones & Harmon, 2002). The advantages of these teaching tools are that they are mobile, accessible, and available 24 hours a day. The Internet, for example, allows the learner to access a vast amount of knowledge from any location at any time. The use of web browsers, audio and video mediated communication (telecommuting, videoconferencing, chat, email exchanges, discussion boards), course management software such as WebCT, can further enhance, guide, and facilitate a learner's educational capabilities and growth (Witte & Wolf, 2003).

Learning Method or Activity Type

Formal. The teaching of adults and the research on adult learning has relied heavily on the minority of adults who attend formal classes. Learning in the formal mode is purposeful and deliberate with the guidance of someone who is responsible for planning and managing instruction using objectives and evaluations. Formal settings provide the learner with a sense of security and structure in their learning. Formal settings are not exclusive to educational institutions. Businesses, churches, factories, private homes, and public institutions are all examples of settings for formal learning (Brookfield, 1984). Distance education is fast becoming an alternative type of formal education (Bhola, 1989). WebCT and other computer-based forums are offering the learner the flexibility of time and the structure of a lesson in any physical environment. The formal method of learning is most familiar in the field of adult education.

Informal. Informal learning takes place for the purpose of learning something simply because the learners want to know more about it. Informal settings require leadership and a continuity of membership who have the same interest. These courses can be found within many groups such as young men's and women's Christian organizations, county and state extension offices, libraries, youth organizations, agricultural groups, business associations, and even high schools and universities (Knowles, 1951). Informal course offerings are flexible and geared toward the learner's needs. Ordinarily these courses may be between six and thirty hours of instruction or learning time. The purpose is not to produce a finished product but to give adults the beginning knowledge needed to guide them in self-learning should they want to pursue the subject area in more depth. Examples of informal course offerings could be: creative writing, photography, music, foreign languages, typing, woodworking, drawing, Bible study, dance, ceramics, electronics, and gardening. It is a functional type of learning and is concerned with issues and real-life activities of people in which learning from their experiences is the main objective.

Non-formal. Non-formal learning is organized learning taking place outside the formal system. It empowers and forces participation for the betterment of the societal whole. Non-formal education emerges from social, political, and cultural issues and changes according to the needs of the time. Agencies that provide non-formal learning include literacy programs, civic and political groups, and religious groups (Ewert, 1989). Learning is systematic, but sporadic (Foley, 2004). The design of the learning is focused on needs, and the implementation of the knowledge is up to the providers and learners.

Learner Motivation

According to Knowles (1951), learning must be purposeful. There is usually an objective in mind and the motivation to acquire knowledge and skills. Three phases in the learning process are: the effort to learn is goal oriented; the desire to learn fuels a lifelong interest in learning; and, the experience of satisfaction and enjoyment with learning. Cyril Houle (1961) offered a framework to understand why adults learn that revealed the adult learner can be goal oriented, learning oriented, or activity oriented. This framework is known as Houle's Typology. According to Rachal (1988), Houle's typology is concerned with the manner of learning and the motivation behind it. Its appeal relies on the simplicity of the typology and provides a basis for the design of curricula.

Goal oriented. Cyril Houle (1961) explained that the goal-oriented learner uses education to achieve specific objectives. There is a goal to be attained at the end of the learning. The goal-oriented learner makes the effort to acquire knowledge to put it to use for some specific purpose. Adults do not, however, solely rely on educational institutions to provide their instruction, but also on private readings and educative visits. They will attend any structured opportunity as long as they can foresee the end result and acquire something for their labor. Several factors influence the decision to keep on learning for the goal-oriented learner. Perhaps an employer requires a new skill to be learned or requests revisiting a skill that was already acquired. Maybe the new knowledge will assure a promotion or allow the person to change their profession.

Whatever the main reason is for reaching the goal, there seems to be other underlying factors that contribute to the decision of learning.

Lifelong learners. Knowles (1951) indicated that everyone has needs that force him or her to do certain things as he or she matures and develops. One of these needs is growth. As people grow and mature the desire for intellectual growth continues. Older adults have the same capacity for learning as they did when they were younger. The rate of learning may decline, but not the capacity. It is the connections they make to the learning already acquired that propel them into learning something new.

Enjoyment. Some people have a social need to be with others who have the same interests. They enjoy being with others for several reasons. Maybe they are escaping a sad or lonely home life, a relationship gone sour, or a family that is not supportive, which propels them into a situation where they are allowed some respite. Some people are involved in the educational process to look for a mate. According to Houle (1961), this could lead to a lengthy educational process just to find that perfect person. Learning can be fun and the knowledge applied to everyday life.

Institutional Type

Wayne L. Schroeder's defines adult educational agencies as entities whose purpose is to develop programs for autonomously controlled adult learning (McCullough, 1980, p. 161). Schroeder (1970) described four types of agencies that provide typically autonomous adult education.

Type I agencies are primarily involved with adult education as their central function. This category includes alternative adult high schools, agricultural extensions, proprietary schools, business schools, residential centers, and nonresidential centers. These adult education agencies exist to serve a specific group of adults rather than the comprehensive whole.

Type II agencies are primarily concerned with youth education, but have adult education as a secondary purpose. Colleges, junior colleges, and public schools are included in this category. Evening or day adult classes, extension divisions, and the Cooperative Extension Service are all included in this type of agency.

Type III agencies attend to the educational and non-educational needs of the community. This includes the health and welfare agencies as well as libraries and museums. The education of adults is only one of their main purposes.

Type IV agencies use adult education as a method to promote self-learning for the betterment of others and the agencies themselves. These agencies are oriented more for the benefit of the organizations or institutions that offer educational services.

Agencies such as business and industry, correctional institutions, armed forces, government agencies, unions, hospitals, trade associations, television, and newspapers use adult education to further their of goals.

Examining Schroeder's institutional types, Rachal (1988) identified reciprocal teaching and learning relationships between providers and learners. This is a more collaborative viewpoint with teaching and learning co-occurring within each program.

Future Implications

Adult education and learning will continue to flourish. Individuals will continue to seek education not only for self improvement but for the benefit of a more global society. People want to learn to work together for the common good of the individual, community, and society as a whole. Knox (2005) predicts that shared values and collaboration will result in global thinking and sharing of knowledge to build a stronger connection among adult educators worldwide. Providers will need to respond and adapt to cultural changes as well as styles of teaching and learning to merge the old ways with the new. Adult educational providers' new outlook toward dealing with collaboration in public issues, community and societal involvement, leadership building, and the encouragement of a team effort are leading to respect for diversity, sharing values, and a joint effort in meeting the needs of all learners. In the future, providers will have to change and adapt to the needs of learners in a global fashion. Providers will be responsible not only for transmitting knowledge but for facilitating inquiry by the learner and for acting as a resource for information.

Conclusion

Organizing the providers continues to be a complicated and multifaceted process. Groups are formed around formal institutions, practices, and distinctive approaches to providing adult education, gaining unity and alliances based on mutual themes, the focus of which sustains the adult learner (Houle, 1961). The challenges would be lessened if the many educational agencies, be they educational institutions, proprietary schools, businesses and industry, cooperative extensions, religious institutions, correctional facilities, or the military were to have a way to communicate and function as a whole instead of as separate entities even within their individual groups. This would allow opportunity for growth, change, and the sharing of knowledge to expand the possibilities of what is available for the adult learner.

The goal of adult education is to facilitate the achievement of the knowledge the learners wish to attain.. The teacher doesn't necessarily create within the student the desire to study or learn something new, but the way the material is presented, the teacher's enthusiasm, the relevancy of the material, how the connections are made to the knowledge the learner already possesses, causes the learner to achieve satisfaction and/or to obtain ownership of the material being taught, building the foundation for them to become lifelong learners. Adult education can be used as a tool to unleash the power of human potential. Lifelong learning is the key to a better quality of life within each family, occupation, and community, developing and producing a more humane global civilization. As the quantity of material to be learned and the number of education-seeking adults increase, the challenge is to provide the possibilities and opportunities in adult education for the benefit of all learners.

References

Beals, R. A. (1936). American association for adult education. In D. Rowden (Ed.), *Handbook of adult education in the United States* (pp. 12-13). New York: George Grady Press.

Bhola, H. S. (1989). *World trends and issues in adult education*. London: Jessica Kingsley.

Brookfield, S. (1984). *Adult learners, adult education and the community*. New York: Teachers College Press.

Bryson, L. (1936). *Adult education*. New York: American Book.

Ewert, D. M. (1989). Adult education and international development. In S. B. Merriam & P. M. Cunningham (Eds.), *Handbook of adult and continuing education* (pp. 84-96). San Francisco: Jossey-Bass.

Foley, G. (2004). The state of adult education and learning. In G. Foley (Ed.), *Dimensions of adult learning* (pp. 3-18). England: Open University Press.

Garrison, D. R. (1989). Distance education. In S. B. Merriam & P. M. Cunningham (Eds.), *Handbook of adult and continuing education* (pp. 221-232). San Francisco: Jossey-Bass.

Hallenbeck, W. C. (1964). The role of adult education in society. In G. Jensen, A.

Liveright, & W. Hallenbeck (Eds.), *Adult education: Outlines of an emerging field of university study* (pp. 5-25). Adult Education Association of the U. S. A.

Houle, C. O. (1961). *The inquiring mind*. Madison: University of Wisconsin Press.

Houle, C. O. (1980). *Continuing learning in the professions*. San Francisco: Jossey-Bass.

Jones, M., & Harmon, S. (2002). What professors need to know about technology to assess on-line student learning. *New Directions for Teaching and Learning, 91*, 19-30.

Knowles, M. S. (1951). *Informal adult education*. New York: Association Press.

Knowles, M. S. (1960). *Handbook of adult education in the United States*. Chicago: Adult Education Association.

Knowles, M. S. (1977). *A history of the adult education movement in the United States (Rev. ed.)*. New York: Robert E. Krieger.

Knox, A. B. (2002). *New realities that frame our futures efforts today. Adult Learning, 12*(4), 27-29.

McCullough, K.O. (1980). Analyzing the evolving structure of adult education. In W. S. Griffith & H. Y. McClusky (Eds.), *Building an effective adult education enterprise* (p. 161). San Francisco: Jossey-Bass.

Rachal, J. R. (1988). Taxonomies and typologies of adult education. *Lifelong Learning, 12*(2), 20-23.

Schroeder, W. L. (1970). Adult education defined and described. In R. Smith, G. Aker, & J. R. Kidd (Eds.), *Handbook of adult education* (pp. 37-38). New York: Macmillan.

Stubblefield, H.W., & Keane, P. (1994). *Adult education in the American experience*. San Francisco: Jossey-Bass.

Tough, A. (1979). *The adult's learning projects*. Toronto, Canada: The Ontario Institute for Studies in Education.

Witte, M., & Wolf, S. (2003). Infusing mentoring and technology within graduate courses: Reflections in practice. *Mentoring and Tutoring, 11*(1), 95-104.

Chapter 2

Community Education

Arlene H. Morris

Introduction

Community is a concept with a variety of meanings. Community may refer to a geographic location, and may be influenced by local, national, and international factors to actually create a mega-community (Galbraith, 1992). However, with the increase of technology, a community may easily exceed a geographic location. Community may be considered in light of how people relate to each other on the basis of shared interests, shared concerns or values, shared roles, or shared demographics such as age or social class. As people form groups of similar identified interests and needs, communities may form in which those involved can grow and develop from shared experiences. Therefore, an expanded definition of community may be "a collection of people who interact with one another and whose common interests or characteristics form the basis for a sense of unity or belonging" (Allender & Spradley, 2001, p. 4).

Education may occur throughout the lifespan. Childhood education is followed by the longer time period of adult or lifelong learning. A continuum of lifelong learning may occur in formal (school or university), nonformal (organizations such as libraries or museums), or informal (workplace, family or friends) settings (Galbraith, 1992). Within each of these settings, the focus may be on either individuals or groups. With each learning experience occur, the individual or group changes or develops a "perspective transformation" (Mezirow, 2000), which then impacts future learning.

The concept of lifelong education is the basis for community education. Galbraith (1992) discusses two dimensions of lifelong education: the vertical and the horizontal dimensions. The vertical dimension refers to the fact that learning is a continuous process throughout life, and that prior learning influences future learning at all age levels. The horizontal dimension refers to the link between education and life events and to the network of all components that influence life. He further proposes that there are psychosocial considerations for lifelong education, which require that it "be flexible enough to accommodate individual options and social differences" (p. 7).

"Community education" is often used as a basis for describing groups for conducting research or planning for traditional kindergarten through twelfth grade public education based on considerations of geographic or demographic factors (Willie, 2000). However, for the purposes of this chapter, the term will be used to refer to educational endeavors to meet the needs of adult learners within various types of groups that may be considered to be communities. This chapter will consider historical perspectives, various types of contemporary community education endeavors in America, and experiences in other countries.

Historical Perspective

The term "community education" is an evolving philosophy (Ward, 2001). In the past, community education was strongly linked with the public schools by using the local school to bring community resources to address community problems (DeLargy, 2002). During the colonial era, the Massachusetts Act of 1642 recommended that school curricula be planned to meet the needs of the community (Solberg, 1970). During the early 1800's, public schools were used for adult education in Providence, Rhode Island and Chicago, Illinois (DeLargy, 2002). In 1845, Henry Barnard's *Report of the Conditions and Improvements of Public Schools in Rhode Island* described a community education philosophy which incorporated the idea that local public schools had a role to play in improving the lives of individuals in the community (DeLargy, 2002), including focusing on the needs of this mainly agrarian society. Barnard's report introduced the concept of social change to the community education curriculum.

In the early 1900s, America experienced a population shift from rural to urban areas in response to industrialism, and public schools were utilized as centers for community education in order to most effectively use public resources. The writings of John Dewey and Joseph K. Hart enhanced the thinking that communities should be more accountable for providing leadership for social change (DeLargy, 2002; Williams, 1998). The public school was viewed somewhat as *pseudo parentis* in that governmental sponsored public schools would now provide for needs of the adult citizens, beyond the function of teaching children. This philosophy of community education applied an agenda to meet community needs that had been identified, at least in part, by those external to the actual community.

During the early twentieth century, the American population also became more mobile. The shift of large numbers of individuals from rural to urban areas, large numbers of immigrants from other countries, and automated transportation necessitated a change in emphasis from the concept of community as a *place* to the concept of community as prescriptive for the specific needs of groups organized around occupations, class, or political views (Williams, 1998).

By the mid-twentieth century, private foundations were involved in funding community education programs. The Mott Foundation Model began by supporting the Flint, Michigan Community Schools Program and spread throughout the United States in the latter half of the twentieth century (Charles Stewart Mott Foundation, 1998). This led to the establishment of community education centers in universities and by state departments of education. The Mott Foundation Outreach emphasized training individuals to work as professional community educators, and recommended placing at least one professional community educator into each public school system (DeLargy, 2002).

Four goals for community education identified by a Delphi study in 1981 were to encourage community development; address environmental, ecological, and energy issues; provide training in community education; and to develop community-based K-12 programs (DeLargy, DeLargy, & Dickey, 1981). Although these goals were intended to continue the community education programs within the local public school setting, a change can be seen in that a new trend or paradigm emerged—specifically, the process of identifying needs of the individual community and identifying the best education methods to meet those needs. This new paradigm eventually evolved into mobilizing the community to seek ways of solving its own problems rather than relying as heavily on external sources for education or funding.

Definitions

Recently, students in an adult education classroom setting were asked to provide personal definitions of the term community education. Some of the responses follow:

- Community education is client-centered, community based programs that meet the unique educational needs of its citizenry, with input and feedback from the people the program serves.
- Community education has moved away from public schools, now being offered by community centers and organizations…It is also something the individual has to want to learn, not be imposed by the state.
- Community education is any program that is taught, funded, organized, or overseen by community leaders or by members of the community. Community is defined by a group of people, not by a regional area.
- Community education should be such that the community states its needs and, together with the public organization, develops a process by which those needs can be met. It should be met in a way conducive to the way those in the community prefer to learn, not forced by an organization, but rather continually evaluated for needs assessment.
- Community education involves using various programs to educate/ 'enhance' the community itself and its people individually.
- Community education addresses the needs of the community to facilitate improvement.

As can be seen in the above quotations, current perceptions of community education are that it is not only for social or recreational programs or only for disadvantaged persons, but rather is focused on meeting identified need(s) of various groups. Community education is a philosophy involved in all educational planning within various communities of interest. This philosophy includes using a systematic method to identify the learning needs of various groups of people and involves those learners in planning for the educational programs.

Galbraith (1992, 1995) discussed five various concepts of community: 1)geographic or locational; 2) communities of interest that may include persons with a common interest such as leisure activities, politics, or religious/spiritual beliefs; 3) communities of function that may include profession/vocation or the function of other life roles; 4) demographic communities that are formed by shared demographic characteristics such as an elderly community or a Chinese-American community; and 5) psychographic communities that are formed by common value system, social class, or lifestyle (such as the rural farming community). He suggests that each of these may overlap or intersect and, thus, form interrelationships that can potentially lead to the growth of the individual or group.

Consideration of the definition of the community impacts the type of education that is most appropriate. Geographic communities can be further identified by demographic variables such as age, race, and gender, locations of population density, or seasonal population variations. These variables may assist in identification of learning needs of the individuals within that geographic community. Available resources such as schools, hospitals, churches, stores, or government agencies within the defined geographic community can be recognized. Discovery of existing institutions within a geographic community may then assist in planning for the most appropriate venue for providing the educational resources needed by the community. Additionally, the community's social system of formal or informal power structure, communication links, and media should be considered to determine their possible impact on any educational endeavor (Allender & Spradley, 2001).

Examples of common-interest communities are members of professional organizations, churches, or individuals linked by a common social issue (for example, environmental protection, services for disabled citizens, political action, or community support after a crisis). The emphasis on a specific issue becomes a motivator for action and, thus, an impetus for community education that will be needed to take action on the issue (Allender & Spradley, 2001).

Galbraith (1992) discussed three types of programs for community education, based on Brookfield's (1983) typology of providers of adult education. Adult education *for* the community includes formal courses for lifelong learning, provided by community schools, the U.S. Cooperative Extension Service (CES), municipal recreation departments, senior citizen centers or older adult activity centers, state or regional colleges or universities, or private or nonprofit educational corporations. Adult education *in* the community includes self-initiated or self-guided efforts by community individuals or groups. The community members determine the planning of the educational content in response to the course of community life. Providers of adult education in the community could be through the influence of community action groups or agencies or through provision of resources for self-directed learning (such as in libraries, CES centers, retailers, or public or private institutions). Adult education of the community occurs when a provider views a community as lacking in some quality needed for improvement or problem resolution in order to be considered a healthy functioning community. Providers of this type of program include the CES, local governments, state agencies and nonprofit organizations.

Community-Focused Versus Community-Based Paradigm

A community education paradigm in which the educational needs of the community are identified by those external to the community could be described as a community-focused approach. Experts in an area of knowledge identify needs of a particular community for education. For example, national health care planners assessing disease statistics may determine that an educational offering should be made available to a particular demographic community group that has a higher than expected prevalence, or government agricultural experts may determine that a higher crop yield would be produced from education regarding an improved irrigation system in a certain area. Community-focused education is therefore similar to the previously mentioned program typologies of adult education for the community and adult education of the community.

However, the paradigm described in the more recent history of community education could be considered to be community-based (Galbraith, 1995). Individuals which make up the community identify needs and participate in the planning and implementing of education that they determine will best meet the needs. The purpose is to meet the needs of the community group as well as needs of the individuals which comprise that group. Examples of this type of community education would be a group of older adults seeking information regarding healthy lifestyle recommendations or a group of people in an area with impure water seeking information regarding the most cost-effective method of water purification for their particular situation. Community-based education reflects the previously mentioned program typologies of adult education in the community.

A community-focused or a community-based approach may be determined by the source of planning for the education as well as the source of funding for the education. Members of a community-based education group who are planning and selecting the education may be providing self-funding or are involved in seeking grant funding. However, a community-focused education endeavor may involve a larger group seeking education to support needed improvements in a sub-group or to share information with a different community group. Additionally, community-focused education may be planned for several sub-groups, with funding received from either the communities themselves or from a larger group such as governmental or non-profit organizations.

A geographic definition of community may lend itself to either community-focused or community-based education, depending on the how the educational need has been identified and how the educational process and program is funded. Conversely, communities who do not share geographic boundaries may be identified by shared interests, goals, or common problems to be solved. Groups with specific interests may be considered community-based because the individuals within the community participate in determining the content and providers for the education needed to meet the self-identified needs of that particular community group. However, schools, health agencies, policymakers, law enforcement, and other groups may collaborate to assess and plan education for issues such as drug-abuse, HIV infection, or disaster response. This collaboration may be either community-focused or community-based, determined by the locus of the planning and the funding source.

Contemporary Approaches

In the United States, innovative methods of promoting community-based education has been emphasized in rural areas, through efforts to potentially impact community development utilizing partnerships of local government, schools, churches, for-profit and non-profit organizations (Doeden, 2001). Additionally, computer mediated communication provides opportunities for urban-rural relationships and for interagency cooperation. Community asset mapping has been used to document resources and empower people to build relationships and vision for community development and education (Kerka, 2003).

Education of an entire state regarding issues that impact the entire population of a set geographic region may be enhanced through cooperation of multiple agencies (Geiger & Smith-Yoder, 2003). Partnerships in planning and in seeking funding and the impact of voluntary organizations will continue to impact community education. Grant-funded community education endeavors frequently seek coalitions that can combine approaches for teaching and reaching population groups (Rollins, 2000). Also, efforts to enhance and reflect the diversity of community participants are encouraged (Bryant, 2002).

Lessons to be Learned From Other Countries

Canada

Cooperation of agencies has proven beneficial in Canada, where Local Further Education councils unite agencies that are involved in noncredit adult education (Galbraith, 1992). Institutions can thereby minimize redundancy, and build on the strengths of each other. However, Galbraith suggests that professional leaders may need to be involved in the program planning (1992).

England

Innovative approaches have been used to provide education for communities that are difficult to reach. Collaboration between municipal organizations and government or non-profit agencies was shown to be effective in reaching a homeless community in central London (Cameron, McKaig & Taylor, 2003). Cummings and Dyson (2007) identified three school models relating to area regeneration which were community resourcing, individual transformation, and contextual transformation. Additional emphasis was needed between schools and communities to improve coordination with national and local policy aspects.

Ireland

In response to erratic community education that included duplication, competition, and lack of connection between formal and informal adult education, the Irish National Association of Adult Education (AONTAS) created a National Adult Learning Council in 2002. This council then established local adult learning boards (LALBs) comprised of representatives from community, education, employers, libraries, health boards, etc., to plan and deliver adult education at the local level. Functions of these local boards include:

- clearly defining outcomes and methods of evaluation.
- collaborating between organized and voluntary providers to meet locally identified needs.
- coordinating services and resources
- ensuring independence and autonomy of the local communities. (Irish National Association of Adult Education, 2002)

An annual area plan from the LALB to the Department of Education and Science would obtain funding, and the LALB would participate in establishing priorities for spending. However, application of the plan led to difficulties in selecting learner representatives for the LALB, maintaining staff and resources, and establishment of working plans and clear lines for reporting (Irish National Association of Adult Education, 2002)

Scotland

Performance indicators (PIs) have been utilized in an effort to have a standardized approach to the quality and effectiveness of community education services in Scotland. Following identification of themes and issues that were needed for national adult education in community groups (rather than by age groups), evaluation statements were developed for use with all community education service activities. The PIs were effective in auditing and financial control purposes, and in establishing educational policy (Karatzias, Power, & Swanson, 2001).

Current and Future Trends in Community Education

Kerka (2003) recommends using a community assessment tool that focuses on a community's assets and resources rather than its deficits. She says the focus is changing from community development to community building, by engaging people as citizens rather than clients. This model provides for more local control as compared to the institutional model in which the funding source often sets the education agenda.

Roberson (2003) emphasizes that new ideas about aging and the older worker will be necessary as the older adult population increases with aging of the baby boomers. By 2030 it is estimated that those age 65 and older will comprise 20 percent of the U. S. population (Roberson, 2003), requiring a revision in community education offerings. Perspectives of older adults must be incorporated into workforce development and community education. Evidence-based suggestions for extending the healthy years of one's life, incorporation of the desire to stay active (perhaps continuing in the workforce) and planning for end-of-life needs are issues to be addressed in planning community education for this growing population.

Communities may include those with specific health care needs. For example, the Robert Wood Johnson Foundation granted funding for the creation of models using coalitions of health care agencies, schools, environmental groups, and public health agencies to accomplish the goal of educating groups of individuals about asthma (Rollins, 2000).

Target audiences may be considered as a statewide community, as in Alabama's 2001 educational initiative for education regarding tobacco use (Geiger & Smith-Yoder, 2003). Collaboration of representatives from state agencies, health care services, education, and community organizations revealed that negotiation of different groups was necessary in addition to specifying the target audience and the logistics of date, location, and promotion in planning.

Conclusion

Our world is rapidly changing, as is evidenced by the demographics of those who populate it. The increasingly mobile society is changing the view of community from a single geographic locale to multiple locations throughout a lifetime. The influence of technology has further broadened the concept of community from geographical areas to the possibility of including persons from all over the world into an internet community. Additionally, as the population becomes older, community education will focus on the needs of this changing demographic population. The past focus of community education as centered in one location to meet the needs of those within that community must be broadened to include communities of common needs or interests. A conceptualization of community education as community-focused or community-based can assist in planning and obtaining funding for community education endeavors. Partnerships and coalitions can also be encouraged to promote effective use of resources and funding sources. Evaluation of the quality of education programs and outcomes can enable replication of educational methods which have been shown to be most successful in meeting the needs of various communities. This can then promote the most valuable and yet most cost-effective methods for community education to be used.

References

Allender, J. A., & Spradley, B. W. (2001). *Community health nursing: Concepts and practice* (5th ed.). Philadelphia: Lippincott.

Brookfield, S. (1983). Community adult education: A conceptual analysis. *Adult Education Quarterly, 33,* 154-160.

Bryant, A. R. (2002). Reverse integration at an adult day health center. *Generations, 26*(3), 59-64.

Cameron, H., McKaig, W., & Taylor, S. (2003). *Crossing the threshold: Successful learning provision for homeless people.* London: Learning and Skills Development Agency. (ERIC Document Reproduction Service No. ED475402).

Charles Stewart Mott Foundation. (1998, September). *Learning together: A look at 20 school-community initiatives.* Retrieved July 28, 2008, from http://www.mott.org/publications/Legacy%20Publications/Learning%20Together.aspx

Cummings, C., & Dyson, A. (2007). The role of schools in area regeneration. *Research Papers in Education, 22*(1), 1-22.

DeLargy, P. F. (2002). Public schools and community education. In J. E. Witte (Ed.), *Providers of adult education* (pp. 13-28). San Francisco: Jossey-Bass.

DeLargy, P. F., DeLargy, C. B., & Dickey, P. D. (1981). *National community education goals: A comparative study.* Valdosta, GA: Valdosta State College, Center for Community Education.

Doeden, C. L. (2001). *Community-based education and rural development*. Washington, DC: Neighborhood Funders Group. (ERIC Document Reproduction Service No. ED478155).

Galbraith, M. W. (Ed.). (1992). *Education in the rural American community: A lifelong process*. Malabar, FL: Krieger.

Galbraith, M. W. (1995). *Community-based organizations and the delivery of lifelong learning opportunities*. Washington, DC: U.S. Department of Education, Office of Educational Research and Improvement, National Institute on Postsecondary Education, Libraries, and Lifelong Learning. (ERIC Document Reproduction Service No. ED385253).

Geiger, B. F. & Smith-Yoder, D. (2003). *Lessons learned planning a statewide conference: Alabama's choice – tobacco or health?* Birmingham, AL: University of Alabama at Birmingham, School of Education. (ERIC Document Reproduction Service No. ED481727).

Irish National Association of Adult Education (AONTAS). (2002). *Local structures in adult education: A discussion paper*. Dublin, Ireland: Author. (ERIC Document Reproduction Service No. ED475692).

Karatzias, A., Power, K., & Swanson, V. (2001). Quality of school life: Development and preliminary standardisation of an instrument based on performance indicators in Scottish secondary schools. *School Effectiveness and School Improvement, 12*(3), 265-284.

Kerka, S. (2003). *Community asset mapping: Trends and issues alert*. Columbus, OH: Center on Education and Training for Employment, Ohio State University. (ERIC Document Reproduction Service No. 481324).

Mezirow, J. (Ed.).(2000). *Learning as transformation: Critical perspectives on a theory in progress*. San Francisco: Jossey Bass.

Roberson, D. N. (2003). *Education and today's older worker*. Athens: University of Georgia. (ERIC Document Reproduction Service No. ED480721).

Rollins, J. A. (2000). Items of interest: Touchpoints changes childhood asthma management. *Pediatric Nursing, 26*(5), 538-540.

Solberg, J. R. (1970). *The evaluation and implementation of the community-school concept*. Unpublished doctoral dissertation, University of Michigan.

Ward, C. M. (2001). Lessons from linking community education and social-work philosophies and practices. *Educational Forum, 65*(3), 262-272.

Williams, B. (1998). *The genius of place.* (ERIC Document Reproduction Service No. ED444793).

Willie, C. V. (2000). The evolution of community education: Content and mission. *Harvard Educational Review, 70*(2), 191-211.

Chapter 3

Colleges and Universities

Tami McCray Olds

Introduction

American higher education has experienced many changes, making classrooms of today much different than those of twenty years ago. One readily recognizable change has been the increasing number of adult students in four-year colleges and universities. With the growing demand for higher education, many returning students no longer fit the demographics of the traditional eighteen to twenty-two year old. Out of the 14.2 million undergraduates enrolled in 1991, 45% were over the age of 25 (Darkenwald & Novak, 1997). These numbers were expected to increase and have a profound affect on colleges and universities. Recognizing the need to attract this increasing population of learners, academic institutions have modified programs formerly tailored to the traditional-aged student. Stanley Gabor, Dean of the Johns Hopkins School for Continuing Studies indicated the needs of these students will be met by proprietary programs if universities and colleges do not (Gose, 1999).

As students change, classroom dynamics change, making it incumbent upon college educators to assess and modify their academic opportunities and methods. To better understand the impact of four-year colleges and universities on adult education, it is important to understand the terminology used, the clientele serviced, the historical background of continuing education, the types of programs currently offered, the attitudes and effectiveness of these programs, and the sources of revenue for the providing institutions.

Definitions

Various terms are used to describe adult and continuing education programs. Those desiring an understanding of adult education in four-year colleges and universities should be familiar with the terminology within this system. Common terminology includes *adult learner, cooperative extension,* and *continuing education.*

Adult education programs are typically designed for *adult learners,* individuals who are usually beyond normal college age or are not regularly enrolled in college or university classes. The regularly enrolled adult student is usually an individual who is taking supplemental course work in addition to their other studies. These adult learners are often times referred to as *non-traditional* students.

Cambridge University is noted as the first university to formally organize an adult education program, which occurred in 1873. Because professors held classes outside the university, these programs were referred to as *extramural*, or studies outside the walls (Welch, 1973). When similar programs were adopted in the United States, the term *extension* was used (Adams, 1901). In 1914, the Smith-Lever Act allowed Congress to create the *Cooperative Extension Service*, allowing for agricultural education. The term *university extension* was used to refer to the nonagricultural extension programs. Recognizing the need to eliminate confusion between cooperative extension and university extension, the term *continuing education* was later adopted to refer to nonagricultural extension programs.

While adult education terminology has been through some changes, knowledge of current terminology is essential to understanding the role of four-year colleges and universities as adult education providers. While continuing education is not a new concept, the demand for it is growing. This demand is due in large part to the increasing number of colleges' and universities' new student clientele.

Clientele

The National Center for Education Statistics (2002) reported that over half the students enrolled in post-secondary education are over the age of twenty-two, and that the adult learner is the fastest growing enrollment category in higher education. Adult students now account for nearly half of all college enrollments, according to the College Board (Gose, 1999). To be able to meet the needs of this growing student population, four-year colleges and universities deal with the unique characteristics of these students, as well as what factors motivate them.

Adult students vary in their learning styles from the traditional-aged undergraduate student. When discussing the concept of Andragogy, Malcolm Knowles, who is known as the Father of Adult Education, asserted that adult students were more self-directed then the younger non-adult learner (Knowles, 1980). Andragogy is defined as the art and science of helping adults learn. Echoing Knowles' view of adult learners as self-directed and internally motivated, Boggs (1981) indicated that instruction promoting self-actualization, critical thinking, application to life, and problem-solving seemed most beneficial to adult learners.

Long (1985) echoed Knowles view of adult learners as self-directed, stating that learning is of increasing importance to adults. Spear and Mocker (1981) suggested adult learning as much more extrinsically motivated than that of younger learners, stating participation as a key element to adults' academic success. Houle (1961) illustrated the diversity of adult learners, identifying their learning motives as activity oriented, goal oriented, and learning oriented.

Adults are returning to the academic setting for a variety of reasons, most of which are centered around some form of professional development. The number of non-traditional students is growing as workers look for ways to improve their jobs skills or move into different professions (Block, 2003). Professionals' careers are changing and they need the educational support to succeed in an entirely new field (Compton & Schock, 2000).

Needing to recruit adult learners, colleges and universities have been forced to recognize these learners have different needs and goals than traditional-aged students. In essence, the adult learner wants a quality education that fits into their schedule (Bowden & Merritt, 1995). While most administrators are reluctant about rearranging scheduling to meet the needs of the adult learners, they also recognize the adult learner will simply find another college that will (Bowden & Merritt, 1995).

In order to market to this new population of learners, academic institutions must understand their unique qualities, as well as what motivates them. Offering non-traditional programs to fit the need of this non-traditional student is an option. Non-traditional courses are usually offered in compressed formats. The history of intensive courses explains that they have existed in various formats.

Historical Overview

Traditional course formats have remained relatively unchanged in American higher education and most colleges and universities schedule courses several times per week for 12 to 16 weeks. Although there has been little evidence to support their use over various alternatives, traditional course formats continue to dominate in higher education, owing to long-standing collegiate and bureaucratic traditions (Hefferlin, 1972). Over the years the number of non-traditional course formats has increased to meet the needs of the adult student. While this approach may seem innovative, the use of intensive courses as effective teaching formats has been patterned after similar courses of the past. Examples of intensive course formats historically used in America include summer sessions, interim sessions, modular calendar systems, and weekend colleges.

Summer sessions were the first form of concentrated study used in American higher education. Present day use of summer sessions has evolved from several sources: teacher institutes, the Chautauqua movement, mechanical and agricultural institutes, the expansion of graduate education, and the growth of university extension programs (Davis, 1972). Teacher institutes appeared in 1839 as a method for enhancing elementary and secondary teaching skills. Later, these institutes evolved into summer normal schools at various colleges and universities (Schoenfeld, 1967).

The Chautauqua movement offered opportunities to study a variety of subjects, study groups, and correspondence schools. Mechanical and agricultural institutes became popular in the 1880s, providing summer sessions for the acquisition of new skills (Davis, 1972). The rise in graduate education, as well as the growth of university extension programs also prompted the addition of summer sessions, beginning in the early 1900s (Davis, 1972).

Harvard University was the first postsecondary institution to offer summer courses, beginning in 1869. These were refresher courses for teachers and were short-term and non-credit (Schoenfeld, 1967). Hatfield (2000) identified Harvard University's leadership in the field of adult and continuing education. In 1910, Harvard University offered bachelor of liberal arts degrees to extension students, featuring open enrollment, coeducation for all ages, modest tuition, and instruction primarily by Harvard-affiliated faculty. In addition to the baccalaureate, a student in Harvard extension can now opt for an associate of arts degree, master of liberal arts in nineteen fields of concentration, and certificates of advanced or special study in administration, management, applied sciences, and public health.

A few decades later, Johns Hopkins University and the University of Chicago followed suit, offering courses for scholarly research and helping to promote the summer session at American postsecondary institutions (Gleason, 1986). In 1892, the University of Chicago formally incorporated extension education into its organization. This innovation is reflected still in many midwestern state universities as strengths to their continuing education programs (Hatfield, 2000).

While private institutions began offering summer sessions, public postsecondary institutions would wait until the late nineteenth century before doing so (Gleason, 1986). Presently, the majority of higher education institutions offer summer terms, most of which adopt an intensive course format. In addition to summer session offerings, interim sessions and modular calendar system were examples of early intensive course formats.

The interim session and the modular calendar system both were developed to offer opportunities to study one subject intensively for a three to four week period. Florida Presbyterian College (now Eckerd College) began the use of an interim session in 1961, offering intensive study between traditional format terms (Conrad, 1978). The modular calendar system was used initially by the post-Civil War Scio College of Ohio and offered students opportunities to master a specific subject before continuing in other fields. In 1877, Williamston Female College used this format, dividing the academic year into seven terms, with one subject being studied each term (Powell, 1976). Hiram College in Ohio adopted a modular calendar system format in the twentieth century; and despite strong student support, reverted to a traditional format amidst pressure from administrators and faculty (Powell, 1976).

A relatively new intensive format emerged in the mid-1960s called the Weekend College, which catered primarily to working adult students. Miami-Dade Junior College introduced the first weekend college in 1965, and its growth gained momentum in the 1970s (East, 1988). Currently, the weekend college course format is popular among adult learners, as well as versions of the summer and interim sessions of the past.

Programs

Because of the growing influx of adult learners, postsecondary institutions are recognizing the need to cater to their scheduling constraints, offering intensive course formats. Also termed continuing education courses, these courses usually exist as three types: credit, for the purposing of obtaining an academic degree or certification; noncredit, for professional development; or noncredit, for personal enrichment. These courses are offered in various intensive course formats, as well as online.

Courses for credit involve individual courses for semester or quarter credit. These courses are often taken by adult students desiring an academic degree or those in need of certification. In addition to the traditional twelve to sixteen week day courses, non-traditional formats are offered to suit the adult student.

Noncredit courses are courses offered for professional development or personal enrichment. Professional development courses exist for professionals who have to continuously update in their fields, such as doctors, lawyers, nurses, and teachers. Participation in continuing education programs relevant to their career fields is required of many professionals in order to maintain their licenses to practice. Additionally, adults who have experienced a change in jobs but who hold degrees, often take professional development courses to receive certification in a new field.

Noncredit personal enrichment courses are taken by adults seeking to expand their intellect with further study. These courses, often offered in the form of life-skills courses, may improve the experiences or relationships of students. Courses teaching First Aid and CPR training, swimming lessons, and financial management are some examples. Many colleges and universities have even offered basic education courses to combat the problem of illiteracy.

Whether for credit or non-credit, intensive courses are becoming more and more common on the college and university campus in an attempt to meet the needs of the growing numbers of non-traditional aged learners. Nixon (1996) found that out of 424 colleges and universities, 217 of them were using accelerated courses and programs. A 1986 survey of two-year and four-year institutions indicated there were approximately 225 weekend colleges nationwide. The student most often enrolled in non-traditional formats is between the ages of twenty-five and fifty years of age (National Center for

Education Statistics, 2002). Non-traditional students typically have a delayed enrollment and did not enter postsecondary education following high school graduation, attend part-time, work full-time, are financially independent, have dependents, and are single parents (Oblinger, 2003). Intensive course formats include summer sessions, interim sessions, and weekend colleges. In addition to these formats, colleges and universities are offering evening and online courses and programs.

Darkenwald and Novak (1997) studied various randomly selected universities and found that nearly all adult degree students were matriculated in the university's adult evening college. Although traditional-aged students were often also enrolled in evening classes, the opposite was not true for day classes, which were almost entirely comprised of traditional-aged students. Evening courses are usually offered one night per week, Monday through Thursday. Darkenwald and Novak (1997) discovered that admission to the day college was highly selective, but admission to the evening college was not. Factors affecting the adult student's admission included previous college experience, a GPA of 2.5 or better on previously taken college courses, or evidence of promise as determined by work or life experiences. While this data suggests potential academic difficulty for the adult learner, research has suggested otherwise. On average, adults over twenty-five years of age perform as well as better prepared young students, and women over thirty years of age seem to actually perform far better (Kasworm & Pike, 1994).

With advances in technology, four-year colleges and universities are increasing their offerings of online courses. In 1995, the National Center for Education Statistics reported that more than one-third of institutions nationwide were offering distance education or online courses while another quarter were planning to implement a specialty course within three years (Compton & Schock, 2000). Adult students enjoy the option of online course offerings because they can be scheduled around work and personal schedules, and students can work at their own pace. These courses seem to work well for the adult, self-directed learner. Whether on the job or during their personal time, lifelong learners will constantly update their skills. The internet brings the classroom to the adult student, on their terms and in their own time frame.

Whether offered as credit or non-credit, for professional development or personal enrichment, nontraditional course formats are increasing in number. Courses are offered at various times of the day or evening, on the weekend, and even on the internet. The number of nontraditional courses is increasing, as well as reaction to them. There has been an increasing body of research concerning the effectiveness of continuing education courses, specifically those offered in intensive formats. Several studies have been done concerning the academic rigor, effectiveness, and student retention of material in these nontraditional courses.

Formats

Intensive or time-shortened courses taught outside the traditional semester or quarter are becoming common at many colleges and universities due to the number of non-traditional students, though many educators are concerned about whether these intensive courses achieve projected learning outcomes (Daniel, 2000). Educators are concerned that creating intensive courses for the convenience of adult learners may be compromising academic rigor and the credibility of such courses (Scott & Conrad, 1992). While much resistance to non-traditional course formatting has been from administrators, most faculty and students endorse them as effective learning programs.

Early research has been accomplished concerning massed versus spaced learning. This research has suggested that distribution of information over longer periods of time is superior than distribution in a massed or compressed session (Ebbinghaus, 1885/1964). Dempster and Farris (1990) concluded two spaced presentations are about twice as effective as two massed presentations. As a result of this knowledge, many educators have been concerned about the effectiveness of compressed courses. Research, however, focusing specifically on intensive courses of study in postsecondary institutions, has produced promising results.

Considering concerns about intensive courses of study, Daniel (2000) conducted a study questioning whether intensive courses allowed students the opportunity to absorb and process subject matter. Daniel discovered that students scored comparably in the intensive courses as those taught in the traditional course equivalent. Data was administered shortly after the completion of the course and again nine months later. While researchers found no significant differences across the classes in terms of their follow-up test scores, the researchers noted that the intensive format group scored slightly higher (Daniel, 2000). Additionally, Lombardi, Meikamp, and Wienke (1992) found intensive course participants made greater gains than participants in traditional length courses and found no significance between the two lengths of courses. Scott (1994) indicated that both students and faculty felt that intensive courses promoted a continuous learning experience that allowed students to synthesize ideas more efficiently.

Other case studies have been done on various intensive course formats: the summer session, the interim session, the modular calendar system, and the weekend college. Concerning summer sessions, most studies found no statistical differences as compared to the traditional course format (Anastasi, 2007; Austin, Fennell, & Yeager, 1988; Kanum, Ziebarth, & Abrahams, 1963; Murphy, 1979). Studies by Masat (1981) and Studdard (1975) indicated no differences in outcomes between interim sessions and a traditional format, while studies by DuVerlie (1973), Tyler (1970), and Wallace (1972) showed more positive results with the intensive interim course over the traditional format. Similar results occurred when comparing the modular calendar system to the traditional format, with three studies (Blackburn, Armstrong, & Dykes, 1977; Haney, 1985; Waechter, 1966) that found no statistical difference between the modular calendar system and the traditional format and two (Kuhns, 1974; Mazanec, 1972) reporting more favorable results for the intensive format.

The weekend college format provides the most intensive course format, with forty hours of coursework often being compressed into two weekends. Much research has concluded no significant differences between the weekend course format and the traditional course format (Austin et al., 1988; Brackenbury, 1978; Doyle, 1978; Doyle, Moursi, & Wood, 1980; Doyle & Yantis, 1977; Shapiro, 1988). All of the above studies reported positive results and endorsed the use of the weekend intensive course format.

Educators, seeking to find a reason for the difference between earlier research and later research, concluded that the demographics of the students may be the determining factor, rather than the lengths of the courses researched. Since many researchers have found that students in the time-shortened classes tend to be older, more motivated, and better prepared, the measures of student success may be biased since students who are more likely to succeed regardless of time format tend to take shortened courses (Daniel, 2000). Smith (1988) suggested that, while administrators were reticent about nontraditional course formats, faculty actually preferred intensive courses. Faculty endorsed intensive course formats because they believed material could be adequately presented in an intensive format, while allowing for more in-depth discussions and more inclusion of supplementary learning activities.

Early research on massed versus spaced learning provided results which prompted concern about the academic credibility of intensive course formats. Further research on these formats in post-secondary institutions did produce favorable results. Most administrators, while recognizing the need to attract the non-traditional student, remain resistant to alternative course formats. However, most faculty and students support them as valid methods of learning. More research is certainly needed, but current results are promising. Studies evaluating the effectiveness of non-traditional methods of learning have found that there is interest in developing other methods of attracting adult students, some requiring the use of alternate sources of revenue.

Resources

Adult education courses tend to be profitable for colleges for a variety of reasons. These courses are often taught by adjunct faculty, who are paid less than full-time faculty members. Instruction occurs in classrooms that would otherwise be empty, at night, on weekends, and during the summer. Adult learners account for over 75% of one college's operating budget and 38% of a university's budget, potentially boosting net profits by 50% or more (Bowden & Merritt, 1995). In light of the increase in nontraditional student enrollment, colleges and universities are motivated to meet the time constraints these students face, offering courses at night, on the weekend, and online (Compton & Schock, 2000).

Four-year colleges and universities are faced with developing accessible undergraduate programs, continuing education programs, and corporate partnerships to meet this demand and secure needed revenues provided by this increased student population. To fund these programs, academic institutions are seeking revenue through a variety of sources. These sources of revenue may be direct or indirect.

With the exception of the Cooperative Extension Service, seldom is there a continuing education program without the requirement of a fee from participants. Often continuing education programs are self-supporting, requiring little additional funding from the academic institution. Indirect sources of revenue often occur in the form of staff benefits, building space, and the use of utilities and janitorial services (Hatfield, 2000). In the case of public institutions, state legislatures may appropriate funds designated for continuing education. In lieu of the fee requirement, subsidies from foundations or governmental agencies may also be sources of revenue for public colleges and universities.

Because a continuing education operation is heavily dependent on participant fees, it is constantly subject to fluctuations in the economy. This means the business of educating adults requires continuous program development, one which is often market-driven rather than academically driven. As a result, many continuing education programs seek funding from additional sources.

More and more private enterprises are competing for the state and federal funding adult continuing education programs provide. Adult basic education program funding has increased 2.5 times between 1980 and 1994, though these programs are currently at risk (Grissom, 1996). As a result, corporate partnerships have become more and more essential. Concerning professional education, Taylor (1998) looked at the issue of corporate partnerships. With shifting professional boundaries and the emergence of new professions, we are seeing a massive increase in claimants to professionalism; that various stakeholders: professional bodies, employers, students, service consumers, and the government have interests which vary in compatibility (Taylor, 1998).

Professional educators face common curriculum issues, often outcome-based. Taylor (1998) indicated that assessment in professional education is an outcome of power sharing between higher education and professional bodies. Higher education dictates the need for standards which can be seen as objective, reliable and fair, and the professional bodies dictate professional requirements for particular learning outcomes. Assessment must have a direct relationship to the way practice is assessed in the workplace and should balance formative and summative assessment. Corporate partnerships provide challenges when these service users want decision-making power concerning course design, delivery and review. Involving service users in the classroom requires clarity and negotiation about roles and responsibilities, power and expertise (Taylor, 1998).

While challenging, corporate partnerships have provided increased opportunities for certificate programs. Facing resistance and apathy from faculty fearing certificate programs would adversely affect curriculum and standards, colleges and universities have sought alliances with corporations offering certificate programs (Gose, 1999). Unlike conventional degree programs, corporations target specific skills needed for their employee's specific jobs (Weber, 1999).

The most successful adult professional degree programs cater specifically to corporate needs, and an educated workforce is attractive to corporate employers. Two motivating factors for employees include potential advancement and increased income. Income generally increases with formal educational attainment, as well as often removing barriers to employment advancement.

Because of the growing demand for non-traditional course offerings and continuing education programs, four-year colleges and universities are seeking alternative sources of revenue. While most of the revenue relies upon direct means, such as participants' course fees, other revenue may be sought through other means. Governmental funding and grants may be sources of revenue for public institutions, while corporate partnerships are becoming sources of revenue for many private colleges and universities. Because nontraditional course offerings utilize various locations, nontraditional scheduling, and adjunct faculty, colleges and universities are finding the development of continuing education programs to be a very profitable endeavor.

Conclusion

With many adults returning to the college and university setting, many academic institutions have felt the need to modify their traditional styles to adapt to the needs of this new student demographic. To understand the role of four-year colleges and universities in adult education, it is important to know the terminology used, the clientele serviced, the history of extension programs, the types of programs currently being offered, the attitudes and effectiveness of adult education programs, and the resources utilized to make these programs possible.

Various terms are used to apply to adult education programs, and, though some changes have occurred, the term *continuing education* currently refers to adult education programs. The adult learner is different from the traditional eighteen to twenty-two year-old student, often more self-directed and intrinsically motivated. In the business of education, colleges and universities recognize adult learners as individuals interested in self-fulfillment and having the desire to invest in academic institutions which are able to meet their needs.

The needs of adult learners, as opposed to their traditionally aged counterparts, involve accessibility and scheduling of programs, making the option for compressed study appealing. While intensive courses have a rich history, their popularity has not been evident until the growing population of adult students. With this growing demand for non-traditional course formatting there were mixed reactions concerning the academic integrity and rigor of these alternative formats.

Concerned about the validity of these non-traditional formats, most administrators have not been receptive to their inclusion as a format of study. Faculty and students, on the other hand, typically support the inclusion of intensive courses as valid forms of study. While initial research on the effectiveness of compressed versus spaced learning suggested spaced learning as better, research done on adult learners in intensive course formats has suggested different, more promising results.

Because of the differences between adult learners and the traditional aged college students, many educators concede that mixed results determining effectiveness of intensive courses is determined most by the intrinsic motivation and self-directed learning of the adult student. These positive results provide support for the addition of other nontraditional options in four-year colleges and universities, motivating them to seek more alternative methods of instruction.

While most of the funding for adult education programs comes from course fees paid by students, other sources of revenue may be used to support these programs. Funding may be provided through governmental grants or corporate partnerships. Allowing others to secure portions of this profitable endeavor, as well as being market-driven by the economy, provides challenges to program offerings and developments. These additional resources, however, are means by which adult education programs are able to flourish.

Statistics suggest the growth of the adult learner is not likely to wane in the future, and most likely will soon outweigh the numbers of traditionally aged students. The survival of four-year colleges and universities may very well depend on their ability to successfully market themselves to this segment of the student population. Most organizations survive based on an ability to adapt to the ever-changing demands of their environments. Academic institutions, in the business of education, are no different. Recognizing non-traditional alternatives for classroom settings, course offerings, course formats, and sources of revenue are means by which four-year colleges and universities will be able to survive and grow in the future.

References

Adams, H. R. (1901). Educational extension in the United States. In *Report of the U.S. Commissioner of Education for 1899-1900*. Washington, D.C.: U.S. Government Printing Office.

Anastasi, J. (2007). Methods and techniques: Full-semester and abbreviated summer courses--An evaluation of student performance. *Teaching of Psychology, 34*(1), 19-22.

Austin, T. L., Fennell, R. R., & Yeager, C. R. (1988). Class scheduling and academic achievement in a non-traditional graduate program. *Innovative Higher Education, 12*(2), 79-90.

Blackburn, R. T., Armstrong, E. C., & Dykes, M. D. (1977). *Evaluation report: UW-O FIPSE project*. Oshkosh: University of Wisconsin-Oshkosh. (ERIC Document Reproduction Service No. ED150 903).

Block, S. (2007, November13). College 529 plan could make great gift for grandkids, but... *USA Today*, pp. 03b.

Boggs, D. L. (1981). *Examining controversies in adult education*. San Francisco: Jossey-Bass.

Bowden, R., & Merritt, R. (1995). The adult learner challenge: Instructionally and administratively. *Education, 115*(3), 426.

Brackenbury, R. L. (1978, Summer). What is more elusive than the learning of philosophy. *Educational Research Quarterly,3*(2), 93-97.

Compton, M., & Schock, C. (2000). The non-traditional student in you. *Women in Business, 52*(4), 14.

Conrad, C. F. (1978). *The undergraduate curriculum: A guide to innovation and reform*. Boulder, CO: Westview Press.

Daniel, E. L. (2000). A review of time-shortened courses across disciplines. *College Student Journal, 34*(2), 298-299.

Darkenwald, G., & Novak, R. (1997). Classroom age composition and academic achievement in college. *Adult Education Quarterly, 47*(2), 108-117.

Davis, J. R. (1972). The changing college calendar. *Journal of Higher Education, 43*(2), 142-150.

Dempster, F. N., & Farris, R. (1990). The spacing effect: Research and practice. *Journal of Research and Development in Education, 23*(2), 97-101.

Doyle, R. J. (1978, February). *Intensive scheduling: The evidence for alternatives in course scheduling patterns.* Paper presented at the Eighteenth Annual Forum for the Association for Industrial Research, Houston, TX.

Doyle, R. J., Moursi, M., & Wood, D. (1980). The effects of intensive schooling: a field experiment. Unpublished manuscript, Central Michigan University, Mt. Pleasant.

Doyle, R. J., & Yantis, J. (1977). *Facilitating nontraditional learning: An update on research and evaluation in intensive scheduling.* Mt. Pleasant Central Michigan University, Institute for Personal and Career Development. (Eric Document Reproduction Service No. ED144459)

DuVerlie, C. (1973). The disappearance of the academic foreign language program. *American Foreign Language Teacher, 3*(3), 16-38.

East, J. R. (1988). *Teaching on weekends and in shopping centers: A guide for colleges and universities.* Indianapolis: Indiana University, Purdue University. (ERIC Document Reproduction Service No. ED291328)

Ebbinghaus, H. (1964). *Memory.* (H.A. Ruger and C.E. Bussenius, Trans.). New York: Dover. (Original Work published 1885, trans. 1913).

Gleason, J. P. (1986). *Economic models of time in learning.* Unpublished doctoral dissertation, University of Nebraska.

Gose, B. (1999). Surge in continuing education brings profits for universities. *Chronicle of Higher Education, 45*(24), pp. A51-A53.

Grissom, B. (1996). Just asking. *Adult Learning, 7*(6), 4.

Haney, J. J. (1985). *A comparison study of modular and semester schedules.* Unpublished doctoral dissertation, Mississippi State University.

Hatfield, T. M. (2000). Four-year colleges and universities. In J. Witte (Ed.), *Providers of Adult Education.* San Francisco: Jossey-Bass.

Hefferlin, J. B. (1972). Intensive courses: An old idea whose time for testing has come. *Journal of Research and Development in Education, 6*(1), 83-98.

Houle, C. O. (1961). *The inquiring mind.* Madison, Wisconsin: University of Wisconsin.

Kanum, C., Ziebarth, E. W., & Abrahams, N. (1963). Comparison of student achievement in the summer term and regular quarter. *Journal of Experimental Education, 32*(2), 123-132.

Kasworm, C. E., & Pike, G. R. (1994). Adult undergraduates students: Evaluating the appropriateness of a traditional model of academic performance. *Research in Higher Education, 35*(6), 689-710.

Knowles, M. S. (1980). *The modern practice of adult education: Andragogy vs. Pedagogy.* Chicago: Association Press.

Kuhns, E. (1974). The modular calendar: catalyst for change. *Educational Record, 55*(1), 59-64.

Lombardi, T. P., Meikamp, J. A., & Weinke, W. D. (1992). Learning gains and course time format in special education. *Educational Research Quarterly,* 33-38.

Long, H. B. (1985). Critical foundations for lifelong learning/lifelong education. *Philosophical and other views on lifelong learning.* Athens: University of Georgia, Adult Education Dept.

Masat, F. E. (1981). An immersion course in BASIC. *Journal of Educational Technology Systems, 10*(4), 321-329.

Mazanec, J. L. (1972). *The effect of course intensity on academic achievement, students attitudes, and mortality rate.* Unpublished doctoral dissertation, Michigan State University.

Murphy, D. R. (1979, Fall). Learning and intensive instruction. *The Journal of Economic Education, 11*(1), 34-36.

National Center for Education Statistics. (2002). The condition of education 2002. Report No. NCES 2002-025. Washington, D.C.: U.S. Department of Education, Office of Educational Research and Improvement.

Nixon, R. O. (1996). A source document on accelerated courses and programs at accredited two and four year colleges and universities. (ERIC Document Reproduction Service No. ED399827).

Oblinger, D. (2003). Understanding the new students. *Educause Review, 38*(4), 36-43.

Powell, B. S. (1976). *Intensive education: The impact of time on learning.* Newton, MA: Education Development Center. (ERIC Document Service Reproduction Number ED 144 195).

Schoenfeld, C. A. (1967). *The American university in summer.* Madison: The University of Wisconsin Press.

Scott, P. A. & Conrad, C. F. (1992). A critique of intensive courses and an agenda for research. *Higher education: Handbook of theory and research, 8,* 411-460.

Shapiro, E. G. (1988). Effects of intensive vs. traditional time formats in IPCD classes. Unpublished manuscript, Central Michigan University, Institute for Personal and Career Development, Mt. Pleasant.

Smith, J. P. (1988). *Effects of intensive college sources on student cognitive achievement, academic standards, student attitudes, and faculty attitudes.* Doctoral dissertation, University of Southern California.

Spear, G. E. & Mocker, D. W. (1981). *The organizing circumstance: Environmental determinants in the non-formal learning.* Unpublished manuscript, , University of Missouri-Kansas City, Center for Research Development in Adult Education, School of Education.

Studdard, A. L. (1975). *A study comparing a regular semester and an interim term college level physical science course based on changes in student attitudes and understanding of science processes.* Unpublished doctoral dissertation, The University of Alabama.

Taylor, I. (1998). Educating the professionals. *Adults Learning, 9*(10), 24.

Tyler, D. (1970). 4-1-4 and the audio-lingual skills. *Modern Language Journal, 54,* 253-54.

Waechter, R. F. (1966). *A comparison of achievement and retention by college junior students in an earth science course after learning under massed and spaced conditions.* Unpublished doctoral dissertation, Pennsylvania State University.

Wallace, J. A. (1972). Three weeks equals thirty weeks? A report on an experimental intensive January language course. *Foreign Language Annuals, 6,* 88-94.

Weber, J. (1999, October). School is never out. *Business Week, 3649,* 164-168.

Welch, E. (1973). *The peripatetic university: Cambridge local lecturers, 1873-1973.* Cambridge, England: Cambridge University Press.

Chapter 4

Community Colleges

Tuboise D. Floyd and Jane B. Teel

Introduction

Community colleges are responsible for providing educational services to approximately one half of the postsecondary students in the United States. The American Association of Community Colleges (AACC) (2008) indicates that the purpose of the community college is to provide open access to enrollment, provide transfer curriculum, provide workforce development and skills training, and noncredit courses such as English as a second language or cultural enrichment programs. The AACC supports the belief that many traditional aged students and adult learners would not be able to further their education to a postsecondary level without the programs offered by the community college.

Baker (1994) considers the community college an important component of the American educational system. Their reputation has been open admissions, geographic proximity, and affordable, quality education. Globalization has impacted the community college system as a provider of adult education. These new challenges have been accompanied by the social, technical and economic trends of the global economy. Community colleges have responded with comprehensive institutions that stand between adult and higher education, industrial training and formal technical education, secondary and higher education.

According to Lorenzo (1994), the creation of community colleges occurred to aid students in overcoming barriers to higher education. In 1973, Bushnell revealed that adult education in the community college should aid adults in adjusting to increased amounts of leisure time, advancing needs for technological skills in the workplace, and developing appropriate knowledge for carrying out civic responsibilities. "The profile of community college students has changed; however, the majority are now part-time students, attend in the evenings, are over the age of twenty-five, and must contend with geographic barriers. Such realities necessitate adjustments on the part of community colleges" (Lorenzo, 1994, p. 119). To understand the role of the community college in providing education for adults, it is important to review the history of the community college, the extensive curriculum offered, the nature of the student population, and the emerging issues faced by many community colleges.

Historical Overview of Community Colleges

The evolution of the community college has added confusion to the institutional mission and the nomenclature of the Community College. The term "Community College" is commonly used to describe all government supported two-year colleges awarding Associate of Arts degrees. The Truman Commission suggested that the named "community college" be applied to the institution designed to serve chiefly local community educational needs (President's Commission 1947, Vol. 3.5). However, many of these institutions do not offer comprehensive programs of study and therefore can not be truly defined as a Community College. More accurately defined, Community Colleges are institutions that provide general and liberal education, career and vocational education, and adult and continuing education.

The term "Junior College" refers to an institution whose primary mission is to provide general and liberal education leading to transfer and completion of the baccalaureate degree. Junior colleges often provide applied science and adult and continuing education programs. The term "Technical College" refer to those institutions awarding no higher than a two-year degree or diploma in a vocational, technical, or career field (Baker, 1994). In addition, Technical Colleges also offer degrees in adult and continuing education and applied science. In reference to all institutions awarding Associate of Arts, Associate of Science, Associate of Applied Arts, Associate of Applied Science degrees, Technical and Para-professional certificates and for increased consistency to the nomenclature, the term "two-year" institution provide a more accurate description.

The passing of the Morrell Act by Congress in 1862 and 1890 paved the way for the American community colleges of today. Although the earliest period of development for two-year colleges began in 1835 with collegiate courses offered in private academies, the private junior colleges continued to develop from 1835 to 1900 (Palinchak, 1973). Late in the nineteenth century, educators such as Henry Tappan, president of the University of Michigan, and William Folwell, president of the University of Minnesota, believed that universities would never become true research institutions until they eliminated the responsibility of teaching the lower level courses (Cohen & Brawer, 2003).

According to Quigley and Bailey (2003) Reverend Frank Gunsaulus could be considered the father of the two-year or junior college in the United States. In a sermon he stressed the need for a two-year post high school institution that offered instruction in engineering, chemistry, architecture, library, and liberal arts. Gunsaulus believed that all these courses should be transferable to a four-year college. Philip Danforth Armour was deeply impressed by Gunsaulus' sermon and pledged one million dollars for such an institution. In 1893 the Armour Institute opened and in 1940 it merged with the Lewis Institute known today as the Illinois Institute of Technology (Quigley & Bailey, 2003).

The two-year normal schools, which focused on preparation of teachers, viewed the junior college movement as a possible means of recognition by higher education. The normal schools received post-high school status as they increased their level of courses offered and introduced general courses. Some colleges began accepting courses transferred from normal schools. Numerous normal schools are included in the early list of junior colleges offering two years of transferable college credit (Fields, 1962).

Established in 1901, Joliet Junior College in Joliet, Illinois, is the oldest existing public two-year college in the United States. University of Chicago president Harper and the principal of Joliet, Illinois' public high school, Stanley Brown, are credited with the origination of this two-year college program which offered a fifth and sixth year of instruction equivalent to the first two years of college (Monroe, 1972). Upon accreditation by the North Central Association of Colleges and Secondary Schools, Joliet's name changed to Joliet Junior College (Fields, 1962).

California led the way among the states known for the rapid spread of the junior college movement. In 1907, the California Legislature authorized high schools to provide post-graduate courses of study equivalent to the first two years of university courses. The next step in California was the establishment of junior college departments in the high schools (Fields, 1962). By 1921, junior colleges in California were a separate institution and they had established 21 colleges (Phillippe & Sullivan, 2005). Alexis Lange of the University of California and Jordan of Stanford University were early supporters of the junior college movement (Ratcliff, 1994). And prior to 1910, Lange was probably the most important person in giving direction to the junior college movement and he emphasized the significance of the junior college in providing students with a general education and a vocational education (Monroe, 1972). As other states followed California, by 1930 there were 200 public and 300 private two-year colleges in the United States (Phillippe & Sullivan, 2005).

In the 1960's 457 public community colleges opened. Creating a national network and growth of facilitates funding by a robust economy and supported by social activism of the time. The 1963 Vocational Education Act and the amendments of 1968 and 1972 vastly augmented the federal funds availability to community colleges. Other federal programs provided additional funds that the community colleges shared: the Comprehensive Training and Employment Administration (1973), Job Training Partnership Act (1982), and Carl D. Perkins Vocational Education Act (1984). Subsequent years saw job Opportunities and Basic Skills, Omnibus Trade and

Competitiveness, Worksite Literacy, and Cooperative Education- programs that were superseded, modified, or extended when the School to Work Opportunities Act of 1994 and the Workforce Investment Act of 1998 were added to the set (Cohen & Brawer, 2003).

In 1947, the Truman Commission in Higher Education concluded that there should be an increase in two-year public institutions called community colleges. The Commission called for free education through the sophomore year of college. According to the Commission, the community college should strive to meet the educational needs of its full-time students, serve a cross section of the population, prepare students to earn a living, prepare students for transfer to a senior college, and provide adult education programs.

The 1947 American Association of Junior Colleges Directory shows that 315 public and 333 privately controlled junior colleges existed. Approximately 65% of the enrollment were adults primarily enrolled in evening classes. By this time, the need to change the name of junior colleges was becoming evident. Originally, the name was appropriate when the primary function was to provide the first two years of a four-year curriculum. However, by this time, a number of junior colleges had developed terminal two-year curricula. Thus, community college became a more appropriate name (Quigley & Bailey, 2003).

The 1981 studies by Breneman and Nelson of Brookings Institution discussed three general strategies for determining the direction for development of the community college. The three strategies were to give equal emphasis to academic, vocational, and community service programs; to place primary emphasis on traditional academic functions; or to create community based learning centers. Their Brookings Institute study revealed the primary direction for community college development was the comprehensive approach with equal attention given to academic, vocational, and community service programs (Breneman & Nelson, 1981).

The end of the twentieth century and beginning of the twenty-first century saw the continued increase in enrollment in community colleges. By 1986, enrollment in community colleges had increased over 35 times since 1936 (El-Khawas, Carter, & Ottinger, 1998). In 1989, Tollefson and Fountain reported 49 states had public two-year community college systems compared with only 38 states in 1963. The 1990's brought another steady increase in high school graduates and again community colleges offered inexpensive and accessible alternatives for higher education (Cohen & Brawer, 2003). In 2005, 6.5 million students were enrolled for credit in community colleges in the United States (National Center for Education Statistics, 2008). Also noted, 2.7 million of those students are adult learners (age 25 years or older).

Today community colleges educate more than half of the nation's undergraduates and since the 1970's, community colleges have steadily grown. According to the American Association of Community Colleges (AACC) there are currently 1,166 community colleges in the United States. Include branch campus and the number rises to over 1,600. Most Americans have the opportunity to pursue lifelong learning due to the close proximity to a community college, the low tuition costs, and availability of financial aid.

General Education

The focus of general education and liberal arts are now typically combined. Early community college leaders such as Eells and Koos supported the importance of general education as a function of the junior or community college. Koos (1925) indicated that junior colleges students should have the opportunity for rounding out their general education even if they are pursuing occupational curriculum. According to Cohen and Brawer (2003), general education is often defined by the competencies mastered by the students. The general education curricula includes "highly prescribed core curricula to nondirective distributional requirement systems to free elective systems" (Zeszotarski, 1999, p. 40). Preparing a student to be a learner and to adapt to the current demands of life is the purpose of general education curriculum (Shaw, 1989).

"The liberal arts curriculum includes education founded on the humanities, science, and social science, the basic studies for most college students, often codified as general education" (Cohen & Brawer, p. 315). Liberal arts originated from "the belief that human knowledge and societal cohesion are grounded in rationality" (Cohen & Ignash, 1994, p. 141). When community colleges were originated, a liberal arts curriculum was put in place as the foundation of the curriculum and remains today as the longest standing curriculum in the community college. The six primary disciplines that make up the liberal arts curriculum in community colleges today are "the humanities, English composition, mathematics, science, social science, and the fine and performing arts" (Brawer, 1999, p.18). In the early years of the community college, 75% of the curriculum was liberal arts. According to the 1998 Curriculum Project directed by Arthur Cohen, the liberal arts courses made up 54 per cent of the curriculum. Even with this change in percentage, the liberal arts curriculum shows exceptional stability. Ninety per cent of the community colleges continue to offer: "history, literature, political science, English, economics, psychology, sociology, biology, chemistry, math, and computer science" (Cohen & Ignash, 1994, p. 143).

Community and junior colleges have embraced five fundamental founding responsibilities to their constituents: to provide a pre-baccalaureate preparation of students (the transfer function); to provide assistance to students through counseling, remediation, and career planning (the student services function); to provide an alternative to students not desiring advanced study, but rather preparation for career (the terminal function); to provide a common liberal arts education to all students for personal growth and civic responsibility (the general education function); and, finally, to provide a variety of service to, and to be in partnership with, the surrounding community (the community services function) (Baker, 1994).

The last decade has been marked with an increase in partnerships between community colleges and government, business, industry and other agencies. These linkages are primarily the result of recognition that together the partners are more productive than if each acted independently. Community colleges have been involved in training and economic development since their beginning. Companies today continue to show an increased reliance on community college training and economic development services. The need for these services is a direct result of company downsizing in attempt to remain globally competitive. The training and development function of community colleges has grown to include custom-tailored and contracted training programs for business, industry, and other agencies. Active coordination with city and state governments allow promotion of business expansion and retention.

There is active pursuit of existing federal and state training funds to buy down training costs for either new or expanding companies or those engaged in retooling or remanufacturing process. In addition, there is close interaction with area chambers of commerce and business to promote economic activity, business and industrial partnerships; involvement in the state legislative process in order to establish training program funds; coordination with the Small Business Development Centers to provide effective and entrepreneurial development services to the communities they serve by assisting existing and new industry, and Job Training Partnership Service Delivery Areas to provide employment training and prescreening (Baker, 1994).

Transfer Function

A primary focus of the community college since its origination has been the transfer function. In 1925, Koos stated that the first function of the community college was to offer "two years of work acceptable to colleges and universities" (p. 19). More emphasis was placed on students going on to a four year institution to receive a baccalaureate degree than going on to immediate employment. Transfer students typically complete the majority of their general education requirements including the liberal arts curriculum and then transfer to a four institution for the baccalaureate degree. However, studies have demonstrated that students enrolled in vocational programs also provide adequate preparation for acceptable transfer (McGrath & Spear, 1994; Monroe, 1972).

In some states, degree programs previously considered as a part of nontransferable curriculum are now being accepted for transfer to a four-year college (Townsend, 2002). After a decline in dominance in the early 1980's due to the influx of part time students, the transfer function reemerged in significance largely due to three factors. Those factors included: the concern for student mobility with their education, the desire by students to attend more than one college or university, and emphasis by state and federal government on accountability of the educational providers (Eaton, 1994).

Literature about transfer coordination has typically focused on articulation which is the most basic type of interinstitutional collaboration (Kisker, 2007). Articulation is defined as the alignment of courses taught and programs offered at different levels to minimize duplication, overlap, and loss of time and credit by students as they move from one educational level to the next. Prior to 1950 formal articulation agreements were basically nonexistent; however after 1970, almost every state had established a formal plan of transfer (Monroe, 1972). Because articulation is predominantly dictated by the four year institution, historically community colleges continually adjusted their curriculum to meet the requirements of the universities.

Vocational/Technical/Workforce Training

Since the passage of the Smith-Hughes Act in 1917 emphasis has increased on improving vocational education programs. By the 1950's occupational or vocational curriculum had become accepted as part of the community college curriculum (Monroe, 1972). From the 1960's and into the 1980's vocational education enrollments grew at a faster rate than liberal arts enrollments due largely to the Vocational Education Act of 1963. There was also an increase in the size of community colleges; the type of students including older students, women, part-time and disadvantaged students; and students with disabilities; and the inclusion of adult education programs (Cohen & Brawer, 2003). Toward the end of the 1980's, student enrollment in vocational education stabilized at 40-50% of the total enrollment (Cohen & Brawer, 2003).

Throughout the years the terms vocational, technical, occupational, terminal, semiprofessional, sub-baccalaureate, and career education have been used to describe postsecondary vocational education. Cohen and Brawer (2003) concluded that although each term had a slightly different definition, they all represented a type of vocational education. In 1941, Eells noted that a semiprofessional should receive more training than a technician and less than a professional and that a certain amount of cultural education should be included to attain a semiprofessional degree. "Real semiprofessional training must be more than mere vocational training" (Eells, p. 7). Semi-professional indicated two years of training while professional required four years. In the 1950's, occupational training at a community college was often referred to as a terminal education. The label, terminal education, quickly lost popularity due to the implication of closing the door to future educational opportunities (Hillway, 1958).

In the 1970's career and occupational education became popular terms for vocational education (Cohen and Brawer, 2003). Sub-baccalaureate refers to the individuals in the mid-skilled labor market with at least a high school degree but not a baccalaureate degree (Grubb, 1996). With the exception of terminal education, most other labels continue in use today.

Workplace preparation and workforce development emerged in the 1990's as the new vocational education. Workforce preparation described the traditional college age students who were preparing to enter the workforce and workforce development was associated with the incumbent worker who desired to upgrade their skills or begin a new career (Bragg, 2001). Grubb and Lazerson (2004) contend that older occupations such as construction, the automotive trades, and food service set the stage for the current image of vocational education; however, the fastest growing occupational course enrollments in community colleges today are biotechnology, business, computer, and information technology.

Older students are typically more interested in specific occupational training than are younger students; but, it is generally the younger students who are interested in exploring various occupations and developing basic skills needed for employment (Warren, 1985). Almost 60 percent of students who attend community colleges declare their purpose for attending as for occupational purposes thus resulting in the need for community colleges to aid in the preparation of the current and future midskilled workforce (Grubb, 1996). Many community colleges today collaborate with local businesses and industries to provide specialized employee training.

Vocational education today differs greatly from the early days of community colleges when the belief was the vocational education should prepare students for immediate employment with less than a baccalaureate degree (Bragg, 2001). Non-liberal arts education should not be viewed as education that leads away from a baccalaureate degree (Cohen & Ignash, 1994, p. 151). Although vocational programs have been typically associated with terminal degrees more adults today want to gain or improve their employment and continue their education.

Remedial/Developmental Education

Although remedial education became the responsibility of two-year colleges after 1920, many questioned the success of those programs (Spann & McCrimmon, 1994). In the late 1960's and early 1970's, remedial/developmental education emerged as a major function of community colleges due largely to some deficiencies of basic academic education at the secondary level and the increased number of people entering college (Cohen & Brawer, 2003).

Developmental education programs were formatted to aid students in acquiring the necessary skills for successful college participation (Tinto, 1993). Originally, remedial/developmental education focused on students deficiencies in academic subjects. Since the 1970's, developmental education curriculum has become a portion of a variety of programs all designed to help the underprepared students (Shaw, 1989).

Cohen and Brawer (2003) conclude that remedial/developmental courses are now designed to teach the basic literacy skills (reading, writing, and arithmetic) and the broader life skills (time management, how to study, coping with family crisis, etc.). According to Spann and McCrimmon (1994) the primary student population in need of the remedial/developmental education includes the: academically underprepared students, learning disabled, visually impaired, hearing impaired, physically handicapped, English as a second language student, and the returning adult student. The community college represents a second chance to learn basic academic skills that were not learned in the public schools.

Community Education

Gleazer (1968) emphasized the importance of the community college to be used by individuals and the general public for community development. Community education is generally the most responsive of all the programs offered to meet corporate and community needs (Lorenzo, 1994). According to Cohen and Brawer (2003), the broadest function of the community college is community education which includes the following categories:

- *Adult education*: Instruction designed for people who are beyond the age of compulsory school attendance and have either completed or interrupted their formal education
- *Continuing education*: The learning effort undertaken by people whose principal occupation is no longer student-those who regard learning as a means of developing their potential or resolving their problems
- *Lifelong learning*: Intermittent education, undertaken in school and other settings
- *Community services*: The broadest term-whatever services an institution provides that are acceptable to the people in its service area
- *Community-based education*: Programs designed by the people served and developed for the good of the community
- *Contract training*: Collaborations between the community college and business and industry to train workers in specific fields

Adult education was the first of the community education services to be readily available at community colleges (Thornton, 1960). Community education may include adult education that focuses on completion of high school curriculum and adult literacy (Cohen & Brawer, 2003). Community education courses can be for credit or noncredit and can require various amounts of time from a one-hour workshop to a semester long course (Lorenzo, 1994). Cross (1988) contends that since the student enrollment in continuing education classes is almost 100% working adults, these programs must be sensitive to their learning needs and work schedule.

Adult and Continuing Education

The literature pertaining to the role of adult, continuing, and community education in the community college presents two conflicting views. On view is that they are adjunct to the principal functions of the college: general and liberal education and vocational and technical education. The second perspective suggests that adult, continuing, and community education, viewed as community services, is not so much a separate function of the college as it is an intrinsic quality that separates it from other forms of postsecondary education (Baker, 1994). The literature also illustrates important demographic changes in America and their associated issues. For example, how will the community college response to an aging population, increased urbanization and immigration?

Over the past decade, the adult learner has been an impetus of change for the community college. According to the American Association of Community Colleges, the average age of a community college student is 29 and over 80% of community college student's work part-time. The adult learner has challenged the pedagogical approach towards education in which society mandates what ought to be learned. Adults have little interest in the many activities and support services provided by colleges outside of the classroom, and are more interested in specific job training. According to Knowles (1978) the adult learner is self-directed and comfortable with taking the initiative, with or without the help of others, in diagnosing their learning needs. The community college can assist the adult learner by providing an enriched environment laden with continued educational innovation aimed at helping the adult reach their learning goals.

Emerging Issues

"Two generations have passed since President Truman's Commission on Higher Education recommended that the door to higher education be swung open. Now community colleges are everywhere" (Cohen & Brawer, 2003, p. 30). However, community colleges are faced with many challenges as they work to meet the educational needs of today's students. Beginning with the original purpose of transfer education, the American community college has included curriculum in general education, vocational and workforce training, developmental, and continuing education. The community college of today is faced with a choice about the future of their programs. Adults desiring to continue their education represent a strong force in shaping the community colleges of the future.

Numerous issues will influence the future of the community college including (Phillippe & Sullivan, 2005):

- More diversity in student enrollments including immigrants, international students, and senior citizens
- Need for basic skills instruction and remediation which is a crucial support service to elevate all students to a level for success with college instruction
- Incorporation of new instructional developments including the learning college concept and application of effective instructional styles based on needs of students and changes in faculty delivery style to include use of technology and individualized instruction personalized to facilitate student learning
- Continued responsibility for workforce development utilizing their ability to design and implement curriculums for emerging careers
- Leadership in the transition of curriculum from the two year institution to the four year institution to aid students in a seamless transition without loss of time and credit
- Addressing the need for funding for education at all levels which is a service for all citizens without regard to age or background in order to produce educated American workers qualified to compete in the world market

In 1986, the Commission on the Future of the Community College emphasized the significance of the community college as a teaching institution with a student-centered focus (Armes, 1989). Through these leaders in higher education, the emphasis was once again placed on determining what works in teaching for most effective student learning. Armes (1989) concludes that with the diverse student population including commuting, part-time adult students with work and family responsibilities, the focus in community colleges must be on the most effective methods for teaching for learning.

Conclusion

Although, community colleges continue to offer curriculum encouraged by the earliest supporters, the curriculum is now designed to meet the varying needs of current students including older adults. Community colleges are post secondary institutions that are government supported to confer degrees in the Associate of Arts and the Associate of Sciences, as well as certificate programs in specialized areas. Through part time and full time enrollment, many adults have completed an associate's degree, trained in a specific skill for local employment, completed advance training for promotions in their current job, completed programs in remediation of skills such as reading, or taken only a minimum of classes for knowledge or enrichment in a specific area.

The new millennium offers a wide variety of opportunities for partnerships between community colleges and government, business, and industry communities. The next generation of community colleges will continue its role as the community service center, distinguishing itsself from other forms of postsecondary education.

References

American Association of Community Colleges. (2008). *Students at community colleges, fall, 2005*. Retrieved May 8, 2008 from www.aacc.nche.edu

Armes, N. (1989). The future of the community college. In T. O'Banion (Ed.), *Innovation in the Community College* (pp. 266-282). New York: MacMillan.

Baker, G. (1994). *A Handbook on the Community College in America: Its History, Mission and Management*. Greenwood. London.

Bragg, D. D. (2001). Opportunities and challenges for the new vocationalism in American community colleges. *New Directions for Community Colleges, 115*, 5-15.

Brawer, F. B. (1999). The liberal arts. *New Directions for Community Colleges, 108*, 17-29.

Breneman, D. W., & Nelson, S. C. (1981). *Financing community colleges: An economic perspective*. Washington, DC: Brookings Institution.

Bushnell, D. S. (1973). *Organizing for change: New priorities for community colleges*. New York: McGraw-Hill.

Cohen, A. M., & Brawer, F. B. (2003). *The American community college* (4th ed.). San Francisco: Jossey-Bass.

Cohen, A. M., & Ignash, J. M. (1994). An overview of the total credit curriculum. *New Directions for Community Colleges, 86*, 13-29.

Cross, K. P. (1988). *Adults as learners*. San Francisco, CA: Jossey-Bass.

Eaton, J. (1991). Encouraging transfer: Its impact on community colleges. *Education Digest, 57*(1), 62-65.

Eells, W. C. (1941). *Why junior college terminal education?* Menasha, WI: Banta Publishing.

El-Khawas, E., Carter, D. J., & Ottinger, C. A. (1998). *Community college fact book.* New York: Macmillan.

Fields, R. R. (1962). *The community college movement.* New York: McGraw-Hill.

Gleazer, E. J. (1968). *This is the community college.* Boston, MA : Houghton Mifflin.

Grubb, W. N. (1996). *Working in the middle.* San Francisco, CA: Jossey-Bass.

Grubb, W. N., & Lazerson, M. (2004, October 29). Community colleges need to build on their strengths. *Chronicle of Higher Education, 51*(10), 16-21

Hillway, T. (1958). *The American two-year college.* New York: Harper & Brothers.

Kisker, C. (2007). Creating and sustaining community college – university transfer partnerships. *Community College Review, 34*(4), 282-301.

Knowles, M. (1978). *The adult learner: A neglected species.* Houston, TX: Gulf.

Koos, L. V. (1925). *The junior college movement.* Boston, MA: Ginn and Co.

Lorenzo, A. L. (1994). The mission and functions of the community college: An overview. In G. A. Baker, III (Ed.). *A handbook on the community college in America* (pp.111-136). Westport, CN: Greenwood Press.

McGrath, D., & Spear, M. B. (1994). The remedialization of the community college. In J. L. Ratcliff, S. Schwarz, & L. H. Ebbers (Eds.), *Community colleges* (pp. 217-228). Needham Heights, MA: Simon & Schuster.

Monroe, C. R. (1972). *Profile of the community college.* San Francisco, CA: Jossey-Bass.

National Center for Education Statistics. (2008). *Enrollment in postsecondary institutions, fall, 2005.* Retrieved May 20, 2008 from http://nces.ed.gov/

Palinchak, R. (1973). *The evolution of the community college.* Metichen. NJ: Scarecrow Press.

Phillippe, K. A., & Sullivan, L. G. (2005). *National profile of community colleges: Trends & Statistics* (4th ed.). Washington, DC: Community College Press.

President's Commission on Higher Education. (1947). *Higher Education for American Democracy*, Volume III: Organizing higher education. New York: Harper & Brothers.

Quigley, M. S., & Bailey, T. W. (2003). *Community college movement in perspective.* Lanham, MD: Scarecrow Press.

Ratcliff, J. L. (1994). "First" public junior colleges in an age of reform. In J. L. Ratcliff, S. Schwarz, & L. H. Ebbers (Eds.), *Community colleges* (pp. 13-31). Needham Heights, MA: Simon & Schuster.

Shaw, R. G. (1989). Curriculum change in the community college. In T. O'Banion (Ed.), *Innovation in the Community College* (pp. 23-45). New York, NY: MacMillan.

Spann, M. G., & McCrimmon, S. (1994). Remedial/developmental education: Past, present, and future. In G. A. Baker, III (Ed.). *A handbook on the community college in America* (pp. 161-175). Westport, CN: Greenwood Press.

Thornton, J. W., Jr. (1960). *The community junior college.* New York: John Wiley & Sons.

Tinto, V. (1993). *Leaving college.* Chicago, IL: University of Chicago Press.

Townsend, B. K. (2002). Transfer rates: A problematic criterion for measuring the community college. *New Directions for Community Colleges, 117,* 13-23.

Warren, J. (1985). The changing characteristics of community college students. In W. L. Deegan & D. Tillery (Eds.). *Renewing the American community college* (pp 53-79). San Francisco, CA: Jossey-Bass.

Zeszotarski, P. (1999). Dimensions of general education requirements. *New Directions for Community Colleges, 108,* 39-48.

Chapter 5

Correctional Education

Melissa Askew

Introduction

Correctional Education began in the 1700's in the United States and 200 years earlier in Great Britain. Since its genesis, correctional education has undergone a myriad of changes, primarily due to variations in philosophy. Prisoners have been seen as deserving of punitive measures or as unfortunates in need of rehabilitation and treatment. The philosophical paradigm has been dependent upon the political climate of the day.

Changes in ideology have not been the only area of debate. Issues regarding female prisoners, their need for and access to prison education, has also been a source of contention. Female prisoners have historically been denied equal educational opportunities to their male counterparts. They are generally offered domestic skills classes rather than taught a trade. Because the majority of single-parent homes are run by women, it is imperative that female inmates receive parenting and life-skill training; however, they must also be afforded vocational skills training, to ensure a legal means of earning money.

Arguments for and against correctional education have been pervasive since its inception, with the major question being whether it works or not. The measure of correctional education's effectiveness is often recidivism rates and is subjective. If an inmate returns to prison because of a lesser crime is he/she deemed a success or failure? If an inmate does not return to prison but fails at becoming a useful member of society, was incarceration and education effective? The dilemma should be obvious. While there is no causal relationship between a lack of education and crime, there is a correlation (Chappell, 2004; Gehring, 2000; Haulard, 2001; Vacca, 2004).

Research has shown a drop in recidivism rates of up to 30% for individuals who participated in any correctional instruction. The rate of re-incarcertion by those obtaining degrees is even lower, with studies claiming a zero percent recidivism rate for prisoners obtaining master's degrees. Programs which offer a General Equivalency Degree (GED) or college degree are most successful and have the lowest recidivism rates (Nuttall, Hollmen, & Staley, 2003).

Opportunities for adult educators interested in this field are virtually endless. New and innovative programs are being developed routinely; however, as is the case with most areas of public education, funding remains scarce. This scarcity of resources means that educators must be all the more creative in order to be effective. Mentoring, peer tutoring, specific practices for the learning disabled, and educational technology are just a modicum of measures used by instructors in prison settings. There are teaching strategies that can be used within the correctional system that are not dependent on the correctional institution for implementation (Zaro, 2007).

History

A rudimentary form of correctional education began in Great Britain in the late 1500's. Prior to this time, prisoners were valued only slightly more than work animals. The main purpose of early prisons and jails was simply to feed, water, and contain. During 1577, there was a shift in philosophy with the creation of workhouses and bridewells. A bridewell was a correctional home used to confine disorderly individuals. Migrating serfs had few or no marketable skills and frequently engaged in unlawful activities in order to survive. Bridewells provided religious and moral education, the hope being that upon release; these migrants would be fit for society. After less than 100 years, bridewells lost their influence in exchange for sending offenders to the New World.

The British ideology assured that once sent to the colonies, criminals would not be heard from again; therefore education and marketability were non-factors. With the onset of the American Revolution, came a revolution of another kind for Great Britain. No longer were British prisoners sentenced to New World exile. Because criminal offenders had to remain within the British citizenry, the evolution of inmate education began.

The late 1700's marked the impetus of correctional education in the United States. The trend began in Philadelphia at Walnut Street Jail. Minister William Rogers provided the instruction. It was required by the warden that class be taught with a loaded canon facing the students, thus preventing a prison riot. As one might guess, all was quiet and uneventful. At its inception, the function of prison education in America was merely to teach inmates to read the bible, preparing them to be saved (Gehring & Eggleston, 1996).

Auburn Prison in New York began what is now considered formal education in May 1826. Although the impetus for inmate education was religious, its continuation was primarily rehabilitative. It was discovered that in order for prisoners to be successful in civilized society, they must be equipped with at least a minimum education. A comprehensive prison act was passed in New York in 1847, requiring the hiring of full-time teachers for each New York prison. Thus began the first weeklong school program for prisoners. New York continued to set the standard for prison reform with the creation of the Elmira Reformatory in 1876. Elmira housed youth and young-adult inmates, aged 16-30, and placed great emphasis on academic and vocational education programming.

Prior to the late 1800's, penitentiaries or prisons were created for the sole purpose of confinement. Although termed correctional facilities, the methods used to correct behavior were purely religious. Any and all education and/or counseling that occurred had a theological basis and was provided to save the inmates' soul (Gehring & Eggleston, 1996). It was theorized that armored with the word of God, prisoners would turn over a new leaf upon release and desist criminal activity. Confinement was for a specific period of time, ignored individual treatment, and disallowed flexible sentencing or parole. The opening of Elmira, the first adult reformatory in the world, changed all of that. Elmira brought corrections into a new age and the impact was felt well into the late twentieth century.

Elmira Reformatory opened in New York in 1876, with Zebulon Reed Brockway at the helm. Brockway was a Connecticut native, with many years of corrections experience under his belt. Brockway's career began at the Connecticut Sate prison in 1848. He moved to Albany, New York where he served as assistant to then county warden, Amos Pilsbury. Brockway moved up the ladder, becoming head of the Monroe County Penitentiary in 1854 and superintendent of the Detroit House of Corrections in 1861. It was in Detroit where Brockway began implementing his innovative correctional ideas, including pre-release halfway housing and non-religious correctional education.

The prison association of New York had a penchant for liberal ideas and became interested in Brockway's theories and practices. The Reverend Enoch Wines, secretary of the New York Prison Association, worked closely with Brockway to create a Declaration of Principles. These principles called for the reformation of criminals through rewards and appeal to the prisoners' self-interest, a system of marks to grade prisoners' progress and indeterminate sentences (Department of Corrections, n.d.). The stage was set for Elmira.

With the end of the Civil War approaching, the prison association made plans to open a new penitentiary to deal with the influx of criminals. Elmira was to be this penitentiary and it opened on July 24, 1876. Being that Elmira was heralded as a reformatory, and an experimental one at that, only first time offenders between the ages of 16 and 30 were permitted. These first offenders, 30 to be exact, were transferred from Auburn Prison and others followed from Sing-Sing.

The next 20 years bore the fruits of Brockway's labors. Many and varied novel programs sprung up at Elmira from classification of inmates, to peer teaching and classes taught by professors from nearby colleges. Courses in ethics, psychology, geometry, and bookkeeping were provided to advanced students, while public school teachers and attorneys taught elementary courses. Brockway constructed a trade school on Elmira's campus, and the purchase of a printing press marked the production of the world's first prisoner newspaper (Department of Corrections, n.d.). To round out these creative practices, Brockway encouraged the use of field sports as inmate therapy.

Because of Brockway's popularity among judges, criminals were routinely sentenced to Elmira. Understandably, overcrowding became a serious issue. What was first built to hold some 500 inmates became an institution occupying about 1500 prisoners. The problem of overcrowding coupled with the creation of probation and accusations of prisoner brutality forced 73 year-old Zebulon Brockway to step down. From his retirement in 1900 to his death in 1920, Brockway continued to consult and lecture on penology and penned his autobiography.

Although Brockway was no longer in charge, Elmira continued to be a reformatory in the truest sense of the word. Brockway's successors took a holistic approach to classifying inmates, using specialists to uncover the origin of individual criminal activity. Prisoners had tests of their mental, emotional, moral, social, and physiological make-up. Results of these tests aided prison administrators in assigning inmates to specific work and school activities. In perusing the results of these tests, it was found that almost 40 percent of the population was mentally defective. Thus began another innovation, whereby mentally challenged inmates were segregated from the general population.

The population of offenders sentenced to Elmira has changed in the last 30 years. It now admits prisoners of all ages, regardless of their status as recidivists. But the core of [Brockway's] program—classification with gradations of freedom and privilege, along with an emphasis on development of the whole person, physical, intellectual and spiritual remains at the basis of modern corrections (Department of Corrections, n.d.).

Momentum for educational prison reform stalled until after World War II, with the formation of the Correctional Education Association in 1945, and the creation of the Journal of Correctional Education four years later. These two major events led to what could be considered the modern age of correctional education. Correctional Education during the 1960's and 1970's focused primarily on vocational education. Like the bridewells of the 1500's, contemporary prisons offered education to inmates in an effort to equip them with marketable skills. The Manpower Development and Training Act and the subsequent Comprehensive Employment Training Act insured vocational education funding for correctional institutions during the 60's and 70's.

The main concern during this period was what to do with the female prisoners, educationally speaking. Because the population of women inmates was significantly lower than that of men, and because work by women was still seen as merely domestic, females were not offered vocational education programs which would prepare them for skilled positions upon their release. They were offered programs such as culinary arts, home economics, flower arranging, cosmetology, and secretarial science. None of these programs prepared women for positions which would bring an income necessary for supporting families (Young & Mattucci, 2006). The only solutions were to create co-correctional institutions where females would be privy to already existing vocational programs, or to cut programs from all-male prisons, thus freeing up money to begin better programs in the women's facilities. In the end it was decided that co-correctional institutions be created, but this was short-lived. The liabilities of sexual assault, pregnancy, and emotional attachment between inmates outnumbered the benefits.

Until the late 1980's and early 1990's, correctional education was federally encouraged and adequately funded. College programs were offered in a variety of subjects, and it was possible for prisoners to be conferred degrees at all levels, Associates, Bachelor's, Master's, and Doctorates. Pell Grants and other forms of financial aid assisted inmates in covering the costs of these programs. This is no longer the case. Over the last decade or two, correctional education budgets have been seriously cut, college programs are available only in rare cases, and federal financial aid to prisoners has been abolished. On a more positive note, the field has grown substantially, and opportunities now exist for educators as never before. The expanded definition for the word literacy is a major reason. No longer is literacy seen merely as the ability to read. It has been shown that for a person to lead a useful and productive life they must also be socially, emotionally, and personally literate. They must be able to face challenges in all areas of life, not just in books. They must learn to properly assess situations, recognize areas in need of improvement, and learn to seek out necessary resources.

Recidivism

The most educationally disadvantaged population in the United States resides in our prisons. Incarcerated adults have among the lowest academic skill levels and highest disability and illiteracy rates of any segment of our society-factors that likely contributed to their imprisonment. Upon completing their sentence, most inmates re-enter society no more skilled than when they left. Frustrated by a lack of marketable skills, burdened with a criminal record and released without transitional services and supports, many return to illegal activities (Klein & Tolbert, 2004).

Research supports the premise that correctional education benefits society by reducing recidivism and transforming criminals into productive members of society, "correctional education programs help inmates to break the cycle of low literacy skills and criminal activity by providing them with the knowledge and skills necessary to succeed in the workplace and in society" (Steurer, 1996, ¶ 2). Prison education participants show a significant reduction in recidivism from that of the general population (Steurer, 1996).

Learned problem-solving and decision-making skills help inmates acclimate to incarceration, thus keeping them from committing infractions while in prison. Prison staff also enjoy a safer, more secure, and structured place in which to work. One school of thought asserts that correctional facilities do nothing more than make inmates better criminals. They have entirely too much idle time, time that could and should be spent in preparation for their release. The opposition asserts that those convicted of a crime should be punished, thereby denying inmates opportunities to better themselves, opportunities a lack of which, probably played a role in their choice to engage in criminal activity in the first place.

There are many research articles espousing the effectiveness of correctional education. One of the best known was prepared by the Correctional Education Association and funded by the U.S. Department of Education. The 2001 *Three State Recidivism Study* involved Maryland, Minnesota and Ohio. This longitudinal study found, "...participation in correctional education reduced the probability of incarceration by 29 percent...correctional education fights crime, cuts the costs for re-incarceration and prepares many adults to return to society as productive citizens, taxpaying workers and positive parents" (Tolbert, 2004, ¶ 3).

Learning Disabilities

While most adult educators deal with students with learning disabilities, it is even more commonplace for correctional educators. It has been estimated that between 30%-50% of inmates suffer from some sort of learning difficulty, and this percentage only addresses students who have been diagnosed. The rate is probably higher when one considers the vast number of students whose disability has gone undetected. In addition, there are certain behavioral disorders that fall within the context of learning disabilities because they impair learning. These behavior disorders are pervasive among prisoners, and run the gamut from attention deficit, hyperactivity, and impulsivity. According to Neil Sturomski's *Learning Disabilities and the Correctional System,* (Tolbert, 2004) correctional educators should have a strong knowledge base regarding learning disabilities to include:

- Characteristics of learning disabilities
- Learning Styles

- Screening and assessment
- Instructional strategies
- Self-esteem and social skills issues of adult learners
- Educational technology

Sheridan and Steele-Dadzie (2005) studied the information processing (learning styles) abilities of incarcerated youth (N=1480) within a correctional center. The majority of their sample was considered figural learners and had enhanced creativity and memory processing abilities. As a correctional educator, it would be relevant to address the cognitive skills needs of these individuals to assist in reducing recidivism within the juvenile justice system. In addition, there are strategies that can be incorporated into the educator's daily practice to aid students with and without disabilities:

- Large print texts and fonts
- One-to-one tutoring
- Talking calculators
- Electronic dictionaries
- Multi media

Technology

There are security issues to be considered when allowing Internet access to inmates. However, these issues may be addressed much the same as they are in public schools. Firewalls and filtering software can insure the Internet is not abused. It is vitally important that students become computer literate, if not computer savvy. Exposure to computers and multi media not only adds to ones list of skills, but can aid and enhance the learning experience. For these reasons, correctional educators should not only be computer literate themselves, but be well versed in the art of integrating technology into the classroom.

The uses of educational technology are almost endless and accessing the Internet is only the tip of the iceberg. There are many software applications that can be used to stimulate the senses, visual, auditory, and kinesthetic, thus attending to a variety of learning styles. Computers can be used to offer Web-based instruction or distance learning. Students can download e-books and audio books from libraries. There are many educational games and activities such as web quests that enhance students' ability to learn and retain information. PowerPoint presentations can lessen the monotony of lectures and use of LCD projectors can aid students with poor eyesight.

Programs

Correctional Education programs generally provide at least the following: ABE (Adult Basic Education); GED (General Education Development); ESL (English as a Second Language); Post-secondary; and Special education. Courses dealing with life skills, vocational training and family literacy are also frequently offered. According to The National Institute for Literacy (Tolbert, 2004), one may define successful programs as Learner-centered; Aware of learning styles and cultural differences; Participatory, engaging students in their own learning; Sensitive to the prison culture; and Linked to post-release services.

LoPinto (2007) recommends that correctional education programs be part of a system-wide education plan and include:

- Recognition of differing learning styles
- Incentives
- Post-release services to reinforce skills that can easily be lost
- Mandatory education
- Special education services
- ESL and bilingual instruction
- Vocational training related to the current market and apprenticeship programs
- Live work programs
- Qualified teachers

There are examples of model correctional education programs in a cross-section of the United States (Prison Literacy Model Programs, n.d.). In addition to the typical ABE, GED, ESL, and literacy courses, these facilities offer specialized classes, which will be addressed. Additional program model information sites are Buena Vista Correctional Facility in Colorado; State Industrial Reformatory in Kansas; Mt. McGregor Correctional Facility in New York; Petersburg Federal Correctional institute in Virginia; Maryland Department of Public Safety and Corrections; Ohio Central School System, Department of Rehabilitation and Correction; and the Texas Department of Criminal Justice.

Buena Vista Correctional Facility is a medium security, male prison. Prisoner's average age is 26 and over 700 inmates participate in correctional education each year. Specialty offerings consist of behavior management, college accounting and electronics, computer education, self-awareness, and social learning. Appliance repair, auto bodywork, barbering, cabinet making, graphic arts and welding comprise just a few of Buena Vista's vocational education programs. The philosophy is that social responsibility, motivation, initiative and learning can be developed within inmates, thus breaking the cycle of crime.

Kansas State Industrial Reformatory is a maximum-security prison for males, averaging 23 years of age serving 500-600 students yearly. A counselor/learning specialist and 17 classroom teachers are employed to facilitate the curriculum. The educational program in Kansas State is made up of academic, vocational and life skills areas. As with most correctional institutions, instruction is individualized. Students are placed in academic courses depending on their Stanford Achievement Test scores, and progress is reviewed on a monthly basis. Improving self-esteem, learning practical living and social skills, and achieving functional literacy skills are among the educational objectives of this reformatory.

Mt. McGregor Correctional Facility, a medium security prison for males, enrolls over 900 students a year. The educational staff consists of more than 20 teachers in the areas of vocational education, GED, ABE, pre-GED, various commercial subjects, and ESL. There are also part-time teachers, volunteer and inmate tutors. Students are assessed according to their results on the Tests of Adult Basic Education (TABE), California Achievement Test, and GED tests. The curriculum is comprised of Adult Functional Competencies including personal, occupational, family, home and social awareness. Substance abuse issues are also integrated into classroom instruction as part of the facilities' substance abuse program. A Volunteer Tutor Program is offered and coordinated by a teacher. Volunteers include inmates, whose function is to enhance literacy skills of students below a 5th grade reading level.

There are also statewide prison initiatives. Maryland state prisons contain about 25,000 incarcerated men and women, 95 percent being male. Three quarters are high school dropouts, and about 20 percent were arrested on drug-related crimes. Over 10,000 prisoners per year receive the services of Maryland's Correctional Education Program. Administration and funding are provided by Maryland's State Department of Education. Employees include approximately 200 full-time teachers, librarians, administrators and secretaries. Community college and contractual employees round out the correctional education staff. Because of space limitations, only about 20 percent of inmates are able to receive services on a daily basis and only 40 percent are provided any services at all. Case managers direct student assessment. Prisoners lacking a high school diploma and are at least 18 years of age are required to participate in educational programs. Priority is then given to younger inmates. Maryland's Correctional Education Program has been nationally recognized for several of its initiatives including peer tutoring and an accountability system.

The inmate population of Ohio has grown from 10,000 in 1971 to about 50,000 presently. Males and females are housed, although males make up the vast majority of convicts at about 94 percent. Seventy-five to eighty percent dropped out of high school, most are guilty of non-violent crimes and have a history of substance abuse. The School System employs over 500 teachers, counselors, and administrators and serves over 13,000 students per year. It is mandatory for inmates who lack a high school diploma to take part in the education program. In addition to academic subjects, The Ohio School System has enacted a Positive Solutions program to address inmate's cognitive and social skills. About 12 sites are equipped for and utilize distance learning.

In Texas nearly 700,000 adults are imprisoned, on parole, probation or are otherwise supervised. Of the 135,000 who are in prison, 94 percent are male and the average educational level is just below the 8th grade. Correctional education falls under the auspices of The Wyndham School District, employing about 1,600 professionals and para-professionals. Nearly 30,000 inmates of prisons and jails are enrolled in correctional education every day.

Not only are convicts enrolled in the more typical courses, but Wyndham also confers career, technical and vocation certificates, GEDs, associates, bachelors as well as master's degrees. The 87 libraries within the system circulated over 1.1 million books, newspapers and magazines in 2001. Job readiness training, job search workshops and job fairs are apart of Wyndham's pre- and post-release employability program, Project RIO. The project has been so successful that Georgia, New Mexico and Oklahoma have followed suit by developing their own inmate employability programs.

Women's Prison and County Jails

Both women's prisons and county jails have traditionally been ignored. While each provides the typical GED, ABE, and/or ESL classes, specialty programs are virtually non-existent. As with most things, there are exceptions to this rule. The Massachusetts Department of Corrections provides a parenting program at two of the women's facilities. The program was created to meet the needs of offenders suffering from mental and substance abuse problems. Participants live in separate dormitory-style facilities, and may have children less than 24 months of age live with them. Inmates learn parenting skills and attend substance abuse groups. The hope is that, upon release, participants will become effective, productive parents and citizens.

The Central California Women's Facility in Chowchilla offers another innovation. Rather than have inmates participate in typical vocational education courses, Chowchilla provides a certification program in the manufacture of dental prostheses. The program receives no legislative funding. It is self-supporting through the inmates' products and services. Not only are students learning useful skills, but the prison also benefits by having participants offer dental prostheses and services to needy inmates.

The specialty program offered at the Plymouth County Jail in Massachusetts is focused on the re-integration of prisoners. Prisoners within 3 to 6 months of release are housed in a separate facility from the general population. They are offered job-training services, and provided with post-release treatment to address problems, which contributed to their incarceration.

Professional Development/Enhancement

The Journal of Correctional Education supplies articles on new and innovative knowledge and practices. The Center for the Study of Correctional Education, California State University, San Bernardino offers professional growth and development courses as well as a degree program for those interested in becoming correctional educators. There are a host of other resources available such as the National Institute for Literacy Education, Correction Connection and the National Institute for Correctional Education (NICE).

The National Institute for Correctional Education (2007) is currently in the developmental stage of, a model curriculum for a master's degree in correctional education…[that] will enable educators to teach more effectively in a correctional setting. Broad competencies would enable educators to more effectively and efficiently understand the discipline and content and plan accordingly; understand the learner and plan accordingly; understand and use appropriate instructional strategies and communication techniques; understand assessment; reflect on his or her performance and seek to grow professionally; and build linkages with others to establish a learning community.

Although there is no certification required for adult educators, a college degree is generally necessary. For those teaching vocational education courses, a background in the field is mandatory. In addition, personality characteristics such as dedication, determination, and patience are essential for correctional instructors. While safety is not an issue, correctional educators do have to contend with learning difficulties, behavior problems, budgetary constraints and frequent interruptions due to lawyer visits, court appearances and lock downs. Professional development and affiliation with professional organizations is of paramount importance for correctional educators. The Correctional Education Association (CEA) (2007) provides workshops, conferences, and professional development opportunities.

The American Correctional Association (ACA) and CEA created standards for juvenile facilities, jails and prisons, which lead to accreditation by the associations. The ACA standards of 2004 include: educational philosophy and goals, communication skills, general education, basic academic skills, GED preparation, special education, vocational education, and postsecondary education. Library services should also be provided in adult facilities, comparable to those found in public libraries:

- Logical organization of materials for convenient use
- Circulation of materials to satisfy the needs of users
- Information services
- Reader's advisory services
- Promotion of library services
- Book lists
- Special programs
- Book and film discussion groups
- Music programs
- A congenial atmosphere
- Educational and recreational audiovisual material

Conclusion

Correctional Education has a long and esteemed history, marked by constant philosophical and ideological changes. Innovators such as Benjamin Brockway set the stage for a demanding yet rewarding profession. Challenges such as under-funded budgets, inequality in educational offerings, misdiagnosis of prisoners with learning disabilities, and technological security issues are very real. These are the same problems faced by almost every other educator whether a prep school teacher, an academician, or a teacher of the incarcerated. The good news is that support networks, as well as professional development organizations, such as the Correctional Education Association (CEA), American Correctional Association (ACA), and the National Institute of Correctional Education (NICE) are available for the Correctional Education professional.

Attributes that are musts for those entering the field include tenacity, flexibility, creativity, and most of all a good sense of humor. Add to these qualities, educational preparation, willingness to develop oneself professionally, and the ability to show respect to incarcerated students. Education just may be the key to changing the lives of prisoners.

References

Chappell, C. (2004). Post-secondary correctional education and recidivism: A meta-analysis of research conducted 1990-1999. *Journal of Correctional Education, 55*(2), 148-169.

Correctional Education Association. (2007). *Performance standards for correctional education programs.* Retrieved July 27, 2008, from http://www.ceanational.org/standards.htm

Department of Corrections (DOCS) Today. (n.d.). *Elmira*. Retrieved July 27, 2008, from http://www.correctionhistory.org/html/chronicl/docs2day/elmira.html

Gehring, T. (2000). Recidivism as a measure of correctional education program success. *Journal of Correctional Education, 51*(2), 197-205.

Gehring, T., & Eggleston, C. (1996). Educational programs. In M.D. McShane & F.P. Williams (Eds.), *Encyclopedia of American Prisons* (pp.180-187). NY: Garland Publishing, Inc.

Haulard, E. (2001). Adult education: A must for our incarcerated population. *Journal of Correctional Education, 52*(4), 157-159.

Klein, S., & Tolbert, M. (2004). *Correctional education: Common measures of performance*. MPR Associates, Inc. Retrieved July 27, 2008, from http://www.mprinc.com/pubs/pdf/common_measures_of_perf.pdf

LoPinto, B. (2007) *Literacy behind bars: Results from the 2003 national assessment of adult literacy prison survey*. Retrieved July 27, 2008, from, http://nces.ed.gov/pubsearch/pubsinfo.asp?pubid=2007473

Prison Literacy Model Programs. (n.d.). Retrieved July 27, 2008, from http://www.tecweb.org/vault/white/prison4.html

National Institute of Correctional Education. (2007). Retrieved July 27, 2008, from http://nicic.org/

Nuttall, J., Hollmen, L., & Staley, E. (2003). The effect of earning a GED on recidivism rates. *Journal of Correctional Education, 54*(3), 90-95.

Sheridan, M., & Steele-Dadzie, T. (2005). Structure of intellect and learning style of incarcerated youth assessment: A means to providing a continuum of educational service in juvenile justice. *Journal of Correctional Education, 56*(4), 347-371.

Steurer, S. (1996). Correctional education: A worthwhile investment. *LINKAGES: Linking Literacy & Learning Disabilities, 3(2)*. Retrieved July 27, 2008, from http://www.nifl.gov/nifl/ld/archive/vol3no2.html#Correctional%20Education

Tolbert, M. (2004). *State correctional educational programs: State policy update*. Retrieved July 27, 2008, http://www.nifl.gov/nifl/policy/st_correction_02.html

Vacca, J. (2004). Educated prisoners are less likely to return to prison. *Journal of Correctional Education, 55*(4), 297-305.

Young, D., & Mattucci, R. (2006). Enhancing the vocational skills of incarcerated women through a plumbing maintenance program. *Journal of Correctional Education, 57*(2), 126-140.

Zaro, D. (2007). Teaching strategies for the self-actualized correctional educator: The inside person vs. the outside person. *Journal of Correctional Education, 58*(1), 27-41.

Chapter 6

U.S. Public Libraries and Museums

Monita G. Hara and Gia D. Johnson

Introduction

The library is an artifact of our historical landscape that offers unique perspectives on important themes in the development of American culture; the history of leisure and work; the emergence of the professions; the formation of gender, class, and racial identities; the evolution of civic architecture; and the organization of knowledge and intellectual property (Carpenter & Augst, 2003). Adult learning extends beyond traditional formal education in schools and universities. Public libraries and museums offer many additional educational opportunities (Humes, 1996). They provide learning opportunities for all types of people with various educational needs and preferences. Throughout this chapter we will explore the various means by which museums and libraries promote lifelong learning for adults.

Libraries: Memory Palaces for All

In the early 1730s America, books were rare and expensive. Even individuals of moderate means could not afford to purchase books. This was soon to change due to the efforts of Benjamin Franklin. In the summer of 1731, Franklin and members of a philosophical association called *Junto* wrote the *Articles of Agreement* to form a library company. The company realized that they could use their combined purchasing power to buy books. So, under the Articles of Agreement, 50 subscribers invested 40 shillings each to start a library, promised to pay 10 schillings more each year, and to maintain the library (The Electric Ben Franklin, 2007).

The earliest works in the Library's collection were books dealing with either religious or educational topics. However, the company's first subscribers were also interested in politics, philosophy, history, geography, poetry, exploration, science, theology and business according to the oldest surviving catalog of the Library Company holdings dated in 1741. The first subscription library was only open on Saturdays from 4 to 8 pm. Members of the Library Company could borrow books freely and non-members could also borrow books, if they put up a surety (The Electric Ben Franklin, 2007). By the 1740s several other American cities had begun forming their own libraries. Benjamin Franklin indicated that Libraries improved the general conversation of Americans (The Electric Ben Franklin, 2007).

Andrew Carnegie should receive the credit for establishing U.S public libraries as we know them today. Born in Dumferline, Scotland in 1835, Carnegie moved with his family to the United States as a young boy. His belief in the value of the library system began when he was young. His father, a weaver by trade, devised one of the first workplace literacy programs where one weaver read aloud while the others worked. After migrating to Allegheny, Pennsylvania, Carnegie also benefited from the free membership of the Mechanics' and Apprentices' Library, which was established by Colonel James Anderson for working class men and boys (Webster & Wilkins, 2000).

Carnegie founded his first free library in the town of his birth, Dunfermline, Scotland, on July 27, 1881. This gift was so well received that Carnegie began to put into motion the giving of libraries to other cities. The second library was built in Braddock, PA in 1889 and was fully funded by the Carnegie Corporation. The Carnegie Steel Company had located its major steel mills in Braddock, Pennsylvania, so the steelworkers and their families were the primary users of this library. The third library was given to Carnegie's adopted hometown of Allegheny, PA.

Unlike the first two U.S. libraries, the City of Allegheny was required to subsidize this library, making it the first publicly funded Carnegie library in the world. On April 20, 1899, Carnegie established his fourth free library in Carnegie Burrough, Pennsylvania by a Declaration of Trust agreement as the Library's legal charter (About Carnegie Corporation, 2007).

Carnegie's philanthropy founded free libraries in the late 19th and early 20th centuries throughout the English-speaking world, including the United States, the United Kingdom, Australia, and New Zealand (Carnegie Libraries of California, 2004). Of these 1,926 were located in the United States (at least one in every state except Rhode Island), 660 in Britain and Ireland, and 156 in Canada. There are a few Carnegie libraries built in places like New Zealand, the West Indies and the Fiji as well, but he built a total of 2,811 free libraries in all (Nasaw, 2006).

Roots of Literacy Education in Library Adult Education

The adult education movement for literacy in libraries evolved from three main sources. First, the 1919 Report of the Adult Education Committee of the British Ministry of Reconstruction gave worldwide visibility to adult education. Secondly, the experience of the American Library Association (ALA) in providing books and advisory services to servicemen during World War I opened public librarians' eyes to the effectiveness of reading guidance. The third source appeared when Fredrick P. Keppel, president of the Carnegie Corporation of New York, commissioned William S. Learned to study the potential of the American public as an agency for adult education. Learned's publication entitled *The American Public Library and the Diffusion of Knowledge* in 1924 set the rationale for the public library to assume its place in adult education. With the Carnegie Corporation being willing to support ALA's Reading With a Purpose program, a series of planned reading programs began which were the first official step in library adult education (Monroe & Heim, 1991).

With Carnegie support, ALA produced a major study of adult education in 1926. This study reported that the field of adult education should include three guidelines:

- the development of consulting and advisory services to those adults that wished to conduct their own education
- the provision of informational services concerning all the adult education available in the community
- and the furnishing of books and other reading materials required by the community providers of adult education (Houle, 1992).

Fredrick Keppel and the Carnegie Corporation were not viewed by everyone as the best ones to lead such a revolutionary concept. Some of the conservative ALA leadership felt that the outside leadership from the Carnegie Corporation was dominating in nature. However, Alvin Johnson's *The Public Library — A People's University*, sponsored by the Carnegie Corporation, was published in 1938 and urged an activist role for library adult education.

The last major effort of the Carnegie Corporation to assist in integrating adult education into library services came during the corporation's 1938 Princeton conference. Monroe and Heim (1991) listed some of the conclusions from the 1938 Princeton conference of the public librarians and adult education specialists:

- The importance of diffusing the adult education responsibility throughout the entire library, rather than relying on a special department
- Offering library services to groups as well as individuals
- Availability of more readable materials for the non-specialist reader
- Addition of films to the library collection
- Community analysis as the basis for planning library activities
- And, the infusion of the adult education point of view into basic library education courses.

In 1939 and 1940, the political events in Europe moved American democracy front and center. A new phase began in adult education in libraries with a focus on citizenship and critical thinking. In June of 1942, the ALA Board approved in June 1942, a new responsibility on the adult reader by proclaiming that books with socially significant questions should be available in abundance. In 1945, the University of Chicago sponsored the Great Books program to promote discussion on war and postwar issues. Monies donated by the Ford Foundation's Fund for Adult Education helped establish the ALA American Heritage Project in 1951, so by 1954, 13 percent of the public libraries were having Great Books discussion groups (Monroe & Heim, 1991).

U.S. Public Libraries

The closest you will ever come in this life to an orderly universe is a good library.
~~ Ashleigh Brilliant

Helen Lyman Smith's 1954 benchmark study compiled a comprehensive list of activities that public libraries used in serving adults (Houle, 1992). Houle (1992) reported that the primary functions of public libraries may be divided into four periods:

- 1854-1875: the Library began as a single purpose institution with education as its central aim
- 1875-1920: the Library became a multipurpose institution where education, recreation, and reference eventually took precedence over education
- 1920-1955: the Library entered a period of appraisal attempts were made to revitalize its educational objective
- 1955-1964: the Library placed major emphasis on its educational aims and less on it recreational aims.

Moore (1963) focused on the third period of the public library's development. Moore maintained that libraries are institutions of learning but set her focus on a framework of the broader adult educational movement. Her work showed two sides: the evangelism of some proponents of library adult education and the antagonism towards the library as a vehicle for adult education in case studies of library programs in California, Maryland, and New York.

Events Shaping Adult Education in Public Libraries

The Adult Education Act of 1966 defined the term adult education as adult basic education, and included programs to develop speaking, reading, writing the English language in order to get or retain employment, and to generally help adults be better able to meet their responsibilities (Adult Education Act, 1966). The Adult Education Act of 1966 (Title III of the Elementary and Secondary Education Amendments of 1966) reinforced a thrust in public library service that began as early as the mid-nineteenth century as the public library tried to meet the diverse need of individuals in the context of social necessities and community readiness.

The purpose of the 1966 Act was to encourage and expand basic educational programs for adults, enabling them to overcome English language limitations, improve occupational competence, and to become more productive and responsible citizens.

Programs were designed for individuals over 18 years of age, with less than 12 years of formal education, and not currently enrolled in school. This act strengthened the role of the public libraries in providing adult basic education. Under the new act, public libraries, in cooperation with public schools were eligible to receive federal dollars to develop adult basic education programs. This partnership proved significant for public libraries and adult basic education (Monroe & Heim, 1991).

Literacy projects in libraries have had various levels of federal support through the Department of Education's Office of Library Programs. Three major programmatic bases of strength for literacy administered by the Office of Library Programs over the last twenty-five years are: the Library Research and Demonstration Program Title II-B of the Higher Education Act (HEA), Library Services Construction Act (LSCA) Title I, and LSCA Title IV.

The following programs funded under Title II-B Library R&D were chosen to demonstrate links between libraries and adult basic education, development of literacy materials, and an understanding of the needs of new readers: The Right to Read for Adults, a cooperative program with Model Cities and Adult Basic Education of the Department of the City School District of Rochester (1972); Cooperative Planning to Maximize Adult Basic Education Opportunities through Public Library Extension in Appalachian North Carolina (1972-73); The Interrelating of Library and Basic Educational Services for Disadvantaged Adults (1972-73); and Libraries in Literacy (1979-80), a survey of literacy programs in libraries to develop a base of information on the nature and extent of literacy activities in libraries (McCook, 1992).

The Library Services Construction Act (LSCA) has supported literacy projects, identified the extent to which libraries were involved in literacy education and supported community-based efforts rooted in an analysis of state and local needs. The LSCA Title I also supported literacy approaches to three programmatic types: community literacy, technology, and one-to-one tutoring. Community literacy, a concept that assumes education is inseparable from students' lives outside the classroom, was the basis for several LSCA supported programs including the Prince George's County (Maryland) Community Library Information Center. Technology-oriented programs focus on the interactive use of computers and videodisc technology as exemplified by the Massachusetts Board of Library Commissioners in their 1987 LSCA plan, which proposed development of literacy programming for grade levels 0 to 4.

One-to-one tutoring models were also given a strong emphasis through the mid-eighties from successful programs which are identified and codified in the 1985 Department of Education supported publication, Effective Adult Literacy Programs: A Practitioner's Guide (McCook, 1992).

Title IV of the LSCA meets the diverse literacy needs in communities and states across the nation through grant programs. They are designed to initiate, continue, expand, or improve literacy services. These projects fall into seven approaches:

1. Collaboration, cooperation, and coalition building. Libraries facilitate involvement with and coordination of literacy activities among various entities such as public schools, community colleges, social welfare agencies, and individual volunteers.

2. Public awareness. Library-based literacy initiatives usually include a public awareness component designed to inform the public of the availability of literacy services or materials, recruit students and tutors, or publicize the effects of illiteracy on the individual and society.

3. Training. Libraries use the LSCA Title VI funds to establish or increase the number of training workshops for volunteers who will provide instruction to adult new learners.

4. Collection development. Librarians constantly monitor their collections, as demand grows for more and better literacy materials suitable for new learners.

5. Technology-Assisted approaches. Electronic media and audiovisual materials offer another means by which adults can improve their reading, writing, and computational skills. Technologically-assisted instruction supplements one-on-one tutorials and workbook approaches are supported by LSCA Title VI.

6. Special instructional components. Tailored to specific community needs, some LSCA Title VI projects have made special use of locally developed ideas and materials.

7. Employment-Oriented projects. An increasing number of LSCA Title VI projects have workplace- or employment-oriented literacy as a focus (McCook, 1992).

National Partners for Libraries and Literacy

The American Library Association supports the achievement of national literacy through educational activities utilizing the historical and cultural experience of libraries and librarians and urges state library agencies to address the problems of illiteracy and give high priority to solutions in their short- and long-range plans for library development and their use of federal and state funds. ALA has alliances with other community agencies involving all family members in a library-based family literacy project and it has been the focus of the Bell Atlantic/ALA Family Literacy Project. The project awarded $5,000 grants to twenty-five libraries in 1990 to enhance family literacy projects. The projects represent a team approach between librarian, adult basic education specialist or literacy provider, and a community representative from Bell Atlantic. The team approach ensures that a network of service providers is established, that several areas of expertise are represented and that local community needs are addressed (McCook, 1992).

The Bell Atlantic/ALA Family Literacy Project grant recipients during 1990-91 represented a wide-range of libraries in the Mid-Atlantic region. For example: (1) the Wilmington (Delaware) Library strengthened an extant Literacy Volunteers of America program; (2) the Martin Luther King Memorial Library (District of Columbia, Anacostia Branch) worked with local public schools to provide individual and shared learning opportunities for parents and children; (3) three counties cooperated through the Southern Maryland Regional Library Association to extend the Mommy Read to Me literacy program; (4) the Books for Babes project through the South Brunswick (New Jersey) Public Library distributed book packets to new mothers; (5) the Free Library of Philadelphia sponsored a book and film discussion series for adult learners and their families; (6) the Rockbridge Regional Library in rural Virginia included sixteen hours of parenting classes at the library using a whole language approach, with transportation and childcare provided; and (7) story times were provided by the Elkins-Randolph Public Library (West Virginia) at the Women's Aid in Crisis, a domestic violence shelter (McCook, 1992).

In 1979, the White House Conference on Library and Information Services (WHCLIS) passed a resolution on literacy, which called for the expansion of literacy programs at community levels, identification of effective library adult literacy programs, coordination of library programs, cooperation among public educational agencies and joint planning (Monroe & Heim, 1991). So to combat illiteracy, the American Library Association formed the Coalition for Literacy in 1981. The goals of the coalition were (1) to inform the nation of the illiteracy problem and solutions and (2) to establish a literacy information and referral service. The National Advertising Council, Inc. joined with the Coalition for Literacy for three years to promote this campaign to recruit leaders, national partners, tutors, and volunteers and to encourage support to eliminate illiteracy (Chobot, 2000).

Outreach Efforts to Serve Special Populations

Today, outreach services are offered free as a way to provide services to targeted populations or to persons that may not have access to traditional library services. The National Library Service for the Blind and Physically Handicapped of the Library of Congress provides books and magazines in Braille and on recorded discs and cassettes free to readers who cannot hold or handle books or see well enough to read conventional print because of a temporary or permanent visual or physical handicap.

In most states there are special libraries that provide the Talking Book Service, such as the Alabama Library for the Blind and Physically Handicapped. Many libraries or state agencies also offer descriptive videos for the blind, which are videos with narration added in the sound track. For blind and visually impaired students of all ages, Brailled textbooks and audiotapes for classroom instruction are available. This service is usually provided through the state schools for the blind. In Alabama, the Instructional Resource Center serves as the resource (Alabama Institute for Deaf and Blind, 2006), which is located on the Alabama School for the Blind campus in Talladega.

In addition to these services, many public libraries have computers that are accessible for the visually impaired. The computers are equipped with special software that reads aloud what is on the screen called screen reader software. The latest versions of Microsoft programs also have accessible screen reading features, as well as, the capability to make the font size very large.

Libraries also supply materials to correctional facilities, to nursing homes, offer book titles for non-English speaking library users, and provide bookmobiles for rural areas. They offer many other programs that reach out to special populations. These include (1) family literacy activities such as the Early Literacy Center at the Framingham Public Library (Massachusetts) and the Homework Center at the DeKalb Library System in Decatur, Georgia; (2) young adult literacy efforts such as peer group tutoring at the Englewood Public Library in New Jersey; (3) disabled literacy efforts such as the TDD (telecommunications device for the deaf) installed at the Contact Literacy Center literacy hotline or extension of services to the developmentally disabled through the Mansfield-Richfield County Public Library in Ohio; (4) institutionalized literacy efforts such as the technology-based Literacy Center at the Oakhill Correctional Institution in Madison, Wisconsin, that was replicated at public libraries throughout the state; and (5) efforts to reach people with limited English-speaking ability such as ESL (English as a Second Language) tutoring through the Bergenfield Public Library in New Jersey (McCook, 1992).

In the mid 1990s, Arlington County Public Library (ACPL) in Virginia launched satellite collections and weekly story times at four of the county's Bilingual Outreach Centers. The Centers are located in apartment complexes with large immigrant populations. They were established by the county to assist with adjustment to life in a new culture. The programs, collections, and services at the Centers acquaint immigrants with the services available through the library system. Initially funded with grants from the Virginia State Library, the U.S. Department of Education, Community Development Block Grants, Friends of the Library, and the Outreach Centers' libraries are now funded by ACPL's operating budget (McMurrer & Terrill, 2001).

Libraries Move into 21st Century Cyberspace

Carnegie changed the physical landscape and made libraries accessible to everyone, but Bill Gates is making the 21st Century libraries available to low income communities. Microsoft Corporation's Bill Gates has emerged as the Digital Age philanthropist, by establishing the Gates Library Foundation and by offering $200 million over five years to bring computers into libraries in poor areas of the U.S. The Gates Foundation has provided computers and software for many public libraries throughout the country (Atkinson, Ryan, Harris & Stack, 1997).

According to the American Library Association there are an estimated 117,859 libraries. This number includes college and university libraries; special libraries such as medical, legal, religious libraries, K-12, and branch libraries (American Library Association, 2007). Nationwide, public libraries had over 711 million books and serial volumes in their collections, or 2.8 volumes per capita (Chute & Kroe, 1999). The 1998 statistics (American Library Association, 2007) on library users show that people 18 years and older nationwide made up 64 percent of the library cardholders. Of the 18 to 34 years age group, 70 percent were library cardholders; of the 35 to 54 years of age group, 72 percent were cardholders; and in the 55+ years of age group, 48 percent held library cards. On the subject of libraries with Internet access, 73 percent were connected, 17 percent were connected but had no public access, and 10 percent were not connected to the Internet (Chute & Kroe, 1999).

The public library of today is once again reaching out to the communities that they serve. Many times the library provides the only access to the Internet available to many low-income families. Across the U.S., libraries also subscribe to premium Web sites and databases that charge fees that few people could afford in their own homes. With technology changes, traditional library values remain such as access to information, intellectual freedom, and protection of privacy. Internet services have actually become a new attraction for libraries by pulling in visitors seeking objective information and by not being subjected to commercialism (Rodger, D'Elia, & Jorgensen, 2001).

In a telephone survey of 3,097 adults conducted by Rodger, D'Elia, and Jorgensen (2001) with funding from the Institute of Museum and Library Services to the Regents of the State of New York in the spring of 2000, it was found that 75.2 percent of Internet users also used the library and 60.3 percent of the library users also used the Internet. Forty percent of the survey participants used both the library and the Internet (Rodger, D'Elia, & Jorgensen, 2001).

A new high-tech trend for library users has emerged. Many libraries across the U.S. are offering 24/7 electronic book (eBook) downloads which the White Plains, New York Public Library introduced in 2004. The Library's eBook collection includes bestsellers, fiction and nonfiction from popular publishers such as Harper Collins, McGraw-Hill, and Jossey-Bass Publishers. In addition to popular titles there are self-help, travel, business, study guides, and more. To date, the Library is loaning about 1,000 eBooks per month (White Plains Public Library, 2007).

According to the White Plains Public Library web site, to check out an eBook one needs a valid White Plains Library card, a device to read the eBook such as a PDA, PC, Mac or laptop computer, free reader software such as Adobe Reader or Mobipocket Reader, and the ability to connect to the Internet from home or work. The lending period is usually 21 days and 10 eBooks can be checked out at any given time. eBooks are checked in automatically at the end of the loan period so a library user never has to worry about late notices or fines. By late 2004, the Library will offer digital audio books for download. This service will allow users to listen to popular audio books on a variety of devices such as PDAs PCs etc. (White Plains Public Library, 2007).

The librarians of today are indeed the ultimate search engines that help U.S. citizens regardless of income, education, age, or hometown. Twenty-first century information services require 21st century librarians (Ercolano, 2007; Minkel, 2004; Steinberg & Mofford, 2006). Librarians of today, just as librarians of past times, continue to serve as the gatekeepers for adult education. Libraries provide a central community location that accepts individuals without conditions. Any individual seeking self-development can use library resources and work with literacy educators in a neutral environment. The supportive reinforcement of materials and individuals willing to provide one-on-one assistance articulates well with programs developed by adult educators. First Lady Barbara Bush in the opening ceremony of the White House Conference on Libraries and Information Sciences on July 10, 1991 said: "Libraries are really one of the greatest gifts that the American people have ever given themselves. They're a gift for all of us----no restrictions of age or gender or class or interest."

Museums

Museums in the United States cover the full range of human thought and emotion. Each museum has its own unique purpose and its own distinctive nature. Museums are inherently education-oriented, just as public libraries; they serve as venues for adult education. Museums provide education to all age groups and backgrounds which is its core mission. Museums are also viewed as centers of learning, civic institutions, as well as protectors of our artistic, historic, scientific, and cultural heritage.

U.S. Museums: Working in the Public Interest to Educate All

According to the American Association of Museums (1999), the federal government in the Museum and Library Services Act defines a museum as a public or private nonprofit agency or institution organized on a permanent basis for essentially educational or aesthetic purposes, which, utilizing a professional staff, owns or utilizes tangible objects, cares for them, and exhibits them to the public on a regular basis. The Institute of Museum and Library Services (IMLS) uses the Museum and Library Services Act definition as the basis for determining which museums are eligible to receive federal funding from IMLS. A museum must:

- Be organized as a public or private nonprofit institution that exists on a permanent basis for essentially educational or aesthetic reasons

- Care for and own or use tangible objects, whether animate or inanimate, and exhibit these objects on a regular basis through facilities that it owns or operates

- Have at least one professional staff member or the full-time equivalent, whether paid or unpaid, whose primary responsibility is the acquisition, care or exhibition of the public of objects owned or used by the museum
- Be open and provide museum services to the general public for at least 120 days a year

The American Association of Museums (AAM) is the accreditation arm of museums. To participate in the AAM Accreditation Program a museum must meet the following criteria:

- Be a legally organized nonprofit institution or part of a nonprofit institution or government entity
- Be essentially educational in nature
- Have a formally stated mission

- Have one full-time paid professional staff member who has museum knowledge and experience. This individual has delegated authority and allocates the financial resources in order to operate the museum effectively
- Present regularly scheduled programs and exhibits that use and interpret objects for the public according to accepted standards
- Have a formal and appropriate program of documentation, care, and use of collections and/or tangible objects
- Have a formal and appropriate program or presentation and maintenance of exhibits

According to AAM, of the nation's nearly 16,000 museums, 750 are currently accredited. AAM also reports that of this estimated number of museums in the United States, there are more than 850 million visits per year (American Association of Museums, 1999).

Types of People Who Attend Museums

Museum programs attract thousands of people each year. Some people are seeking experiences that can lead to personal growth and transformation, while others come to learn something new, to be entertained, and/or to socialize. Knowledge seekers, socializers, skill builders, and museum lovers are also among those who are attracted to museums. Knowledge Seekers demonstrate a strong desire to learn new things. They seek challenging content, a broad array of learning activities, and additional resources that allow them to follow up their interests.

Socializers attend museum programs for social interaction. They attend programs to get to know people with similar interests. Skill Builders like to learn by doing and want high-quality training. Their goal is to improve specific skills and gain new ones. Museum lovers involve a distinct group of adult museum program participants who love the museum and everything it stands for. They also volunteer in several areas of the museum (Burton, Fellenz, Gittins-Carlson, Lewis-Mahony, Sachatello-Sawyer, & Woolbaugh, 2002).

Museum Programs

Museums offer valuable learning activities. With every activity adults learn from the variety of programs offered at these museums. Burton et al. (2002) outlined some of the programs offered at museums and included the following:

- Lectures are the most common type of adult programs offered in museums. They are the easiest to plan, economical to run, and can efficiently meet the museum's educational mission by presenting relevant material to large numbers of adults over a short period of time. For example, the National Gallery of Art

Friday evening lectures introduce a provocative idea in thirty minutes, followed by a reception that allows participants to discuss ideas.

- A guided tour in the museum is one of the most distinctive, long-standing educational programs offered by American museums. A staff member, docent, or volunteer usually conducts a guided tour. A brief overview of the entire museum or a more intensive tour of a mini gallery, exhibit hall, or special event may be offered for the participants.

- The Historic Alexandria Candlelight tours in the Washington DC area invite adults to explore five historic homes decorated for the holidays.

- Gallery Demonstrations are presentations given within a museum gallery or exhibition hall and may or may not be directly related to an exhibit. They are generally open to all visitors regardless of age. Some programs even provide a hands-on learning experience by allowing observers to try an activity themselves.

- The Buffalo Bill Historical Center offers demonstrations on a daily basis through their summer artists-in-residence programs. Artists are situated in various galleries and exhibition halls to demonstrate their crafts.

- Docent training is critical because the docent may be the only museum representative with whom visitors interact, apart from the person who collects their admission fee. Some docent-training programs emphasize personal development, while others focus on content. Some programs are quite structured, while others are more flexible and rely on docents to be self-directed learners. The objective of the training is to educate docents about the museum's collections and to train them in the best ways of presenting that material to the public.

- The McNay Art Museum in San Antonio once offered a mini-course, Low-Fat Art History, that consisted of a series of eight evening programs surveying art through history. The participants could receive twelve hours of graduate credit for completing the course.

- Teacher workshops offer some type of teacher-training programs. Programs may include weekend courses, one-day workshops, or one- to three-day conferences. Most programs offer teacher certification or graduate credit hours.

- The National Gallery of Art in Washington, D.C., offers a six-day interdisciplinary course for both teachers and administrators. Courses address a central topic, bringing together educators from across the country to study, reflect, and learn with colleagues.

- Collaborative programs offer arrangements between museums and businesses, schools, community groups, government agencies, other organizations and often lead to innovative and successful programming. By sharing staff, resources, and clientele, collaborators can produce community-wide events that would otherwise be beyond reach.

- In Tacoma, Washington, the Consortium Partnership linked the Washington State Historical Society, KCTS-Seattle Public TV, and the University of

Washington Press for the purpose of producing products related to the centennial celebration of Mt. Rainer National Park. Working together, they created an exhibit with related educational programs, a documentary film, and a book.

- Some other programs include: workshops for the general public, performing arts, seminars, film series, classes, community service, outreach programs, programs for adults with special needs, virtual travel programs, theater programs, festivals and special events, travel and adventure programs, certificate programs, books signings, discussions, and readings.

These programs can motivate adults into learning new activities, enhance awareness of museums, and will continue to influence adults' future decisions about learning long after the program's end (Burton et al., 2002).

Prominent Museums

The art museum has had a rich literature so far as lifelong education is concerned.
~~ Cyril O. Houle

Huntington Library, Art Collection and Botanical Gardens

One of the most famous museums in the Unites States is a legacy left by Henry Edwards Huntington — the *Huntington Library, Art Collections and Botanical Gardens*. Huntington was born in Oneonta, New York in 1850 and moved to California in the early decades of the 20th century. Huntington's good fortune came from his Uncle Collis P. Huntington, who was the founder of the Southern Pacific railroad. Collis mentored and supported his nephew, Henry, by giving him his first important job as supervising railroad construction. In 1892, Collis brought Henry to California as his assistant to the Southern Pacific Company.

Later on in 1902, attracted to the beauty of the San Gabrial Valley, he purchased the current *Huntington Library, Art Collections, and Botanical Gardens*, then called the San Marino Ranch for citrus producing and selling. A few years later, he built an elegant mansion to house his rare collection of art and books that he had been assembling since the 1880s. In 1919, Henry said that he wanted to give something to the public before he died, so he bequeathed the 207-acre estate of the mansion, gardens, and library into a public trust to promote and advance learning, the arts and sciences and to promote the public welfare.

In 1920, the library building was built to house Henry's outstanding collection. This includes treasures for research and exhibition such as Ellesmere's manuscript of Chaucher's *Canterbury Tales*, a Guttenburg Bible on vellum, the double elephant folio edition of Audubon's *Birds of America,* and the early editions of Shakespeare's works

(Thorpe, 1994). Inside the mansion are European Art, French and English furniture collections, and many famous works of art from British masters. Two works of art that are housed there are: Sarah Barrett Moultin: Pinkie by Thomas Lawrence (1794) and Jonathan Buttall: The Blue Boy by Thomas Gainborough (1770) (Beard, 2003). The gardens themselves are exquisite with an estimated 15,000 varieties of plants and shrubs. Following the deaths of Henry and Arabella Huntington the institution was then opened to the public. The holdings of furniture and art were enriched even further by bequests and gifts from other wealthy donors (Beard, 2003). "The Huntington" is now one of Southern California's most popular tourist attraction attended by hundreds of thousands of visitors each year from all over the world (Thorpe, 1994).

The Getty Museum

J. Paul Getty was another wealthy businessman that viewed art as a civilizing influence on society and believed in making art available to the public for its edification and enjoyment. Getty made his fortune in the oil industry. He founded the J. Paul Getty Museum in 1953. This museum, established in his ranch house in Malibu, CA, housed collections of Greek and Roman antiquities, 18th century French furniture, and European paintings.

Most of Getty's personal estate passed to a trust in 1982. The trustees sought to make a contribution to the visual arts, so the planning for the Getty Museum, now known as simply the Getty, began when property high atop a hill side in Los Angeles, CA was purchased near the Roman style villa, designed after the 1st century AD Villa dei Papiri. The Getty is 1.2 million square feet and is surrounded by one hundred and ten acres of land. The Italian travertine marble structure offers a panoramic view of the Pacific Ocean, San Gabriel Mountains, and Los Angeles. The Getty is comprised of five interconnected two-story pavilions with natural lighting as an important architectural feature. The exterior courtyards include fountains, Mexican cypress trees, cacti gardens, botanical trees and numerous unusual plants in all sizes, shapes, and species.

The Research Library at the Getty Research Institute focuses on the history of art, architecture, and archeology with relevant materials in the humanities and social sciences. There is a general library collection, which includes more than 800,000 volumes of books, periodicals, and auction catalogs as well as a special collection, known as the Photo Study Collection, which contains rare books, prints, maps, photographs, optical devices, manuscripts, and an archival collection. It also contains around two million study photographs of art and architecture from old world to the 20th century (Research Library, 2007).

The Getty also houses a provenance index. This index compiles databases from the U.S. and Europe that contain transcripts or material from auctions and archival inventories of European works of art. In addition to the beautiful spaces of the Getty, there is a 225-seat restaurant and a 415-seat Café. There is also a 450-seat auditorium where visitors can attend films, lecture colloquia, and musical performances (The Getty Center, 2007).

The Art Institute of Chicago

A museum is known to the world through its treasures. The Art Institute of Chicago's collections of 19th and 20th century European and American art, Japanese woodblock prints, old master prints and drawings, and much more have helped rank this museum as one of the world's most important. In 1879, through the initiative of private citizens, the Chicago Academy of Fine Arts replaced the failing Academy of Design (founded in 1866). Within three years of its founding, the Academy changed its name to The Art Institute of Chicago. In 1887 the museum and its school move into a new building, designed by the Chicago firm Burnham and Root, on the southwest corner of Michigan Avenue and Van Buren Street, to accommodate its growing needs (Wood, 2000).

The museum offers many free programs to the public: the escorts for the blind, lectures, galleries talks, and voices. There are escorts and free guided tours of the museum for visitors with visual impairments. The lectures offer many aspects of the museum's collection, which include slide-illustrated presentations, panel discussions, or conversations, hosted in one of the museums numerous audience halls. The Gallery Talks involve a tour of the highlights of the Art Institute and a thematic talk about one specific area of the museum collection, such as Impressionism. The Lectures make connections between time periods, artists, or a special exhibition. Voices is a regular series in which participant's come to hear locally and nationally known actors read scripts from artists' letters, journals, and writings. Slides and music accompany each reading (The Art Institute of Chicago, 2007).

The museum also offers three programs for Seniors (55 years +): Elderhostel, Art Insights, and Senior Celebrations. Elderhostel is a program that offers stimulating, museum-based exposure to art from around the world. The weeklong program includes gallery talks, thematic lectures, and viewing special exhibitions. Art Insights brings slide talks to senior centers, groups, residences, and nursing homes. The presenters offer talks about the museum's masterpieces for seniors living in the Chicago area. Senior Celebrations is an annual kick-off day held in September for the Art Insights program. Senior Celebrations offer a variety of programs throughout the day, such as slide talks and performances. There are small informal talks in the galleries, painting in the galleries by School of the Art Institute artists, and live music and sketch classes. The programs and collections from The Art Institute of Chicago reveal more than the history of one city's taste; they create a vivid portrait of a museum's ongoing attempt to achieve balance between age-old traditions it preserves and the new ideas and challenges that confront it in our ever-changing world (The Art Institute of Chicago, 2007).

The Smithsonian Institute

In 1846, James Smithson established The Smithsonian in pursuit of the increase and diffusion of knowledge." The Smithsonian Institute is the world's largest museum complex. It houses 16 museums and galleries, and holds more than 142 million artifacts and specimens in its trust for the American people. The Institution is also a center for research. According to the Smithsonian Annual Report for 2003, the Smithsonian website has had 73 million visitors, 24 million visitors to the actual Smithsonian museums, 3.9 million Traveling Exhibition Visitors, 17 museums and galleries, 9 research centers, and 140 affiliate organizations.

The Smithsonian also promotes lifelong learning with many programs, tours, and educational seminars (Smithsonian Education, 2007). Some of the Smithsonian Outreach Program includes: the Asian Pacific American Program (whose purpose is to increase understanding of the Asian-Pacific American experience in Smithsonian exhibitions, programs, and research); Center for Education and Museum Studies (which offers many courses in arts, film, music, performing arts, philosophy, religion, humanities, literature, sciences, personal development, and many more); Center for Folklife and Cultural Heritage (which promotes the understanding and continuity of cultures); Latino Initiatives (which is dedicated to studying the Latino culture); National Science Resources Center (which seeks to improve the teaching of science in the nation); Regional Programs (which takes Smithsonian scholars to schools); Traveling Exhibitions (the largest traveling exhibition service in the world); and many more outreach programs (Smithsonian Education, 2007).

Many research centers also contribute to lifelong learning among adults. Research centers include the: Archives of American Art (maintains materials on the history of the visual arts); Astrophysical Observatory (studies astronomy, astrophysics, earth and space sciences); Center for Materials Research and Education (studies the conservation and analysis of museum collection items); Conservation and Research Center (preserves threatened species and habitats); Environmental Research Center (examines linked ecosystems at the land-sea interface; Marine Station at Fort Pierce (studies the marine ecosystems of Florida); Migratory Bird Center (studies and protects bird migration); and the Tropical Research Institute (studies ecology, behavioral and evolution of tropical organisms) (Smithsonian Education, 2007).

The Smithsonian Institution preserves and showcases the nation's treasures. It presents history in ways that inspire learning. It creates new knowledge through scientific research and exploration and most importantly it brings the Smithsonian experience into communities across the country. Museum professionals use the latest conservation and preservation techniques developed by the Smithsonian. Many students and adult learners participate in Smithsonian research through online field trips, as well as, planned field trips to actual museums. The Smithsonian Museum serves the nation and directly touches American lives (Smithsonian Education, 2007).

Special Museums

There are at least 1,000 museums in this category in the U.S. These museums can also be learning palaces due to their abundance of historical factoids and the entrepreneurial spirit for which they have been established. If nothing else, these museums indicate that if someone is interested in something sooner or later they will probably dedicate a museum to it (Bond, 1995).

There are museums that are small and not so small in virtually every state in the U.S. For example, if one is a music lover then a visit is in store to the *Miles Musical Museum* in Eureka Springs, Arkansas. Here one can meet the family of Floyd Miles and have them fire up everything from a Wurlitzer organ to a Coinola Nickelodeon (Arany & Hobson, 1998). The *Rough and Tumble Museum* in Kinzers, Pennsylvania is where farmers were described in the old days as rough and tumble by being able to fix anything with a little spit and baling wire. The *Ice House Museum* in Cedar Falls, Iowa is where many of the docents are retired icemen (Bond, 1995). Or, if one likes computers, the *Computer Museum of America* in La Mesa, California is where one can find seven decades of computer technology (Arany & Hobson, 1998). Or, the recently moved from California, *Roy Rogers and Dale Evans Museum* located in Branson, Missouri where a lifetime of memorabilia of costumes, stuffed animals, cars, guns, Remington sculptures etc. are on display and where Roy Rogers, Jr. and a new band perform old western songs.

The civil rights struggle in the U.S. is of interest to many that visit America and also Americans themselves. The Birmingham Civil Rights Institute (BCRI) in Birmingham, Alabama is an excellent example of a museum that strives to reach out for diversity and understanding of various cultures and groups and their struggles for civil rights. At the BCRI one can actually relive the civil rights movement via historical information on this era in America's past. Many of the docents are themselves foot soldiers of the Civil Right Era. In addition to the African-Americans struggle the BCRI is also interested in other groups. The BCRI recently hosted a traveling exhibit from Gallaudet University in Washington, D.C. (the only university in the world for deaf students) entitled, History Through Deaf Eyes, which depicted the pictorial history of deaf individuals for education, equality, employment, family, and communication options, as well as, highlighting the tremendous accomplishments that have been made by deaf individuals contributions to the arts. In conjunction with this event, the book entitled *Deaf Artists in America: Colonial to Contemporary by* Deborah M. Sonnenstrahl, winner of the 2003 Benjamin Franklin Award for Education, Teaching, and Academics was formally presented by the author in lecture format at the Birmingham Museum of Art.

Museums and Formal Education Planning

The trend in U.S. museums is to adopt an array of offerings, which can vary with the audience, and to create engagement with the audience such as proposed by The Toledo Museum of Art in Toledo, Ohio. Their approach to planning public offerings addresses different levels of visitor knowledge through the following steps. Step 1 would be to identify the audience group and their current level of involvement or understanding of art based on a community profile/needs and market research. Step 2 is to identify the type of engagement desired from audience group based on the Museum's strategic plan and goals and audience needs. Step 3 refers to determining the interpretive approach and content or idea to be delivered based on audience level of involvement, their likes, needs, and past successes of previous programs. Step 4 would be to select or develop a format to deliver content in a way that produces the desired result based on knowledge of educational theory, learning styles, past program successes, and audience information.

The last step refers to indicators that identify the result is being achieved and evaluating the end result. For example, if there was a total uninitiated general visitor, a goal would be to create a social interaction around the works of art. This could be accomplished through the use of an audio tour and informal, story-telling approach that relates to a central theme. An indicator would be whether or not people talked with each other in the galleries. The end result could be measured through observation and user surveys.

Another example that would use this approach to planning public offering steps would relate to the interested and knowledgeable visitor. The goal could be to inspire deeper connection with the Museum beyond gallery visits. One method to reach this goal would be to encourage participation in Gallery Talks and provide experiences in the galleries and related artist demonstrations or hands-on activities. The indicator for this example could be whether there are regular participants in the Gallery Talk series and enrollment in art classes. The results could be measured through an analysis of class registration roles.

America's museums present the best of the world's culture, heritage, and achievement. They are the nation's premier cultural and educational institutions. Museums provide an opportunity for individuals to discover, learn, remember and have fun. They help define the present, educate for the future and preserve the past (American Association of Museums, 1999). In essence, museums are birthplaces, as well as, life-sustaining paths to lifelong learning for adults or adult education programs.

Conclusion

Libraries play many roles within their community. They provide learning opportunities through library collections, programs, internet access, and outreach services. Libraries make up the only educational system that supports a person from infancy to old age. The core purpose of many museums is to acknowledge and celebrate the people, history, and accomplishments of an area or an era. All types of museum programs have the potential for creating memorable experiences for effective change in participants (Burton et al., 2002). A museum opens the doors to all people to the treasures that it holds inside.

Museums and libraries support the educational goals and needs of the community they serve. They provide lifelong learning while promoting community-based education. People are allowed to access technology and offered many lifelong learning activities at museums and libraries. Museums and libraries offer a wide range of materials and collections to observe or view. They serve as readily- available, valuable and accessible resources for adults to be able to remain engaged in learning at various stages of their lives. Future technological advances will provide the adult learner with even more opportunities for learning within and outside of the walls of both libraries and museums.

References

About Carnegie Corporation. (2007). Retrieved on December 1, 2007 from
http://www.carnegie.org/sub/about/biography.html

Adult Education Act of 1966, Public Law. No. 89-750, § 301-315, Vol. 80.

Alabama Institute for Deaf and Blind. (2006). Retrieved on December 1, 2007 from
http://www.aidb.org/

American Association of Museums. (1999). *About AAM*. Retrieved on December 1, 2007
from http://www.aam-us.org/aboutaam/index.cfm

American Library Association (2007). *Number of Libraries in the United States*. Retrieved
on December 1, 2007 from
http://www.ala.org/ala/alalibrary/libraryfactsheet/alalibraryfactsheet1.cfm

Arany, L., & Hobson, A. (1998). *Little museums over 1,000 small (and not-so-small)
American showplaces*. New York: Henry Holt and Company.

The Art Institute of Chicago. (2007). *Calendar: Featured events*. Retrieved on December 1,
2007 from http://www.artic.edu/aic/calendar/

Atkinson, J., Ryan, P., Harris, P, & Stack, S. (1997). Alabama libraries team up with Gates Foundation to provide computer and internet access in public libraries. Retrieved December 25, 2007 from http://www.gatesfoundation.org/UnitedStates/USLibraryProgram/Announcements/Announce-80.htm

Beard, G. (2003). English furniture at the Huntington library, art collections, and botanical gardens. *Magazine Antiques, June,* 70-79.

Bond, C. (1995). If you can't bear to part with it, open a museum. *Smithsonian, April,* 90-97.

Burton, H., Fellenz, R.A., Gittins-Carlson, L., Lewis-Mahony, J., Sachatello-Sawyer, B., & Woolbaugh, W. (2002). *Adult museum programs: Designing meaningful experiences.* Walnut Creek: AltaMira Press.

Carnegie Libraries of California. (2004). *Andrew Carnegie (1835-1919).* Retrieved on December 1, 2007 from http://www.carnegie-libraries.org/

Carpenter, K., & Augst, T. (2003). The history of libraries in the United States: A conference report. *Libraries & Culture, 38* (1), 61-67.

Chobot, M. (2000). *Public libraries and museums.* In J. Witte (Ed.), Providers of Adult Education (pp. 71-86). San Francisco: Jossey-Bass.

Chute, A., & Kroe, P. (1999). Public libraries in the United States: Fiscal year 1996. *Education Statistics Quarterly, 1*(2), 99-101.

The Electric Ben Franklin. *The Library Company.* Retrieved on December 1, 2007 from http://ushistory.org/franklin/philadelphia/library.htm

Ercolano, A. (2007). But it's not my job...The role librarians play in library development. *Bottom Line: Managing Library Finances, 20*(2), 94-96.

The Getty Center. *Architectural Description.* (2004). Retrieved on December 1, 2007 from http://www.getty.edu/news/press/arch/archdesc.html

Houle, C. (1992). *The literature of adult education.* San Franciso: Jossey-Bass.

Humes, A. (1996). *Public Libraries and Community-based Education: Making the Connection for Lifelong Learning.* Washington, DC: Office of Educational Research and Improvement, U.S. Dept. of Education: U.S. G.P.O., Supt. of Docs.

McCook, K. (1992). Where would we be without them? Libraries and adult education activities: 1966-91. *RQ, 32*(2), 245-253.

McMurrer, E., & Terrill, L. (2001). Library literacy programs for English language learners. National Clearinghouse for ESL Literacy Education, Washington, DC.

Minkel, W. (2004). Tell the world who you are because your community needs to know. *School Library Journal, 50*(1), 31-32.

Monroe, M., & Heim, K. (1991). *Partners for lifelong learning: Public libraries & adult education.* Washington, D.C: U.S. Government Printing Office.

Moore, M. E. (1963). *Library Adult Education: The biography of an idea.* New York: Scarecrow.

Nasaw, D. (2006). *Andrew Carnegie.* New York: Penguin Press.

Research Library. (2007). Retrieved on December 1, 2007 from http://www.getty.edu/research/conducting_research/library/

Rodger, E., D'Elia G., & Jorgensen, C. (2001). The public library and the internet: Is peaceful coexistence possible? *American Libraries, 32*(5), 58-61.

Sonnenstrahl, D. (2003). *Deaf artists in America: Colonial to contemporary.* San Diego, CA: Dawn Sing Press.

Steinberg, M., & Mofford, K. (2006). Librarians as partners. *Teaching Professor, 20*(10), 3-5.

Smithsonian Education. (2007). Retrieved on December 1, 2007 from http://smithsonianeducation.org.

Thorpe, J. (1994). *Henry Edwards Huntington: A biography.* Berkeley, CA: University of California Press.

Webster, L. & Wilkins, B. (2000). A lasting legacy: Florida's Carnegie libraries. *Florida History & The Art, Summer,* 6-18.

White Plains Public Library. (2007). *Digital downloans ebooks & more.* Retrieved on December 1, 2007 from http://www.wppl.lib.ny.us/

Wood, J. (2000). *Treasures from the art institute of Chicago.* New York: Hudson Hills Press.

Chapter 7

Religious Institutions

Robert J. Griffith

Introduction

Butts (1955) indicated that not only schools but the culture educates people through the institutions that they live by and through the guiding beliefs that they come to accept. This is certainly the premise by which today's religious affiliates develop educational programs, although there are multiple motives involved. The church was probably the most influential institutional force for the education of adults in the first two centuries of our national life (Knowles, 1977). Brubacher (1966) reported that religious and moral influences have made themselves felt in educational aims, curriculum, methods of instruction, educational philosophy, and the issue of public versus private schools. Our educational society has been molded from the beginning of this nation until present by religious principles and reason. This chapter reviews the history of religious institutions, examines the framework of religious institutions, and discusses some current programs and content.

History

Pilgrims came to America in search of religious cultural freedom that did not exist in their homeland. Even though many of our politicians and judicial figures in this country choose to forget it, this country and government was founded on religious precepts and statutes. Thus, our educational history is deeply rooted in religious motives and purpose.

During the Roman Empire, Christianity became the official religion. During this time, the Christian Church had all pagan schools either closed or changed into Christian institutions. The Christian Church claimed to be divinely instituted as a teaching agency, from Jesus's mandate to his disciples to go forth and teach all nations. Christianity reoriented the aim of religious and moral instruction and restated the theory of human nature (Brubacher, 1966). Additionally, Christianity exalted the church rather than the state as the principle educational agency. According to Christian principles, a man's relationship with God was more vital than his relationship with the state.

The sixteenth and seventeenth centuries were the backdrop for the religious reformation. Many religious revolts took place to oppose the Catholic Church in Europe. As a result of these revolts, sects such as Lutherans, Calvinists, Puritans,

Presbyterians, and Methodists were born. Those that opposed the Catholic Church or protested were labeled Protestants. This religious reformation in Europe undoubtedly had an impact on America. After all, the colonists that founded this country were ethnically Europeans. The nature of education during this era was due to the predominantly Protestant character of the American colonization (Knowles, 1977). The Puritans settled in New England with a Calvinistic doctrine of theocracy. The Puritans viewed the state as the protector and supporter of the church, thus to do its bidding and enforce its pronouncements (Butts, 1955).

The state of Connecticut imposed the death penalty as instituted from the Bible for various crimes. This theocratic conception of the state made it appropriate for the civil authority to require and support religious education as considered by the Puritans (Butts, 1955). During this era, laws gave voting privileges to males who were both landowners and church members. As a result, the government took on a flavor of those who were religious and landowners. The religious education in this era had but one agenda, teach people how to read. The book used to teach was the Bible, thus two goals were accomplished with one action. Society was learning how to read as well as learning the Gospel. The Bible became the most widely read piece of literature (Sidwell, 1968).

As a result of this literacy movement, the famous Massachusetts Law of 1642 was passed. This law essentially ordered the teaching of all children to read, and parents and masters that did not comply were fined. Many other colonies followed Massachusetts with similar laws. By 1776, most skilled white males in New England were literate.

In 1636, the Puritans founded Harvard College in Massachusetts. Initially the college was not intended for formal education; rather it was a school for training ministers. Many other colonies began institutions of higher learning. William and Mary College was founded in Virginia in 1696 with religious motives. The curriculum at these universities was well versed in religious and moral rhetoric. Many of the materials used consisted of catechism, psalmody, and the writings of early church fathers. Many clergy made their mark on society by becoming authors of religious writings. The educational aim was also to learn more secular wisdom such as respect for individuals and property, courage, self-sacrifice, and truthfulness. Harvard College owned the colonies' only printing press for more than 30 years beginning in 1638. The Harvard press published both secular and religious works.

In this early beginning of our country, adult education and learning occurred as part of the process of cultural transmission (Stubblefield & Keane, 1994). During this cultural era, the colonies witnessed a literary explosion. New England gave way to a growing number of bookstores during this time as well. The first newspaper was published in Boston in 1690. Newspapers provided local information as well as reprints from English papers; letters from readers; sermons; essays; advertisements; and reports on inventions, discoveries, and experiments (Stubblefield & Keane, 1994). Many parish libraries were established during this time; however they were primarily accessible by the clergy. The public had limited access to these libraries. Most families did not have access to books and literary works or could not afford to purchase them. Access to these works was reserved for a small elite population. The most common literary productions in homes during this era were the Bible, other religious pamphlets, and newspapers and magazines.

As a supplement to the literate public, public lectures became popular in the early 1700s. Subjects such as astronomy, electricity, religion, pneumatics and hydraulics, anatomy, and medical topics were common among the public lectures (Stubblefield & Keane, 1994). The public lectures were given by the clergy, scientists, engineers, and professors such as John Winthrop of Harvard College. Boston, New York, Philadelphia, Newport, and Charles Town developed into a regular circuit for these public lecturers.

The 19th century witnessed the establishment of many religious and secular educational institutions. These institutions were prefaced by religious societies as early as 1700, such as the Society for Promoting Christian Knowledge and the Society for the Propagation of the Gospel in Foreign Parts founded by Thomas Bray. The most famous secular adult institution of this era was the Junto, a men's club started by Benjamin Franklin in 1727.

By 1831, voluntary agencies and institutions were very prevalent within this country, and became one of the most significant aspects of the development of adult education (Knowles, 1977). The French observer Tocqueville (2004) revealed that Americans of all ages, all conditions, and all dispositions constantly form associations and through these they serve as entertainment, to construct churches, to diffuse books, and in this manner hospitals, prisons, and schools were founded.

Other religious institutions included the American Bible Society (1816), the American Tract Society (1824), the American Sunday School Union (1824), the Young Men's Christian Associations (1851), and the Young Women's Christian Associations (1855). As Tocqueville observed, the cultural climate was affected by a growth of voluntary associations. As a result the religious climate changed as well. The spirit of the churches became more conducive to voluntary citizen participation (Knowles, 1977). The churches themselves took on the characteristic of voluntary associations such as interdenominational organizations, charity agencies, and hospitals (Knowles, 1977). Many Catholics developed reading circles that were founded within the parish libraries.

The New York City Catholic Library Association was developed in 1854, and by 1860 it had a historical section, a debating club, a mechanics' society, and a library with more than 1,000 volumes. The Xavier Alumni Sodality began in New York in 1863. It brought the alumni of all the Catholic colleges together to promote the study of good books and foster a taste for the sciences and arts (Knowles, 1977).

In the late 19th century, reading circles developed rapidly and were widespread. In 1889, the Reading Circle Union was formally organized. Probably the most significant institution developed in the late 19th century is the Chautauqua Institution. The Chautauqua Institution was originally established in 1874 by Dr. John Vincent, secretary of the Methodists Sunday School Union. It was conceived to be a summer educational program for Sunday school teachers. The Chautauqua Institution became the most influential adult educational institution of this era. In 1878 the first integrated core program of adult education organized in this country on a national scale came into being, the Chautauqua Literary and Scientific Circle (Knowles, 1977). This was a four year program of home reading in history and literature, carried on by the local reading circles.

The Chautauqua Institution pioneered new forms and methods such as the correspondence course, book clubs, summer school, and university extension. As a result of the foundational work of the Chautauqua Institution, the Catholic Summer School of America was established in 1892. Additionally, William Harper founded the American Institute of Sacred Literature in 1889. The institute contained popular Bible studies, summer schools, and extension courses.

As identified from this brief history of the religious institutions, there has been a continuous dynamic relationship between individual, community, society, religion, and culture. Havighurst (1965) revealed that religion is always in the process of being translated into the language of a particular social environment and will be adapted to the needs of a given time and place in history. Religious communities act upon and are acted upon by the larger society in response to changes in the larger culture, and sometimes in response to the ethical and social challenges of the day (Berger, 1967; Glock & Stark, 1965; King, 1958).

Religious communities are fundamentally involved in cultural change, both as recipients of change and causal agents of change. Elias (1985) reinforced Havighurst's point by indicating that religious traditions are strongly influenced by the development and refinement of cultural circumstances.

Framework

Havighurst (1965) proposed a thoughtful and sensitive approach to religious adult education, but an aggressive one. He urged institutions to develop programs that seek to develop a religious mind and personality fit for the end of the twentieth century. Havighurst (1965) considered that adult religious education has a crucial role to play in the stimulation of conscious motivation for the adult learning experience. Havighurst (1965) stated:

> If the adult has not found their way to adult educators, the adult educator must find their way to him or her, establish lines of communication with those institutions and organizations that have meaning for him [her], letting them serve as the familiar and tested link between him [her] and further education. (p. 65)

This is where the modern religious institution shines above other forms of education. Religious institutions look for ways to find the adult. The adult learner seeks knowledge for immediate use and application within his or her current social role (Brookfield, 1986). Religious adult educators can provide new avenues for personal and social growth through fellowship, worship, social services, and religious courses. Havighurst (1965) wrote:

> Consequently the churches may be unusually good agencies for adult education. A program set up under the auspices of a church might have more chance of success than the same program set up, for example, under a junior college, or under the public library. This type of conclusion would have to be qualified by considering that some kinds of educational programs may not be considered suitable for church sponsorship. A church might be timid about setting up a study group on civil liberties, and it would probably regard a class in accounting as out of its field. (p. 65)

Schroeder (1970) classified church organizations as Type IV agencies, in addition to government, hospitals, and voluntary agencies. Table 1 presents Schroeder's classification schema for adult agencies. Peterson (1980) identified five factors that contribute to the religious community's ability to provide adult education.

1. Because of their availability, religious communities are the most accessible providers of adult education in America. There are more churches, synagogues, and mosques than all the other types of adult education agencies combined.
2. The religious community relies on volunteers from within the community to conduct adult education offerings. There are generally enough adults to lead the educational programs.
3. Adults of all socioeconomic levels are involved in the religious community.

4. Religious communities are the principle center of activity for many people, especially older adults.
5. In many small towns and rural areas, religious communities are multipurpose organizations, combining religious, social, and educational functions.

Table 1

Schroeder's Classification of Agencies in Adult Education

Types	Explanation
Type I Agencies established to serve the educational needs of adults. Adult education is a central function.	Usually associated with the educational needs of a special group of adults rather than development of comprehensive programs to satisfy the unfilled educational needs of all adults in the community. Two examples are proprietary schools and independent residential and nonresidential adult education centers. Proprietary schools include business schools, correspondence schools, and technical schools.
Type II Agencies established to serve the educational needs of youth which have assumed the added responsibility of at least partially serving the educational needs of adults. Adult education is a secondary function.	Included here are the public schools (adult evening or day programs), junior colleges (community service or adult education divisions), and colleges and universities (general extension divisions, evening colleges, residential centers and Cooperative Extension Service).
Type III Agencies established to serve both educational and noneducational needs of the community. Adult education is an allied function employed to fulfill only some of the needs which agencies recognize as their responsibility.	Libraries. museums, and health and welfare agencies constitute examples of agencies which though established to serve the more general needs of a community, become involved with adult education as a means of satisfying part of their total purpose.
Type IV Agencies established to serve the special interests (economic, ideological) of special groups. Adult education is a subordinate function employed primarily to further the special interests of the agency itself.	Examples include business and industry, labor unions, government, hospitals, churches, and voluntary associations which are concerned with adult education to the extent that such education contributes to the effectiveness of the agency in fulfilling its primary purpose.

Note. Adapted from W. L. Schroeder, In R. M. Smith, G. F. Aker, and J. R. Kidd (Eds.), *Handbook of Adult Education*, 1970. pp 37-38. New York: Macmillan.

Peterson (1980) contended that these factors make the religious community the single most preferred, most comfortable setting outside the home for almost any organized activity. Havighurst (1965) considered that the church is one of the principle educative agencies for all ages. For adults, it may become *the* principle agency.

Current Programs and Content

There are a great number of religious institutions in America. They provide services ranging from private schools to pre-marital counseling to lay leader training. There are many programs available within religious institutions. The programs presented here are not intended to be an exhaustive summary of the religious programs available but rather a discussion of some of the common ones available across this country. When reviewing these various programs, one should notice the personal appeal to the individuals needs, the practicality of the program offered, the flexibility of the programs, and reflect on Peterson's five factors that make these programs successful.

Counseling

Many religious denominations offer pre-marital and post-marital counseling. This is usually conducted by the rabbi, priest, pastor, minister, or preacher, depending on the denomination. Some denominations actually require pre-marital counseling by the minister or the church will not allow them to be married under the purview of that assembly. Most ministers of these denominations will provide counseling to members that request it. Other churches will hire professional counselors for families who are in distress.

Another program that is popular for many denominations is marriage seminars, workshops, or classes. This type of training is not necessarily designed for struggling marriages but rather to support and enhance current marriages. Seminars and workshops will typically be for 1-2 days over a weekend, and classes will usually meet once a week for a number of weeks. Many times the church will use teachers or facilitators from within their own assembly, or sometimes they will hire professional teachers or speakers. Additionally, these services are often free or at a minimal cost to cover expenses with no profits.

Financial Planning

Financial planning is good stewardship. This is the belief of many religious institutions; therefore they provide financial planning services. Some denominational churches will offer a class on budgeting and estate planning. Others will incorporate it into Sunday morning Bible classes and use a financial planning curriculum as a guide or use a book such as *The Financial Peace Planner: A step-by-step guide to restoring your family's financial health* by Dave Ramsey. Some assemblies will keep detailed records of individual monetary gifts for tax purposes, and provide tax tips and tax filing advice in the local church bulletin.

English as a Second Language (ESL)

In today's culture, there is a rapidly growing population of Americans that speak English as a Second Language (ESL). Providing ESL classes is an ideal way to reach these adults. Some type of ESL class or service is offered in most all religious institutions. Some churches provide regular ESL classes for a couple of hours per day. For example, there is a church in Los Angeles that offers ESL classes Monday through Thursday from 9:00 A.M. – 12:00 P.M. They also offer three different levels of these classes: beginner, intermediate, and advanced. Another example is a synagogue in New York that provides ESL classes on Wednesday nights and Saturday mornings. Other churches simply read the English bible to members that do not read or speak English natively. This seems primitive, but as discussed in the history section, this has been occurring for hundreds of years in this country.

Many college campuses and Christian student centers provide ESL services to their International students. For example, there is a church in Auburn, AL that reads the Bible to Chinese International students on a regular basis. This simple program accomplishes both the need of the student to learn English and the desire of the church to teach its religious theology.

Social Groups

A rapidly growing trend in this country among all religious communities is the idea of social groups, sometimes called interest groups, small groups, share groups, community groups, etc. Small groups can help you get to know other people, offer encouragement during difficult times, and become a major part of one's spiritual journey. Social groups meet many personal needs and are important to the adult maturation process. Additionally, they are important to the religious maturation.

Most religious communities that use social groups provide a variety to choose from. They range from college students, young married couples, single adults, groups with and without children programs, middle age groups, and senior citizen groups. This enables the institution to meet more specific needs of the members within each group.

Formal Education

There are a plethora of religiously based colleges throughout this country. There is a college for every major religious theology practiced in this country. Some examples are Trinity Christian College, Gratz College (Jewish), Southern Catholic College, Brigham Young University (Mormonism), and the American Islamic College. These colleges offer many different degrees. These degrees range from very common degrees such as Bachelor of Science in Business or Bachelor of Arts in History to more religious specific degrees such as a Bachelor of Arts in Islamic Studies or a Bachelor of Arts in Jewish Studies. Additionally, many of these colleges offer technical and professional degrees such as nursing and engineering. If you attend a religious institution to obtain a non-religious oriented degree, you will still be required to take courses with religious content. The minimum number of theological classes required is typically contained within the core curriculum required for all degrees. You will take more religious oriented classes if your degree is religious in nature.

Most of these colleges or universities offer graduate education. The graduate opportunities include both masters and doctorate degrees. Additionally, many other professional certifications and qualifications can be completed at these colleges, such as a state teaching certification. Most individuals that attend religious graduate institutions do so at seminaries. There are many Jewish and Christian seminaries throughout this country. Seminaries primarily offer graduate degrees of religious content; however, some offer bachelorate degrees. Most individuals that choose to attend a seminary do so with the intent of a leadership career within their religious faith.

Religious Training

There are numerous avenues through which religious sects provide religious training. It can range from subtle guidance from a priest, to leadership training courses. Most Christian and Jewish denominations provide religious training through what is typically referred to as lay leader training. Lay leader training enables clergy to strengthen ministries by increasing the number of active lay leaders in their church or synagogue. The word lay or laity comes from the Latin word *laicus*, which means not belonging to the clergy. In other words, lay leader training is for the non-clergy and is used to develop and strengthen leaders within the assembly to assist the clergy. This training can be developed from within the congregation, or there are curricula designed and developed by professionals from all orders of faith that can be purchased and used on a local level.

Men's and Women's Retreats

Another popular social program among all religious groups is retreats. These retreats typically have a specific agenda and are held in numerous locations. Most of these retreats are on a weekend so that they are practical and fit into most adults' schedules. Sometimes these retreats offer child care options as well for those that need them. Many religious denominations have privately owned getaways that are used for their own purpose or leased out to other religious institutions. Retreat agendas range from religious training, marriage enrichment, budget planning, mission planning, spiritual enrichment, or just purely fellowship. For example, there is a denomination in Auburn, AL who has a men's retreat every year at a nearby deer hunting camp. Some other retreat examples are:

1. A women's retreat at Emerald Island North Carolina designed to foster renewed spiritual and life commitment. The retreat includes fresh flowers, a full body massage, live music, and vibrational healing.

2. A men's retreat at Sea Brook Island in South Carolina designed to improve the husband's spiritual leadership within his family. The retreat has a professional guest speaker for the weekend hired specifically for this event. The retreat was prefaced by a series of lessons using Steve Farrar's book *Point Man: How a man can lead his family.*

3. A women's retreat at Camp Qwanoes on Vancouver Island in British Columbia composed of many choices for the weekend. The retreat has a diversity of workshops to discuss relevant issues and learn new skills. Areas of focus are crafts, family life, marriage, inter-personal relationships, spiritual enhancement, and practical personal development.

4. A men's retreat at Crooked River State Park in St. Marys Georgia organized for the men leaders of a local denominational chapter. The purpose of this retreat is to review last year's budget, prepare next year's budget, and develop some future goals of the assembly in the area of local growth and missions.

Conclusion

Religious education has had a long historical impact on this society and culture and it will continue to have lasting implications on our present and future societies. This chapter is not intended to be a comprehensive review of religious institutions, but rather a brief introduction. The material presented is merely a small portion of information within a vast ocean of information. One only needs to perform an internet search of religious institutions to understand the variety and complexity of this area of study. As Knowles and Havighurst aforementioned, religion has been one of the most influential forces on adult education in our history, and will probably continue to be *the* principle educational agency for adults.

References

Berger, P. (1967). *The sacred canopy: Elements of a sociological theory of religion.* Garden City, NY: Doubleday.

Brookfield, S. (1986). *Understanding and facilitating adult learning.* San Francisco: Jossey-Bass.

Brubacher, J. (1966). *A history of the problems of education* (2nd ed.). New York: McGraw-Hill.

Butts, R. (1955). *A cultural history of western education* (2nd ed.). New York: McGraw-Hill.

Elias, J. L. (1985). *Studies in theology and education.* Malabar, FL: Kreiger Publishing Company.

Glock, C., & Stark, R. (1965). *Religion and society in tension.* Chicago: Rand McNally.

Havighurst, R. (1965). The *educational mission of the church.* Philadelphia: Westminister Press.

King, M. (1958). *Stride toward freedom.* New York: Harper and Row.

Knowles, M. (1977). *A history of the adult education movement in the United States.* Malabar, FL: Krieger Publishing Company.

Peterson, R., & Associates (1980). *Lifelong learning in America.* San Francisco: Jossey-Bass.

Schroeder, W. L. (1970). Adult education defined and described. In R. M. Smith, G. F. Aker & J. R. Kidd (Eds.), *Handbook of Adult Education* (pp. 37-38). New York: Macmillan.

Sidwell, R. (1968). Writers, thinkers, and fox hunters: Educational theory in the almanacs of eighteenth century colonial America. *History of Education Quarterly, 8*(3), 275-288.

Stubblefield, H., & Keane, P. (1994). *Adult education in the American experience.* San Francisco: Jossey-Bass.

Tocqueville, A. (2004). *Tocqueville: Democracy in America.* Publisher: Library of America.

Chapter 8

Proprietary Schools

Nora Gerdes Stevens

Introduction

A proprietary school is simply a school run for profit. This often means the institution has a different philosophy from a school supported by the government or one run under nonprofit status. Proprietary schools must attract students as their customers and make money for their investors. Government-supported universities often place greater emphasis on research than teaching.

The History of Proprietary Schools

Since the founding of the United States, there has been disagreement about the correct form of public education. Thomas Jefferson was a proponent of a classical liberal arts education. Benjamin Franklin, on the other hand, was out-spoken in his belief in a pragmatic and utilitarian education. He considered experimental science a source of practical applications that would impact every area of life and increase profitability and comfort for all (Gillett-Karam, 1999). This basic distinction of two of the nation's earliest leaders has distinguished the controversy between traditional and proprietary schools ever since.

The first proprietary schools were correspondence schools, arising in the mid-1700's. An advertisement in the *Boston Gazette* in 1728 offered instruction in shorthand, promising students will be "as perfectly instructed as those that live in Boston" (Katz, 1973, p. 6). Residential proprietary schools became common shortly thereafter (Hittman, 1999). As early as the mid-1800's, there were multiple proprietary schools in diverse cities under the umbrella of a single corporation. Bacon's Mercantile Colleges opened schools in Madison, Cincinnati, and Cleveland in 1850 and the Bryant-Stratton chain, organized in 1852, had grown to more than 50 schools in as many cities by the end of the Civil War (Hittman, 1999). Some of the growth of such schools around the time of the Civil War can be attributed to the movement of women into the marketplace. With men away at war, businesses were forced to hire women. Since women were often untrained in business, proprietary schools filled the need by offering courses in shorthand and typewriting (Lee & Merisotis, 1990).

The Serviceman's Readjustment Act of 1944, now known as the GI Bill, greatly altered higher education and proprietary schools. Money was available for any academic institution to which veterans could gain admission (Greenberg, 2004). As adults, veterans were more demanding about the practical content of their coursework. J. Jorge Klor de Alva, founder of the University of Phoenix, reported this as the rationale behind providing practical, convenient education (Fischetti, Anderson, Watrous, Tanz, & Gwynne, 1999). Adult students were reluctant to accept course requirements apparently unrelated to their study simply because they were required for the degree. This assertive attitude required a paradigm shift from instructors who were accustomed to the unquestioning compliance of traditional young college students.

During the 1980s, numerous private career colleges were available to serve students who chose not to enter traditional public schools. These colleges had little or no accreditation or federal oversight. In response to complaints that students were not receiving the training for which they were paying, evidence of mismanagement of monies, and anger from traditional trade associations, the federal government tightened its requirements for accreditation. The change in accreditation standards eliminated more than 1,500 schools during the 1990s, leaving institutions with stronger curricular content, higher quality of instruction, and better student support. Those surviving schools make every effort to match the needs of employers. However, for-profit schools are still somewhat plagued by a public perceptions of a lack of credibility (Meers, 2002).

Despite more stringent accreditation standards, proprietary schools have been growing. For example, two-year, degree-granting institutions grew 78% from 1989 to 1999 while four year institutions grew 266% during the same time (Milshtein, 2003). The Chronicle of Higher Education reported that Laureate Education, a proprietary education company, increased its enrollment 62% in 2004 and the University of Phoenix Online enrollment increased 52% (Money & Management, 2004). In 2003, the number of students at 70 University of Phoenix campuses around the country and online was 213,000, up from 80,000 in 2000 (Blumenstyk, 2004).

Several national factors have contributed to the growth of the proprietary school market. Global competition between corporations means employees can expect to change careers several times during their lifetimes. Additionally, employers are looking for job skills, not just credentials; therefore, job skills must be continually updated. Also, the enormous growth in the field of information technology requires employees to have and maintain education at higher levels than ever before (Perez & Copenhaver, 1999). The growth of high technology has also spawned the need for more skilled management and customer service personnel (Carnevale & Strohl, 2001). Taken together, these circumstances make certificates and training more desirable to the workforce.

At a time when up to 90% of college graduates have reported that their bachelor's degrees did not prepare them with the skills they needed in new jobs, proprietary schools are shining. Even though liberal arts programs are generally desirable for teaching the ability to think, employers are concerned that new graduates

102

lack critical thinking and writing skills (Newman, Couturier, & Scurry, 2004). Academic institutions such as the University of Phoenix are successfully measuring learning outcomes, unlike many traditional schools who claim the process is too difficult or expensive or face enormous resistance to change from faculty and staff (Fischetti, Anderson, Watrous, Tanz, & Gwynne, 1999; Newman, Couturier, & Scurry, 2004). "The measures of success for career colleges are retention, completion and placement" of their students (Meers, 2002, p. 23). This attitude forces proprietary schools to remain current on the needs of the employing industries.

Types of Proprietary Schools

Proprietary schools vary widely in their offerings. "Topics range from the physical to the metaphysical, from behavioral skills and attitudinal change to every conceivable aspect of management, from esoteric scientific interests and technical fields to the sublime and the ridiculous" (Eurich, 1990, p. 29). Students can find courses relating to any interest or in almost any field. Many of these institutions rely heavily on the adult student for their tuition income and have degree offerings that accommodate the differing needs of adults.

Some of the original proprietary schools were the beauty schools and technical schools and both types of institutions continue to thrive. The Beauty School Directory online describes cosmetology, esthetics, electrolysis, nail technology, and teacher training as the main programs offered by today's beauty schools (Beauty Schools Directory, 2007). Many programs can be completed in six months to two years of full time study and schools often offer job placement services. Some states require a high school diploma as a prerequisite to beginning beauty school but some, like Texas, only require that the student be over 17 and have a seventh grade education (Beauty School.com, 2007).

Technical schools are even more diverse in their offerings than beauty schools and are expanding. In a recent online search, Career Education Search listed the following degree paths: automotive and diesel technology, marine mechanics, electrical engineering, certified quality engineer, electrician, industrial instrumentation, plumber, robotics, game design and development, computer networking, e-commerce, programming and software, web site development, cable network technician, and architectural engineering, among others. They also listed institutions that will train workers for careers with specific companies like Cisco Corporation and Oracle (Career Education Search, 2007).

Another large sector of post-secondary education is art and culinary instruction. One example is the Art Institutes, owned by the Education Management Corporation (EDMC). The Art Institutes specialize in creative and applied arts. Its 31 campuses offer degrees in design, media arts, fashion and culinary programs (The Art Institutes. 2007).

Alternatively, Johnson & Wales University specializes in culinary arts and business training around food service and hospitality (Johnson & Wales University, 2007).

A relative newcomer on the scene is the proprietary competitor for bachelor degrees in areas traditionally supplied by public or private, non-profit institutions. Companies like University of Phoenix and DeVry Institute have been expanding their offerings to support the adult student who desires a four-year or graduate degree. For instance, in addition to offering more traditional business classes, the University of Phoenix has expanded into graduate education and nursing degrees.

Proprietary Schools and Adult Education

The adults who attend proprietary schools tend to be career-focused and thus willing to work hard toward their academic goals. Generally, the population is comprised of recent high-school graduates and adults looking for a change from their current careers (Meers, 2002). Proprietary schools offer a route to education unavailable to those who cannot enter the traditional university pathway for whatever reason.

Proprietary schools closely follow the employment needs of the nation. Employees with skills in areas such as management, finance, marketing, business services, and the education and health care professions can either come out of a liberal arts background with a focus on broad thinking skills or a proprietary school background with a focus on practical skills and job placement. While the value of a liberal arts education is widely known, even its proponents agree that a bachelor's degree from a liberal arts institution is often not the best stepping-stone to the job market, even if the graduate would eventually do very well (Carnevale & Strohl, 2001). It is into this gap that proprietary schools slip and there they thrive. For the person wanting a secure career outcome from his college studies, the narrow offerings of the proprietary school may be ideal.

The biggest challenges for adults returning to school are time and money (Notebook, 2002). Traditional liberal arts colleges and universities are accustomed to students who have just emerged from high school, are often supported financially by their parents, and can attend classes when they are offered. Adult students, on the other hand, are often working and taking care of a family as well as attending school. They need classes during evening and weekend hours to accommodate their jobs. They also want to finish their education expeditiously so that they can begin to make more money in their new careers. Many students of proprietary schools are the first generation of their families to attend college (Burd, 2003; Meers, 2002; Schmidt, 2003).

As pioneers in their families, first-generation students cannot rely on educational advice from their relatives and sometimes even emotional support is lacking (Schmidt, 2003). Some social groups, particularly Hispanics and blacks, are not so accepting of the value of education, potentially creating a schism of educational haves and have-nots who compete for higher level jobs (Eurich, 1990). Hispanics, in particular, are not being retained by traditional higher education providers. Proprietary schools that can appeal to these minorities both open a market of customers for themselves and help to close this socioeconomic gap. Proprietary schools have become adept at assessing adult students' needs and offering appropriate classes and services.

Classes at for-profit schools are often unlike traditional colleges. Instead of taking several classes at once, the student takes one course at a time with great intensity, frequently including hands-on laboratory work. These training cycles are often shorter than traditional semesters or quarters, lasting only 10-12 weeks. The Art Institutes follow this schedule, offering 11-week quarters (The Art Institutes, 2007). In some schools, students can progress at their own pace, starting a new class whenever they complete the previous one. This building-block style of training can be especially efficient in technical training where a student needs to master one skill area before moving on to the next (Meers, 2002).

As the technology becomes more affordable and accessible, many proprietary schools are also offering courses either partially or completely on-line. This allows adult students to get the courses they need without traveling to a campus and without needing to schedule their lives around classes. They can study during the time they have available between their other obligations. This is particularly helpful to Hispanics who are culturally less likely to travel far from their families to find the most appropriate educational opportunities. For-profit schools with flexible schedules and online offerings allow them to stay closer to family and jobs while working on a degree (Schmidt, 2003).

Not all students are sufficiently self-disciplined to tolerate the autonomy of classes that are completely online, however. To overcome this problem while still reaping most of the benefits of online education, some schools offer combination courses. The University of Phoenix, for instance, has intensive weekend sessions once a month at a local building but otherwise students work through online resources (Meers, 2002; Olsen, 2002). Local meetings between students also help overcome issues of student isolation and the social interaction increases student retention. When students are working with a supportive team, they are more likely to continue and finish their degrees (Olsen, 2002).

Ironically, adults can be intimidated by the idea of putting themselves back into a learning environment. In traditional higher education settings, there is a remaining strong bias against older students returning to school despite the fact that they are now a majority of college enrollees (Quinnan, 1997). Proprietary schools work to make the transition back to school as smooth as possible. For instance, the Art Institute of Seattle offers an 11-week First Quarter Orientation curriculum to help students acclimate to their new situation. For students coming straight out of high school, this can include assistance in finding an apartment, while for adult students; this can take the form of assistance in time management skills for balancing work, school, and familial obligations. The Art Institutes also offers tutoring, math and English workshops, assistance for non-native English speakers, and testing supervision (The Art Institute of Seattle, 2007). As another example, the University of Phoenix uses conservative technology for the online aspects of its courses. Their online courses require only a 56K modem, Windows applications, and offer text-only lectures. This helps lessen the computer/Internet aspect of the intensive learning required and removes the need for more expensive computer access (Olsen, 2002).

Even small barriers, like having to attend an orientation, can be enough to keep adult students from returning to school. A study presented at the American Sociological Association in 2004 reported that needy students are more likely to finish their degrees if they have access to: "one-stop-shopping" for administrative hurdles like enrolling, registering for classes, and financial aid; predictable and stream-lined curricula; and low counselor-student ratios (Glenn, 2004). Proprietary schools have made it a priority to provide these services.

Proprietary schools are also good at providing career and educational counselors from the outset to guide students from starting back to school to eventually finding a job (Burd, 2004; Glenn, 2004). Since many proprietary school students' main goal is greater employability after graduating, the number of those employed post-graduation becomes a main selling point when proprietary schools are advertising for new students. Especially when there is a downturn in the economy, there is an increased focus on short-term returns from education (Hebel, 2003). The Art Institutes, for instance, boasts that 89% of its graduates are working in a field relevant to their degrees within six months of graduation (The Art Institutes, 2007).

Immersion in their chosen field, with flexibility to handle their other life requirements, like family and job, works well with adults' schedules. They see no use for the general education requirements of traditional degree programs. Proprietary schools develop schedules that fit the lifestyles of their students, offer quality instruction, and do not have many extraneous requirements (Meers, 2002). Also, because they offer classes year-round and in a more focused manner, students can arrive at a degree more rapidly, hence losing less earning time and money in the long run. Public colleges often are not so organized and students take longer to complete degrees when they take unnecessary classes, or even drop out (Glenn, 2004). Students also receive more individual attention at proprietary schools than at community colleges because they are paying for it (Eurich, 1990).

106

While the focus of a proprietary school may be singular—to get a student prepared for a successful career—there are many academic facets to be covered in the process of education. The Art Institutes, for instance, advertise learning real-world methods with deadlines, ideas proposed in front of classmates, and projects done with teams (The Art Institute of Seattle, 2007). Proprietary schools have often used the final career goal as a central theme when teaching such courses. Students report more ease with math, for instance, when it is taught in the context of the machine calibrations that the student will be using in her or his career (Milshtein, 2003).

There are even some excellent teachers from liberal art colleges are choosing to shift to for-profit universities because they really get to teach and there is no pressure to do research or publish (Borrego, 2002). The University of Phoenix requires its on-line faculty to be working in the field in which they teach and to have at least a masters degree. Teachers who are working in the field that they teach have up-to-date, hands-on experience in their subject (Olsen, 2002). The Apollo Group, for instance, employs over 17,000 part-time faculty, as compared to fewer than 400 full-time faculty (Money & Management, 2004). Proprietary schools argue that liberal arts programs, bowing to the independence of professors, can lose sight of the interconnectedness of subjects, forcing students to make their own connections (Gaff, 2004).

Are They Here to Stay?

There is pressure on traditional universities to put resources toward educational realignment since 90% of students and employers are seeing a distinct disconnect between the skills of graduates and the requirements of jobs. Since for-profit colleges assess themselves largely on graduation rate and subsequent job placement, they are often more in touch with current job needs of students and employers (Newman, Couturier, & Scurry, 2004).

Some traditional institutions are seeing the value of the for-profit strategy. Bellevue University in Nebraska operates just like a for-profit institution, providing year-round, accelerated courses to adult students who usually have full-time jobs. The current president of Bellevue, John B. Muller, admits that the change to a for-profit strategy saved the school from closing its doors but "our ability to tell students what is good for them is limited" (Van Der Werf, 2003, p. A24).

Johnson & Wales University, America's Career University, acts like a proprietary school in many ways but is officially nonprofit. For instance, it offers: three 11-week terms per year for flexibility, an upside-down curriculum that offers students classes in their majors during the first year so they can determine if that major is right for them, and a four-day school week that allows students to maintain a job on the weekends. Johnson & Wales boasts that 98% of its graduates are employed within 60 days of graduation. Similar to the University of Phoenix, Johnson & Wales also offers lots of hands-on experience, faculty who usually work in their areas of instruction, and strong links to the industries that their students will be entering. Johnson & Wales also fosters multiculturalism by offering international educational opportunities through its association with IHM Business School in Goteburg, Sweden (Johnson & Wales University, 2007).

The quality of proprietary school programs can be high. For-profit institutions are closely aligned with the relevant industry and employers of their graduates. If a program is not meeting the needs of employers, it is quickly replaced by new programs or new training methods (Meers, 2002). However, there is some question about how much rigor for-profits can demand from students who are also their paying customers. Some critics of online degrees wonder if an academic institution can demand the effort required to get a good education when they are also businesses trying to please customers (Olsen, 2002). There have also been accusations of high-pressure tactics to assure enrollments when recruiters are compensated by the number of students they recruit (Blumenstyk, 2004). Proponents of for-profit schools rebut questions of quality by arguing that quality of traditional programs can also be quite variable. For instance, there has been a recent upsurge in graduate teaching degrees offered by for-profit institutions. Some school districts have become so disappointed with the quality of teaching candidates emerging from public colleges that they now educate their own teachers and principals (Newman, Couturier, & Scurry, 2004). This kind of atmosphere is ideal for proprietary school exploitation (Blumenstyk, 2003).

Currently, proprietary school students can receive federal aid money but the institutions themselves cannot receive money to improve their properties or expand offerings. The ability of for-profit schools to receive federal money is hotly debated by public and non-profit education institutions. They argue that for-profit institutions do not have public education as their sole priority and that money for public education is stretched too thin without the for-profit schools being able to compete for improvement grants. One suggestion was to allow monies to follow students, regardless of the accredited institution they choose, rather than sending money to schools (Burd, 2003). Tuition at a public two-year college averaged $1,685 in the 1995-1996 academic year compared to $7,302 at a proprietary two-year school; at four-year colleges, tuition averaged $3,594 at a public school and $9,153 at a for-profit school (Burnett, 2003). Per-term costs may be higher but often the for-profit is more focused, allowing students to more efficiently obtain their degrees (Olsen, 2002).

As governments give less money to public schools, forcing them to increase tuition, students of lower income families will be priced out of liberal education programs. Since minorities comprise more lower income families, the socioeconomic gap between attendees of public schools and proprietary schools will widen (Carnevale & Strohl, 2001). According to the Chronicle of Higher Education, in the 1999-2000 school year, 80% of students of for-profit, private institutions received federal financial aid of some kind whereas 20-40% of students of public institutions received aid and about 55% of students of nonprofit, private institutions received aid. Of two-year, for-profit schools, 54% received loans while 72% received loans for four-year institutions (The 2004-5 Almanac, 2004).

Conclusion

In spite of growing pains and opposition from traditional schools, proprietary schools clearly have their place within higher education. The value of a practical education will always importance and traditional schools would do well to learn some teaching and administrative techniques from proprietary schools. However, the traditional liberal arts curriculum also has a place and hopefully will maintain its ability to produce students trained to think, unencumbered by the vicissitudes of its student customers.

References

The 2004-5 Almanac: Proportion of undergraduates receiving financial aid, 1999-2000. (2004). *Chronicle of Higher Education, 51*(1), 13.

The Art Institute of Seattle. (2007). Retrieved December 28, 2007, from www.ais.edu

The Art Institutes. (2007). Retrieved December 28, 2007, from www.artinstitutes.edu

Beauty School.com. (2007). Retrieved December 28, 2007, from www.beautyschool.com/index.cfm

Beauty Schools Directory. (2007). Retrieved December 28, 2007, from www.beautyschooldirectory.com/faq

Blumenstyk, G. (2003). Companies' graduate programs challenge colleges of education: for-profit institutions find a new market: schoolteachers. *Chronicle of Higher Education, 50*(2), A30.

Blumenstyk, G. (2004). U. of Phoenix uses pressure in recruiting, report says: institution disputes charges that it pumps up enrollment through illegal tactics. *Chronicle of Higher Education, 51*(7), A1.

Borrego, A. M. (2002). Trading ivy for an office park: why 3 liberal arts scholars moved from traditional academe to for-profit institutions. *Chronicle of Higher Education*, A10.

Burd, S. (2003). For-profit colleges want a little respect. *Chronicle of Higher Education, 50*(2), A23-25.

Burd, S. (2004). Choices limited for needy students. *Chronicle of Higher Education, 51*(6), A26.

Burnett, S. (2003). What are they doing right? *Community College Week*, 6-9.

Career Education Search. (2007). Retrieved December 28, 2007 from www.collegesurfing.com/ce/search/technology

Carnevale, D., & Strohl, J. (2001). The demographic window of opportunity: Liberal education in the new century. *Peer Review, 3*(2).

Eurich, N. P. (1990). *The learning industry: Education for adult workers*. Lawrenceville, NJ: Princeton University Press.

Fischetti, M., Anderson, J., Watrous, M., Tanz, J., & Gwynne, P. (1999). University of Phoenix: Beat 'em or join 'em. In J. L. Bess & D. S. Webster (Eds.), *Foundations of American Higher Education* (2nd ed., pp. 414-419). Needham Heights, MA: Simon & Schuster.

Gaff, J. G. (2004). What is a generally educated person? *Peer Review*, 4-7.

Gillett-Karam, R. (1999). Community colleges and proprietary schools. In J. L. Bess & D. S. Webster (Eds.), *Foundations of American Higher Education* (2nd ed., pp. 403-405). Needham Heights, MA: Simon & Schuster.

Glenn, D. (2004). For needy students, college success depends on more than access, study finds. *Chronicle of Higher Education, 51*(2), A41.

Greenberg, M. (2004). How the GI Bill changed higher education. *Chronicle of Higher Education, 50*(41), B9.

Hebel, S. (2003). Public colleges emphasize research, but the public wants a focus on students. *Chronicle of Higher Education, 49*(34), A14.

Hittman, J. A. (1999). The impact of proprietary schools on the viability of community colleges. In J. L. Bess & D. S. Webster (Eds.), *Foundations of American Higher Education* (2nd ed., pp. 407-413). Needham Heights, MA: Simon & Schuster.

Johnson & Wales University. (2007). Retrieved December 28, 2007, from www.jwu.edu

Katz, H. H. (1973). *A state of the art study of the independent private school industry in the state of Illinois*. Springfield: Illinois Advisory Council on Vocational Education.

Lee, J. B., & Merisotis, J. (1990). *Proprietary schools: Programs, policies, and prospects* (ASHE-ERIC Higher Education Report No. 5). Washington, D.C.: George Washington University, School of Education and Human Development.

Meers, G. (2002). Exploring sources of career and technical training: For-profit career colleges--A part of the future. *Techniques: Connecting Education and Careers, 77*(8), 22-25.

Milshtein, A. (2003). What makes for-profits so successful? *College Planning & Management, April,* 24-26.

Money & Management: The Chronicle Index of for-profit higher education. (2004). *Chronicle of Higher Education, 50*(48), A26.

Newman, F., Couturier, L., & Scurry, J. (2004). Higher education isn't meeting the public's needs. *Chronicle of Higher Education, 51*(8), B6.

Notebook: Weekend classes are the key to attracting nontraditional students, a study finds. (2002). *Chronicle of Higher Education, 49*(5), A53.

Olsen, F. (2002). Phoenix rises: the university's online program attracts students, profits, and praise. *Chronicle of Higher Education, 49*(10), A29.

Perez, S. A., & Copenhaver, C. C. (1999). Certificates on center stage: Occupational education for a working economy. In J. L. Bess & D. S. Webster (Eds.), *Foundations in American Higher Education* (2nd ed., pp. 427-429). Needham Heights, MA: Simon & Schuster.

Quinnan, T. W. (1997). *Adult students "at risk": Cultural bias in higher education.* Westport, CT: Bergin & Garvey.

Schmidt, P. (2003). Academe's Hispanic future: the nation's largest minority group faces big obstacles in higher education, and colleges struggle to find the right ways to help. *Chronicle of Higher Education, 50*(14), A8.

Van Der Werf, M. (2003). Acting like a for-profit college. *Chronicle of Higher Education, 49*(47), A24.

Chapter 9

Business and Industry

Shannon Hogg and Debbie E. Stone

Introduction

Business and industrial training and education programs are characterized by great diversity in both type and methods used to achieve business objectives. Technological innovation has fueled this dramatic growth by changing the way business is conducted and products and services are provided. The task of keeping adults current in the skills and knowledge base they need to successfully perform their jobs has become more complicated (Cross, 1981). There are new skills to learn, as well as new equipment and software to be mastered by employees. The obsolescence of skills is occurring at increasingly shorter intervals, while the total variety and range of skills needed for employment is expanding rapidly.

Management within companies and organizations has recognized the need to create, support, or facilitate employee training and educational programs in order to fill positions with competent and adequately trained workers (Lang & Wittig-Berman, 2000). There is general recognition and acceptance of employees' desire to advance and progress. Companies struggling with increased demand for employee training are forced to search for a much broader range of options. There is an increased inventory of tools at the disposal of the workforce educator. Research within the field of adult education over the last few decades has also provided insights leading to improvements in educational approaches and alternative solutions. The environment of workforce education within business and industry is evolving through the efforts of companies to meet dramatic change.

Trends in Industry Related Education and Training

A perspective on the size of workforce education is provided by a look at the annual expenditures of businesses in the United States reported in the American Society of Training and Development State of the Industry report. In 2006, they estimated 129.6 billion dollars was spent on the employee learning and development (State of the Industry Report, 2007). In 2004 companies spent an average of 2.3% of their payroll costs on training and educational programs, which averaged to be $955 per person (State of the Industry, 2004). The large size of workforce education is a result of the rapid introduction of change and the recognition by companies that skilled employees provide better work at a lower cost.

One of the major changes in today's economy is the increasing need for highly skilled employees. The ability of a company to quickly train employees in our rapidly evolving economy and technical environment is recognized as a competitive advantage in business. For a historical comparison, the skill levels needed in the job market during the 1970s consisted of roughly 20% of employees with a four year degree, 20% with high skills and 60% unskilled labor (basic skills to be taught by the hiring company) (State of the Industry, 2004). Projections for the year 2012 show that the job ratio is leading towards a differing focus, with 16% of jobs requiring a four-year degree, 24% in the low skilled sector, and the remaining 60% of jobs requiring high skill levels (Horrigan, 2004).

One factor contributing to this shift is the decline in low skill manufacturing jobs, due to both technology improvements and global competition. Companies in many countries with well developed economies are shifting to higher technology based markets because of the inability to compete with the hourly wages of unskilled labor costs in developing countries. This technological shift helps fuel the increased need for educational and training programs to develop the high technical skills required for those jobs (Desai, Richards, & Eddy, 1999). This situation is widespread, with most jobs being altered by changes in equipment, technology, processes, business applications, computers and software. The employee in almost any position and in every organization is facing the necessity of learning something new in order to stay current with job requirements (Ponton, Derrick, & Carr, 2005).

Types of Training and Education within Business and Industry

There are many different approaches used by companies to assure their employees have the appropriate skills required for their jobs. Some organizations deliver training and development using programs managed within the company, while other businesses outsource training to external suppliers. Training in many small companies is usually informal, mostly on-the-job training and often dependant to some degree on self-directed study by the employees (Guglielmino & Murdick, 1997). The different approaches used are almost as diverse as the description of different organizations, which range from Fortune 500 corporations to small family-owned businesses. The large amount of variety in workforce training approaches across business and industry reflects the vast differences in the size, mission, philosophy, and scope of organizations. There are generalities within the training approaches used by these diverse groups, which are discussed in the next sections from two of the approaches: conducting the training internally and externally.

Internal Sources

It is common for many companies to manage and administer training within their organization. This is particularly true for those companies requiring specialized skills not commonly found in their geographic region. For example, automotive companies relocating or building new production facilities in parts of the country where that type manufacturing has little history often find they are better equipped to provide the specialized training needed to bring in new employees than the local vocational schools and colleges. The use of internal sources allows the training to be specifically focused to the localized operation. A wide variety of programs are employed to conduct on-site training within business and industry. Some of the common practices organizations manage for providing education and training are described in the following sections.

On-the-Job Training

Without question, on-the-job training (OJT) is the most commonly used type of training in business and industry. From small companies to large industrial giants, in some form or another, OJT is a part of every employee's training. It can come in several forms, from being given a few minutes of basic information to supplement a set of work instructions before being turned loose to do a particular job, to the structured assignment of an experienced employee, so that he/she can perform the job tasks. On-the-job training is often a formal process where there is a standardized checklist for employees and supervisors to use, with verification of skills through demonstration. Some organizations have clearly defined criteria for both training and evaluation of the new employee's ability to perform the tasks. In other instances the process is much less formal.

In a small business, such as a flower shop, training a new employee would not consist of sending them off for training, but would be an informal process that would begin with teaching simple tasks, such as cutting flowers, or wrapping stems with floral tape and then move to more complex tasks until they can arrange floral creations by themselves within cost constraints.

Advantages of OJT include specific hands-on focus on tasks within the work environment and cost savings from not taking the employee away from work. A disadvantage to the process is the inconsistency of the training experience, unless the organization has a well defined and developed curriculum to guide on-the-job training (May & Kahnweiler, 2000). Companies have long recognized advantages in the use of on-the-job training over the academic model for many employee roles. One proposal asserts that the academic model is not appropriate in the enterprise, and that learning while doing creates enormous competitive leverage for the corporation that empowers its workforce to have the knowledge – both human and digital – that they need, when they need it, the way they understand it, in the amount they require (Davenport, 2006).

Instructor-Led Programs

Larger companies tend to have training programs which are developed specifically for their needs, with an internal training staff. Instructors who are employed within a large and well funded company section usually have greater opportunities to develop their own skills in conducting training. Often the instructors in such an environment have a formal education to support their role as an instructor or have shown a natural talent for conducting a class. Larger companies also have the ability to invest time and resources into developing well structured curricula to provide consistency in delivery. According to the 2005 State of the Industry Report from the American Society for Training and Development, live instructor-led training still accounts for over 70% of all education and training provided by business and industry. This includes instructor-led classrooms, instructor-led online courses, and self-guided remote training (State of the Industry, 2005).

Until recently, when one referred to instructor-led training it meant a classroom setting with an instructor using traditional teaching methods. Now it means much more. The term blended learning describes the type of program most instructors wish to provide in their training. This approach combines classroom time with one or more non-traditional teaching methods. It often incorporates some form of hands-on instruction and is accommodating of a larger diversity in student learning styles. Examples of this include: computer based assessments as pre-work, field assignments, and simulations.

For example, a group of operators learning how to successfully operate a new piece of equipment might do the following: participate in a web-conference with the manufacturer's technical people and then spend a few hours in the classroom reviewing what they've learned. They might then go into a training lab and run a simulation of the equipment, followed by hands-on operation of the actual equipment on the floor. This process of learning would all take place under the watchful eye of instructors. This was the normal training experience in the past.

Subject Matter Experts

Subject matter experts (SMEs) are employees who are good internal sources of information for a given technical process, machine or system. They are individuals who are used to improve the training within companies in a number of ways, since they are often the only personnel within the organization with the requisite background in their area of expertise to conduct training. The area of expertise is not necessarily deeply complicated but is usually limited to a few individuals and to a particular job or task, which may have serious consequences if it is performed incorrectly. Subject matter experts are the only internal resource available to provide instruction, if the training is conducted for the purpose of obtaining certification through a governing professional organization.

One disadvantage sometimes experienced with this process is that the SME may not have the experience and skills in delivering the training. Many organizations use "train-the-trainer" programs to improve those skills in their personnel. Enhancing the educational delivery skills of the technical expert has the added benefit of improving the quality of work instructions and training manuals developed to supplement and reinforce employee training. In other situations the SME works with the trainer to assist their efforts in acquiring the requisite background in the subject content so they can deliver the instruction. SMEs may also provide support in developing the curriculum and course materials used in the instruction to insure it is both adequate and accurate. This practice allows a person who has good skills and experience in teaching techniques to deliver the training program, while retaining the SME as a resource in the class for clarification and expertise when it is needed.

Computer-Based Instruction

A growing trend in business and industry involves computer-based training and educational programs. In 2004, 28% of learning hours in business and industry involved technology-based delivery, with approximately three quarters of this based on the use of computers (State of the Industry, 2004). This is up from only 8.4% in 1999. Computer-based instruction initially took the form of stand-alone curricula developed for self-directed study. There is a current shift towards interactive web-based programs and classroom simulation of work situations.

An advantage of computer-based training is the ease of updating content, allowing the employees to develop new competencies, as they are needed. There is an increased acceptance of the practice of blending computer based instruction with other types of instruction. An instructor-led course can be reinforced with simulations and trial exercises on a computer, or supplemented with additional subject related resources through internet access. Programs can be developed specifically for the requirements of company job tasks and then made available to the affected employees for self-directed learning scenarios. The flexibility with setting time and locations for conducting the training is another advantage. This allows individuals to adapt a self-paced program to their own schedule or for companies to plan training around the work schedule. Many jobs today require the employee to use a computer to perform tasks, or at least allow access to one as a resource or for communication. Often, this same computer can be used to deliver training at the site the employee's work is performed, rather than in a classroom away from the work environment.

A wide variety of technologies support computer-based training including: remote classrooms, self-contained curricula, web-based discussion groups, and streaming video live lecture presentations. There is a movement towards using computer gaming processes and simulation to facilitate different learning styles and generational learning differences. The options for providing relatively low cost and current computer-based training today are much broader than they were just a few years ago and are continually expanding.

Corporate Universities

The term corporate university is used to describe the groups established within corporations for the purpose of providing both work related training and educational programs (Corporate University Xchange, 2007). An example of the corporate university is the educational and training system developed by Motorola in 1980, called Motorola University. Motorola developed an extensive and comprehensive collection of courses and curricula to cover a broad range of skills needed by their employees and mandated 40 hours of training per year as a minimum for each of their employees as part of a continuing education program (Miraglia, 1994). The curriculum expanded to cover business education similar to formal education classes but was structured to fit standard practice within Motorola.

Beginning in the 1970s there was wide spread movement towards cooperative collaboration with local colleges and universities to jointly develop curricula and courses oriented towards the needs of private companies and organizations. Many of these partnerships evolved into corporate universities under the primary control of the sponsoring company. None were ever actual universities, although some classes conducted by the college or university at the company's facility are accredited for application towards a degree at the school. In 1997 there were over 1,200 corporate universities recognized (Ryan & Lane, 1998).

The growth of corporate universities within business and industry was strong for about 20 years. More recently, colleges and universities have become involved in orienting their curriculums towards programs focused more specifically on employment, which has the effect of reducing the need for companies to develop comprehensive approaches to educating employees. The use of the term corporate university is becoming less common as the opportunity for pursuing formal education through flexible hours and internet based curriculums increases and corporate training becomes more focused on programs tailored for the particular work environment of the company. Today the corporate university still exists but is more common within larger companies and organizations.

Mentoring

The term mentoring has been given various definitions by differing authors in a wide array of fields. The exact description of the process is dependent on the circumstances of the environment where it takes place and the background and personalities of the individual participants. As mentoring applies to workforce education it can be described in general terms as a personal interaction between the mentor, a person with experience and knowledge and a protégée, who is in need of that knowledge and background. It generally involves trust between the participants and a genuine desire from both parties to make the exchange of knowledge happen. The scope of the task of mentoring usually goes beyond the mere exchange of information to include personal development of the novice and nurturing of his/her path to successfully using what he/she learns in both life and work.

Mentoring is often one of the most effective methods of workforce training, when the needed skills and background are not easily put into a traditional curriculum. The practice may be formally utilized by an organization or may be the result of an individual's efforts to progress. An employee may look for a mentor to accelerate their acquisition of critical skills and background in the processes used by the workforce. In another situation, an experienced person may seek out someone to mentor as a means of allowing their own movement into an area of interest, when the mentor's current responsibilities can be passed on. Companies often develop mentoring programs for the specific task of developing an employee with the potential to assume management responsibilities.

There are many reasons mentoring is fostered and often formally organized within companies. The wide scope and great complexity of job tasks, such as management responsibilities, require an equally wide array of skills and background from personnel. The process of waiting for individuals to progress through traditional paths into positions of authority is often too slow today to allow rapid reaction of the company to dynamic change. A more responsive approach often involves planned mentoring programs to develop potential candidates, who already have the skills and education needed for new technology, to rapidly become knowledgeable about company practice and develop competency in the management operating systems of the group.

Mentoring is used at every level in some companies to help employees work effectively within the group. It is effective as a form of on-the-job training in providing new employees with rapid assimilation of company practice and policy. The process often involves rotating assignments with different employees to familiarize individuals with a broad spectrum of job responsibilities within the organization. This may include assignments at different facilities within a corporation. In each new job the employee is assigned to an experienced individual, who assists in providing a clear understanding of how the system works and how different employees and groups work together to achieve the organization's objectives. This practice helps employees in different company departments and sections to understand the roles and responsibilities of the groups and individuals they work with and fosters better cooperation.

External Training Sources

The ability of a company to develop and implement a training program is dependent on many factors, such as budget constraints and size. Another significant factor is the great diversity and specialization of the curricula needed to cover a range of job tasks, which is constantly increasing in numbers and technical difficulty. It can be difficult to find trainers with both a satisfactory ability in delivery and the specific current technical expertise in a large diversity of high skill areas. It is often less expensive for a company to hire an external supplier to provide a limited one time training program than it would be to maintain a larger in-house training staff. External sources for training come in many forms in today's market, from non-profit organizations to companies established to meet specific training needs for a segment of business and industry.

Equipment/Software Manufacturer's Training

One source of external training is provided by companies, which produce specialized equipment and software and offer proprietary training programs in the use their systems. The training package is usually included in the purchase price of the equipment, along with initial set-up and use, and supplemented with follow-up training packages available for more advanced applications. It is common for these programs to include technical certifications, which may occasionally be tied to warranty claims on the equipment. Training programs offered in these arrangements are normally very flexible since it is in the provider's best interest to promote the use of their equipment over a competitor's. Both on-site and off-site training programs are common.

An example of this would be Allen-Bradley's training for the Programmable Logic Controllers it manufactures. These are used to operate a large variety of industrial equipment. The difficulty of learning a new piece of equipment's operating controls can greatly impact how quickly it can be put to use and the cost involved in using it through the years of service, as new people have to be trained to operate it. It is in the best interest of equipment manufacturers to develop effective training programs. Allen Bradley has developed a competitive advantage in selling their systems and equipment by developing effective self-directed training manuals and programs, which make it easier for companies to train employees in operating the equipment.

Training programs developed by companies can be beneficial to both the company and the learner, providing additional incentive for their development. A training curriculum focused on a proprietary product can serve to expand the market base for it by making it more useable to the consumer. Microsoft has developed web-based curricula for many of their software systems and combined them with certification programs to provide learners with a measure of their gained expertise. The presence of a large pool of potential employees familiar with their product makes it easier for companies to use Microsoft and improves their position in the market. The individual benefits because the certification program developed by Microsoft provides evidence to potential employers of the skill level and experience they obtained by completing the training.

Professional Organizations and Standardization

The growth of professional organizations has been driven by the increased need for work-related instruction, which is current and relative to the employment tasks and to universal standards. Most business and industry related professional organizations now support certification programs within their various fields and offer training curricula to obtain qualifications. Today's greater access to communication and information through the internet has provided an environment which makes developing and obtaining membership in a group designed to advance knowledge and skills in particular disciplines much easier. The scope of these professional organizations has expanded beyond the general curriculum associated with four year college degrees, to include specialized instruction focused on occupational skills. Companies often support professional affiliations, since this usually results in an employee who has training more specifically focused on the requirements of the job. Often the company will pay the annual dues for their employee's membership in these occupational and professional societies and cover the cost of the training offered through these associations. The company often is better able to sell their product or service if there is evidence of well trained employees.

An example is provided by the collection of web based training programs designed for certifications with the American Society for Quality. The curriculum is segmented and self-directed to accommodate a broad range of students at differing levels of competence. The program includes on-line seminars, moderators and class discussion groups, where students can exchange ideas, opinions and ask questions. There are formal on-line classrooms, as well as entire curricula developed for self-directed study. This professional group provides certification exams in a broad range of industry related specialties.

Another benefit of professional organizations with certification programs is the establishment of standards which match job skill requirements across professions. A company looking for an employee specifically trained in a particular discipline has evidence that the individual has the needed background and skills for the position, if they possess a certification from a widely recognized professional organization. Because professional certifications are more closely designed to business and industry standards, they are often seen as a better indicator of competence than the technical school diploma or college degree, which offer a more generalized curriculum.

Companies and organizations, which are the customers of manufactured product, often require critical portions of the work to be performed by workers holding specific certifications. The certifications obtained through educational programs and examinations developed and administered by professional organizations often meet those requirements.

Private Training Companies and Consultants

Private training companies and consultants are often employed to provide training and educational programs for a variety of reasons. The growth in the use of external companies to provide training curricula is driven in part by the dynamic change within most fields of knowledge and professions. The task of providing adequate and current training becomes more difficult as technology increases in complexity. There is often insufficient time for a company to develop internal programs to provide instruction in recent innovations. External sources, who offer their services for a price, are usually available in almost any field requiring specialized knowledge to provide training. The organization with workers that require training benefits because it is not burdened with the costs of retaining a full-time employee to provide a one-time training session. Many smaller companies may not have the resources to sustain a full time training section or enough employees to require one.

There has been a recent growth in the use of external companies to provide training. The percentage of expenditure for external sources has risen steadily since 2003, with the average now at 27 % (State of the Industry, 2004). The use of external sources for training is in part due to the need to cut costs. Increased specialization of job tasks requires more internal resources to cover these evolving training requirements. Outside sources can offer the narrow focus and short duration training without the overhead associated with maintaining internal programs. The areas most commonly addressed by these external sources of training include technology, content design, development and delivery (State of the Industry, 2004).

Private training sources often provide standardized training materials and a course curriculum, which is designed to be used by an in-house trainer at a reduced cost. This approach might be appropriate for a company needing to develop and implement a new internal training program for a domain of knowledge not previously covered there. An advantage of using an external company's training material and developed curriculum in such cases is increased flexibility for delivery and consistency to industry standards.

Partnerships with Educational Institutions

Many different business and industry entities work with educational institutions to provide training that is prepared with that particular employer's needs in mind. It could be a local technical college providing instruction for a group of employees to prepare them for jobs in skilled trades. Many companies find their own employees are more likely to stay with them if they are provided with educational opportunities that provide advancement opportunities within the company. It's a win-win situation for everyone: the company, the employees, and the school. Some companies, if large enough, provide college credit courses on their site, so that employees can continue their education without even leaving the office. One of the latest additions to the partnership process is the use of university portals on the World Wide Web for use by employees from their own company intranet.

Partnership between companies and organizations on the one hand, and colleges and universities on the other, for the purpose of developing and conducting educational and training programs is a growing trend. This partnership usually represents a benefit to both the educational institution and to the organization receiving the training. Educators experience first hand what the job requirements are for employment in the field and see some of the problems associated with actual practice. The recipients of the training benefit from having the instruction presented by professionals in the field of education and the curriculum can be designed specifically to meet the needs of the organization.

Governmental Agencies

The federal government is involved in developing and supporting a variety of training programs within business and industry. One of the primary goals of this effort is the retraining of the unemployed, who need to learn new job skills to reenter the workforce. Federal grants to colleges and universities are used to promote specialized training in support of the expansion of a business into an area, which is in need of development and jobs. Some support is given to companies in the form of tax incentives for the company's sponsorship of formal educational programs for employees. The federal government indirectly aids business and industry through its training of military personnel. Much of what is taught within the branches of the military has direct application in the civilian job market.

Local and state governments often provide tax incentives and assistance in developing training programs, as an incentive to attract new business into their area. This can represent substantial incentives when large corporations are considering sites for new plants. The local and state governments benefit from the increased tax revenues resulting from new jobs and the decrease in costs associated with unemployment.

Federal and State governmental programs also contribute to workforce education through sponsorship of basic literacy and high school equivalency educational programs. Many of these are conducted at company facilities in a partnership with governmental and educational organizations.

Growing Emphasis on Self-Directed Learning

Companies recognize the advantages of utilizing training and education programs designed for the self-directed learner. A shift is taking place from training (a top down intervention initiated by the organization) to learning (an ongoing process that lies in the domain of the individual) (Cranton, 1994). In 2004, companies reported approximately 23% of their training programs were based on self-paced curriculums (State of the Industry, 2004). A curriculum can be made as specific to work functions as needed and the learner can proceed at their own pace. Adult employees are often very receptive to programs designed for self-paced learning and flexible hours. The company benefits because the cost of providing self-directed learning is frequently only half of what is required for a stand-up instructor based program, especially if an instructor has to be brought into the facility or the employees sent to an outside source for training.

A key component in the effectiveness of self-directed learning is the ability of individuals to self-regulate their behavior to perform the necessary actions for success (Candy, 1991). The degree of a person's self-regulation is in turn influenced by motivational factors (Carlson, Bozeman, Kacmar, Wright, & McMahan, 2000). Zimmerman and Schunk (1989) summarized the leading theories related to self-regulated behavior from the perspectives of operant views, phenomenological views, information processing views, social cognitive views, volition views, Vygotsky's views, and constructivist views. Each approach has its own set of strengths and controversies and each has a common element in that they describe human behavior as a process apart from the perspective of psychological dualism, although they do incorporate some elements from it.

Much of the focus of a company's effort to encourage and develop self-directed learning programs for their employees involves the creation of choices, in the form of supporting material and curricula the employees can choose from to facilitate their personal efforts towards learning. Educational requirements are often met at the company level with just-in-time training of context-specific learning designed to support a particular work assignment (Ryan & Lane, 1998) Training in industry is often seen as a commodity, which needs to be tailored to meet a company's specific needs and should be available just as it is needed in the workforce. The process of accomplishing that objective can be a challenge.

Conclusion

A large amount of education within the workforce today is a result of the individual effort of employees who are self-motivated to improve themselves and advance their own careers. In some instances employee surveys rate the opportunity for self-improvement in a company a higher priority than compensation (Shah, Sterrett, Chesser, & Whitmore, 2001).

Traditionally educational programs within industry have been modeled on curricula within the formal university, where an instructor presents decontextualized material to students without a realistic correlation to problems encountered at work. Some of the larger corporations, which have the manpower and resources to support large scale training programs, are developing their own programs. A necessary condition for widescale and effective incorporation of effective training programs will involve inclusion of a curriculum for teaching instructors in methods for conducting and managing educational programs and employees in techniques for becoming more self-directed.

Today there are a myriad of sources within business and industry for implementing flexible training curricula designed for adult learners, ranging from plans totally developed by the employees who know what information they need, to packaged curricula provided by an external supplier. The adult learner is frequently self-motivated and capable of researching a subject field without outside guidance and direction. Companies are recognizing new and different ways an employee can acquire competence in a field and are striving to develop resources to meet the continually changing demands for staying current with fields of knowledge and expertise.

References

Candy, P. C. (1991). *Self-direction for lifelong learning*. San Francisco: Jossey-Bass.

Carlson, D., Bozeman, D., Kacmar, M., Wright, P., & McMahan, G. (2000). Training motivation in organizations: An analysis of individual-level antecedents. *Journal of Managerial Issues, 12*(3), 271-288.

Corporate University Xchange. (2007). About Corporate University Xchange. Retrieved December 29, 2007 from http://www.corpu.com/default.asp

Cranton, P. (1994). Self-directed and transformative instructional development. *Journal of Higher Education, 65*(6), 726-744.

Cross, Patricia K. (1981). *Adults as learners: Increasing participation and facilitating learning.* San Francisco: Jossey-Bass.

Davenport, R. (2006). Future of the profession. *Training and Development, 60*(1), 40-47.

Desai, M., Richards, T., & Eddy, J. (1999). Training systems management implications. *College Student Journal, 33*(4), 501-510.

Guglielmino, P., & Murdick, R. (1997). Self-directed learning: The quiet revolution in corporate training and development. *SAM Advanced Management Journal, 62*(3), 10-19.

Horrigan, M. (2004). Employment projections to 2012: Concepts and context. *Monthly Labor Review, 127*(2), 3-22.

Lang, D., Wittig-Berman, U. (2000). Managing work-related learning for employee and organizational growth. *SAM Advanced Management Journal, 65*(4), 37-43.

May, G., & Kahnweiler, W. (2000). The effect of a mastery practice design on learning and transfer in behavior modeling training. *Personnel Psychology, 53*(2), 353-373.

Miraglia, J. (1994). An evolutionary approach to revolutionary change. *Human Resource Planning, 17*(2), 1-24.

Ponton, M., Derrick, M., & Carr, P. (2005). The relationship between resourcefulness and persistence in adult autonomous learning. *Adult Education Quarterly, 55*(2), 116-128.

Ryan, C., & Lane, J. (1998). Education initiatives inside business today. *Business Communication Quarterly, 61*(4), 124-129.

Shah, A., Sterrett, C., Chesser, J., & Whitmore, J. (2001). Meeting the need for employee development in the 21st Century. *SAM Advanced Management Journal, 66*(2), 22-28.

State of the Industry. (2004). American Society for Training and Development (ASTD). Alexandria, VA: Author.

State of the Industry. (2005). American Society for Training and Development (ASTD). Alexandria, VA: Author.

State of the Industry. (2007). American Society for Training and Development (ASTD). Alexandria, VA: Author.

Zimmerman, B., & Schunk, D. (1989). *Self-regulated learning and academic achievement: Theory, research, and practice.* New York: Springer.

Chapter 10

Cooperative Extension

Holly Holman

Introduction

Formally organized in 1914 by the Smith-Lever Act, the Cooperative Extension Service is a partnership between Land-Grant institutions and the U.S. Department of Agriculture (USDA) focusing on the education of America's farming population. Over the last ninety years, there has been a reduction in the number of farmers; however, the Cooperative Extension continues to deliver quality information and programs on agriculture improvements and farming techniques. The decrease of farms and farmers has been caused by the development of better machinery, farming techniques, and other technological and research advancements. Another reason for the diminishing interest in farming topics is the progression from a rural based society to an urbanized country. By recognizing and acknowledging the trends of the nation, the Cooperative Extension is developing innovative resources to address the topics and issues that American society faces in the technological age. However, the Extension is true to its farming roots and continues to serve today's farming population.

The Cooperative Extension has a rich history of educating the masses on topics and issues that are relevant during the time period at hand. Although the Extension was not formally organized until the early twentieth century, its origins date back to the founding of the United States. Agricultural societies and influential leaders delivered the latest technological advances and farming methods to rural residents. Agricultural fairs grew out of the popularity of agricultural societies. This revolutionary approach began the employment of special agents of the USDA to develop initiatives that promoted improvements in agricultural methods. The concept of employing special agents was integral in establishing the Cooperative Extension Service.

The Cooperative Extension Service fulfills the educational needs of the people through Land-Grant institutions. In today's society, the Cooperative Extension continues to use the 76 Land-Grant universities and colleges to carry out agricultural education to the community. The objectives of the Cooperative Extension are expanding due to the trends in technology and urbanization; however, the Land-Grant institutions and county agents remain the administrative body closest to the identifying the people's needs and developing educational vehicles to solve them.

The United States was founded primarily as an agrarian economy. Due to this economical specialization, many of America's early influential political leaders had a deep interest in agricultural growth and development. Before becoming the United States' first President, George Washington was a successful farmer in Virginia who experimented with soil conservation, new crops, tools, and farming methods (Brunner & Yang, 1949). Other influential leaders such as Thomas Jefferson and Daniel Webster established interest in promoting better practices of agriculture. The desire to promote agriculture developed a society that valued the advancement of farming.

One of the earliest organizations to form was an agricultural society in Philadelphia during 1785. The primary focus of this group was to educate the masses on agriculture (Sanders, 1966). The concept of this society quickly spread to other parts of the country. These societies organized at local and county levels with the intent to exchange ideas on agriculture practices and promote agriculture within the community. The widespread acceptance of these societies contributed to the organization of two-to-three day community meetings focused on discussions of agricultural problems and home economics, which later became known as farmers' institutes (Sanders, 1966).

With the success of these individual societies, a group of representatives from twenty-three states and territories organized in 1852 to form a national society entitled the United States Agricultural Society (Brunner & Yang, 1949). The members of the national society were composed of men associated with public affairs and practitioners of farming. The society expanded on the local societies' mission by including field experiments. It is believed that the United States Agricultural Society was influential with the development of the USDA (Brunner & Yang, 1949).

Demonstration Work

Demonstration work was also a vital player in the formation of the Cooperative Extension Service under the USDA. During the late 1890s, the Southern states were plagued with the issue of milling rice. Technological advances in the machinery of milling was too powerful causing cracking or crumbling for the species of rice currently being grown in regions of the South (Bailey, 1945). The Secretary of Agriculture, Jim Wilson, employed Seaman A. Knapp to research ways to solve the problem. Knapp had proven to be an asset to the Agricultural System in the past by being an active part in agriculture research and lobbying for farmers (Bailey, 1945). Explorations in Japan were funded by Wilson for Knapp to study and test various types of rice. The outstanding research of Knapp led to the discovery of a species able to be grown in Louisiana. The success of this mission led the USDA to value Knapp as a leader, researcher and teacher in agricultural affairs.

At the turn of the twentieth century, the USDA began a campaign for the Promotion of Agriculture in the South. The plans for this promotion were no small feat.

Under the leadership of Beverly T. Galloway, the Chief of the Bureau of Plant Industry, rice testing such as species breeding, fertilization, and rotation was the focal point of the push. Also, foreign seeds and plants as well as domestic plants were tested in order to determine the durability of each species under the conditions of the South.

The promotion expanded its objectives of propagation to include agronomics by locating accessible farms near large-scale agricultural problem areas to perform demonstrations of best practices in unfavorable conditions. These farms were to serve as examples to local communities on how to overcome undesirable results by incorporating crop rotation and diversification with better farm management techniques and the use of up-to-date seed selection and cultivation methods (Bailey, 1945). Knapp was appointed the Special Agent for this project.

Knapp's most prevalent work under the Promotion of Agriculture in the South was the evolution of demonstration techniques. Demonstration farms were operated under government subsidy. Labor costs, seed, fertilizers, and expert advice on farming techniques were furnished at no cost to the impoverished farmers. The land and capital was loaned or leased to the government by the owner; therefore, making the government the tenant of the land. The crops were divided equally between the tenant and the owner of the land (Bailey, 1945). The demonstration farms were seen as a way to exhibit the successful methods of a few outstanding farmers while teaching crop rotation and general farming to the Southern population. The effectiveness of the demo farms was short-lived due to the scattered locale and the perceived notion of "government farms operated by salaried managers" (Bailey, 1945, p. 148). Although the farms did not last, Knapp received valuable insight on valid methods of demonstration, which he utilized in a later project.

The experience with demonstration farms in the Promotion of Agriculture led to Knapp's idea of community demonstration farms. In 1903, the community of Terrell, Texas commissioned Knapp to organize a demonstration farm. Due to the budgeting for the demonstration farms under the Promotion of Agriculture, the USDA did not allocate any funds to the Terrell project; therefore, governmental influence was eliminated from the farm. Restrictions to Knapp's commitment level caused Knapp to employ the same methodology of the community demonstration farms; however, one distinct difference was made. Clear guidelines for the operation of the Terrell Farm were given to both the farmer and the local community.

The first provision defined was the establishment of an executive committee to ensure that the community's interests were well-served. The elected committee was responsible for ensuring that the farm selected for the project followed through with the plans outlined by Knapp.

The parties responsible for the financial obligations of the demonstration farm were outlined in the second condition. The community was responsible for all expenses associated with the farm. The community of Terrell proposed to "raise by subscription a suitable amount to cover any losses that might be sustained by the owner and operator of the farm by reason of following the directions of the Department in the matter of planting and cultivation" (Bailey, 1945, p. 153).

The responsibility for following the instructions laid out by Knapp was completely given to the farmer. By placing this accountability on the farmer and removing all governmental influence, the attitude towards this experiment was in contrast to the attitude of the community in the other demonstration farms where the farms were seen as government run enterprises. The commitment of the farmer to dedicate his farm for experimental research that would solve a regional farming problem in the community fostered a mindset of cooperation for the good of all.

The townsmen on a contingency basis established a guarantee fund. The fund covered the farmer in the event of loss if the committee felt the farmer made an acceptable effort to follow the instructions set up by Knapp and a loss was still incurred. At the time of harvest, not only was the fund untouched, but the farmer reported a $700 gain due to the improvements made during the experiment to his usual farming methods. The success of the Terrell community demonstration farm strengthened Knapp's guiding philosophy for pedagogical learning: "What a man hears he may doubt, what he sees he may possibly doubt, but what he does himself he cannot doubt" (Bailey, 1945, p. 155).

The Boll Weevil

During the same year as the success of the Terrell farm, the cotton boll weevil devastated the state of Texas. The boll weevil wreaked havoc on the cotton industry in Texas. It caused a loss of fifteen million dollars in one season. The counties of Limestone and Robertson were some of the worst hit areas by the destructive insects. Almost half of the cotton farms in this area were abandoned and about one-third of all stores closed. The annual average of cotton production in Limestone County fell from 50,000 bales to 17,025 bales in 1903 (Bailey, 1945). While touring the infested area, Knapp wrote "I saw hundreds of farms lying out; I saw a wretched people facing starvation; I saw whole towns deserted" (Woodward, 1951, p. 410).

The fear of the boll weevil destruction spreading across the Cotton Belt prompted Congress to develop an emergency plan for the areas infested. A joint plan by the Department of Entomology and the USDA was presented to Congress and signed by Theodore Roosevelt in January of 1904 (Bailey, 1945). The appropriation of $250,000 was divided between the two bureaus for research of and defense against the boll weevil. Knapp received $40,000 of the appropriation to establish cotton demonstration farms across Texas to educate farmers on the continuing of cotton production with improved methods of farming despite the presence of the boll weevil. With only six weeks until planting, Knapp organized the Farmers' Cooperative Cotton Demonstration Work in Houston with the support of railroad agents, farmers, merchants, professors and farmers' institute workers (Bliss, Symons, Wilson, Gallup, Reese, & Schruben, 1952).

Knapp first commissioned the aid of the railroad presidents whom he considered agents. Knapp placed great value on the influence of the presidents due to their work with the farmers' institute and their acquaintance with the people along their railroad tracks. After careful explanation of the Terrell demonstration farm plan, each railroad representative was asked to promote a sixty-day campaign that encouraged the continued production of cotton despite the boll weevil. Each railroad agent was directed to act as a lieutenant-general in charge of the territory along his road, an average of over 800 miles of land (Bailey, 1945).

The duties of the railroad agents were narrow in scope. The agents traveled along their lines on a lecture train with Texas Agricultural College professors and farmers' institute workers to solicit interest in community demonstration and initiate the organizing of this effort (Bailey, 1945). The most important mission of the railroad agents was to locate influential men with farming experience within a community to recommend as a Special Agent for the USDA. These Special Agents would work under Knapp to promote participation in the demonstration movement and organize local committees to aid in the work. Other assignments of the Special Agents consisted of visiting demonstration sites once a month, urging other farmers to sign up, distributing free selected corn and cotton seeds, and soliciting support from local businessmen (Bailey, 1945). The Special Agents were influential in educating farmers on farming methods, crop rotation and seed selection.

The success of the campaign for demonstration throughout the infested areas of the South attracted the interest of the General Education Board. The purpose of the Board was "the promotion of education within the United States of America, without the distinction of race, sex, or creed" (Bliss et al., 1952, p. 37). This mission led the Board to undertake the philanthropy of educating the people of the South. The demonstration method was seen as a useful way to accomplish this goal.

The initiative to educate the South was met with opposition. The federal government was apprehensive about supplying funds solely on the basis of education. The current funding was focused on the continual budget for combating the boll weevil. In 1906, an agreement between the General Education Board and the USDA opened the expansion of the demonstration work to states not infected by the boll weevil. The Board funded the educational efforts in the non-infected states; however, the USDA dictated the educational movement. With the additional funds for demonstration work, its efforts were expanded to Mississippi, Alabama, and Virginia (Woodward, 1951).

Due to the efforts of the Board, demonstration work was expanded to all Southern states by 1913 (Woodward, 1951). The widespread acceptance of demonstration work in the South led to the concept of county agents. The demonstration work in each state was directly supervised by a district agent that was responsible for demonstration education of six to twenty counties. The district agent's expertise was in high demand leading Knapp to propose the appointment of an agent in each county to aid in the demonstration method. Through this recommendation, the use of county agents became prevalent.

With the appointment of the county agents, the use of community demonstration farms was suspended. The concept of demonstration was redefined as the visiting of the county agent to the farmer's farm to give demonstrations of farming principles at the expense of the farmer (Brunner & Yang, 1949). This model of demonstration was the guiding theory of the Cooperative Extension System.

Development of the U.S. Department of Agriculture (USDA)

Before the development of the USDA, a governmental branch housed under the federal patent office emphasized the importance of farming and agriculture and the consequential influence these had on the U.S. economy. The first commissioner of the patent office, Henry L. Ellsworth, possessed a strong background in farming. Ellsworth requested funds for collecting and distributing seeds and compiling agricultural statistics (Sanders, 1966).

In 1839, the division of agriculture was assembled under the patent office. The continual growth in agriculture and farming led President Abraham Lincoln to establish in 1862 an independent branch without cabinet entitled the United States Department of Agriculture (USDA). Lincoln declared the USDA as the people's department (Conner, 2005). In 1889, Congress elevated the USDA to cabinet status.

The same year that the USDA came into existence, Congress passed the Morrill Act, commonly referred to as the Land-Grant College Act. The act established institutions in each state that would provide agricultural and mechanical education to the communities within that state. The primary objective of the institutions "shall be, without excluding other scientific and classical studies and including military tactics, to teach such branches of learning as are related to agriculture and the mechanic arts, in such manner as the legislatures of the States may respectively prescribe, in order to promote the liberal and practical education of the industrial classes on the several pursuits and professions in life" (Cooperative State Research, 2004, ¶ 4). Higher education in the United States was turning its focus from the classical studies to applied disciplines. The applied subjects led the way to teaching techniques that carried a student beyond the classroom.

The Morrill Act opened the door of higher education to middle and lower classes of society. The Morrill Act established a college system of fifty-one colleges and universities for the common people. A ternary education under the Morrill Act was no longer a privilege for the elite few.

The establishment of experimental farms on select land-grant colleges was revolutionary in the educating of the community as well as students on the practices of agriculture and mechanics. The farms served as research laboratories and educational classrooms for the land-grant colleges and community farmers. With the success of the experiment farms, Congress passed the Hatch Act of 1887 to establish experiment stations at each land-grant college. The Hatch Act provided Federal funds to assist in farm research, investigation and experiments in order to "assure agriculture a position in research equal to that of industry" and "to promote the efficient production, marketing, distribution, and utilization of products of the farm as essential to the health and welfare of our peoples" (Cooperative State Research, 2002a, p. 8).

The Smith-Lever Act of 1914

The Cooperative Extension Service was formally organized in 1914 by the Smith-Lever Act. The bill highlighted a cooperative partnership between the Land-Grant colleges organized under the Morrill Act and the USDA. Through the partnership, a third arm of the colleges, extension, was organized to focus on "reaching out" on the part of the colleges. The Extension was to provide cooperative agricultural extension work to the community as well as teach agricultural, home economics and related subjects to all people (Simons, 1962).

Three distinguishable constituents of the bill were outlined within the context of the Act. The first component focused on the cooperation between the USDA and the land-grant colleges. The 2002 revision of the Morrill Act continues to recognize the importance of agriculture and home economics and includes a newer concern of today, renewable energy. The 2002 revision states that the USDA and the land-grant colleges participate in "diffusing among the people of the United States useful and practical information on subjects relating to agriculture, uses of solar energy with respect to agriculture, home economics, and rural energy" (Cooperative State Research, 2002b, p. 13). This cooperation aims to serve the local people not attending or in residence at the colleges.

The second section of the Act outlined the mode of instruction to be used to publicize and teach the subject matter of importance. The 2002 revision of the act states that the "development of practical applications of research knowledge and giving of instruction and practical demonstrations" in the areas of agriculture, home economics, solar energy, rural energy and related subjects will be fostered (Cooperative State Research, 2002b, p. 13).

The last important feature addresses the issue of budgeting and reporting of the monetary funds. In order for the college to receive funding for the fiscal year, the college officials submit a plan detailing the extension work for the upcoming year. The plan is reviewed by the Secretary of Agriculture to ensure that the appropriate guidelines "to minimize actual or potential conflicts of interest among employees of such college whose salaries are funded in whole or in part with such funds" are in place (Cooperative State Research, 2002b, p. 13). Reports detailing finances of the fiscal year as well as quarterly reports are also submitted to the USDA for accountability and public record.

Cooperative Initiative

With the formation of the Cooperative Extension Service, a collaborative effort of educating the people of rural communities was set forth by the federal, state and county governments. Each level of these governmental branches contributes to the funding of programs under the Cooperative Extension Service. The portion of funding provided by each level of government varies by state. The portion that the federal government provides has decreased over the decades, while many state governments have increased their percentage of funding for the Extension (Warner & Christenson, 1984). By contributing to the budget, each level is instilled with the feeling of ownership over the program.

The federal contribution to the Cooperative Extension Service is administrated to states through formula and earmarked funds. Formula funding was established through legislation to appropriate funds based on a formula calculated by the ratio of the rural population of the state to the total rural population of the United States according to the latest census report (Smith & Wilson, 1930). The overall federal budget amount is determined each year and then distributed using the above funding formula. The funds based on this formula do not have to be specified to a program; however, through annual reports of programs, the federal government is able to ensure that the funds are used for appropriate educational objectives. Through the formula funding initiative, most states are required to match the contribution with non-federal dollars (Cooperative State Research, 2006a).

Earmarked funds are appropriations set aside for the use of a specific program. In order to receive funding for these need-based programs, each state applies for funds that are usually received in the form of grants. Accounting for the earmarked funds requires a cost analysis of the program along with the reporting of its implementation and effectiveness. Through the two funding sources, the third arm of the land-grant institutions, extension, is able to reach the communities needs.

Impact of World War I

The birth year of the Cooperative Extension Service also marked the beginning of World War I in Europe. Three years later, the United States entered the war. This commitment had a great affect on the focus of the USDA and Cooperative Extension Service. The war effort to increase production and preserve certain agricultural products pressed the Cooperative Extension into full service. New programs were introduced to educate the rural and urban populations on food issues associated with the switch to an "emergency state." At the Land-Grant College Meeting in 1914, President A. M. Soule, stated, "the word emergency implies a need for haste. This is further emphasized by the great importance of food in this World War" (Bliss et al., 1952, p. 117). To carry out these important new programs, the Extension's workforce was expanded. The number of counties employing Extension agents grew from 928 counties in 1914 to 2,435 in 1918 (Rasmussen, 1989).

The Cooperative Extension geared up to take on the daunting task of marketing and educating the rural communities as well as the urban neighborhoods on the goals of the Extension during the War. The main goal of the Extension was to "increase the nation's production of food, particularly wheat, even as people were leaving the farms to join the armed services or to work in war industries" (Rasmussen, 1989, p. 71). The production of wheat was crucial due to a poor harvest in 1916 coupled with increased demand by the United States allies of World War I (Rasmussen, 1989).

Another campaign that focused on increasing the supply of wheat for allies was the Safe Farming Program. This program targeted the Southern states. It encouraged this population of the United States to grow more consumable commodities. During the early twentieth century, cotton and tobacco were the major crops of many Southern farmers. County Extension agents within these states focused on educating the farmers on diversification of agricultural products. The program informed farmers on measures to take to provide the farmers' family and community with products such as corn, peanuts, potatoes, meat, milk, and other consumables. This program was able "to improve [the regions] standard of living by expanding local food production" instead of depending on other regions of the country to provide food (Brunner & Yang, 1949).

Other goals of the Extension during World War I focused on sustaining the level of labor on farms, the preservation and canning of foods, increasing home and community gardens, and employing demonstration methods at the club level. Agents were also called to act as propagandist to inform the rural communities on issues concerning the war. The central purpose of most of the goals was to increase food production for the war and to provide alternatives to the crops usually grown for the population on the home front. The Cooperative Extension met the challenges of World War I with great success. The accomplishment of the Extension in promoting war based programs and campaigns gained it a good reputation with the citizens and political leaders of the United States (Brunner & Yang, 1949).

The 1920s and the Great Depression

The 1920s and the Great Depression signaled a time of change for the Cooperative Extension Service. The Extension was considered a successful governmental service at the end of World War I in 1918. Even with this heightened success, many political leaders felt that the end of World War I also marked the end of the Cooperative Extension. Many governmental programs that were viewed as useful during the war received little to no funding after the ceasefire. With the declining economic state of many farmers in America after the war and with local support, the Cooperative Extension's services continued to be of use (Rasmussen, 1989).

World War I marked the end of a propitious era for most farmers in America. The demand for and price of crops were high during the war; but, shortly after the end, the price of crops dropped significantly while the price of farming supplies continued to rise. Many farmers were no longer able to provide a decent level of life and went into foreclosure. This economic state led to an agriculture depression that began in the early 1920s before the world-wide Great Depression.

In order to help curb the effects of the agriculture depression, the Cooperative Extension continued educating and promoting techniques to improve the economical viability of farms. Two methods, farm management and the use of cooperatives, were employed to combat the depression. The county agent would work with a local farmer to develop a farm management plan on efficient use of available resources and new technologies such as the tractor.

The Cooperative Extension had an active role in initiating local cooperatives. The American Farm Bureau Federation, the USDA and many farmers believed that cooperatives would be a vital part in overcoming the depression (Rasmussen, 1989). Farming cooperatives were set up usually with the help of a county agent to buy and sell farm products. One of the biggest cooperatives was located in the cotton belt of the South. The cotton cooperative in the South also helped with the marketing issues (Gee & Terry, 1933).

The Cooperative Extension also used home demonstrations to teach the wives of farmers about various domestic activities such as home economics, nutrition, canning and preserving foods, gardening and sewing (Rasmussen, 1989). Another important service the Extension provided during this period was 4-H clubs for youth development, nutrition, programs on water quality, and agricultural development

(Applebee, 2000). These 4-H boys' and girls' clubs were, and are still today, influential in connecting the youth with hands-on application of agricultural and home economics methods. The Extension believed that in order to improve farming techniques and the quality of life the future residents as well as the adult generation had to be targeted (Schwieder, 1993). Another purpose of the clubs was to provide youths with a method to explore better farming methods. By providing this exploration, it was hoped that the youth would encourage their parents to adopt better farming methods (Schwieder, 1993).

Impact of World War II

The United States entered World War II in December 1941 after the bombing of Pearl Harbor. The Cooperative Extension once again was a major player in delivering political agendas and implementing educational and service programs to the rural communities during wartime. The USDA at the end of 1940 requested an increase in production. This plan was formally put into action on March 11, 1941 with the passing of the Lend-Lease Act which allowed the United States to export supplies to Britain (Rasmussen, 1989). The Cooperative Extension was asked to carry out this objective to the farming population (Rasmussen, 1989). However, there was a distinct difference between this campaign and the campaign ran during World War I. The government assured farmers "that they would not be faced with unreasonably low prices or unmarketable surpluses during the war or immediately following the end of hostilities" (Rasmussen, 1989, p. 108).

During World War I, county extension agents were influential in helping farmers harvest crops by finding able-bodied individuals to assist during heighten periods of production. During World War II, this informal recruiting process became a formalized federal farm labor program. The program recruited men, women, and youth from surrounding areas and countries to work "year-round, seasonal or emergency short-term assignments on farms" (Rasmussen, 1989, p. 110). County agents were a vital part of recruiting, training, and placing the farm laborers. Two influential programs, the Victory Farm Volunteers consisting of youth and the Women's Land Army, were responsible for half of the farm workers (Brunner & Yang, 1949).

Another significant program that emphasized increasing food production was the victory garden program. A collaborative effort between the USDA and the Office of Defense Health and Welfare Services introduced a gardening program that was led by Extension agents, home demonstrators, and 4-H leaders. These leaders instructed urban families on raising vegetables and tending the gardens. County agents also set up programs to provide seed, fertilizer, and gardening tools to individuals participating in the programs. Over 15 million families participated in the victory garden program in 1942. The program grew to over 20 million in 1943. It contributed to more than 40 percent of the fresh vegetables grown for use in the United States during 1943

(Rasmussen, 1989). Other topics that the Extension education numerous individuals on involved canning, freezing, and dehydrating of fruits, vegetables, and meats (Rasmussen, 1989).

4-H clubs were instrumental in educating youth and participating in community service projects during wartime. The 4-H branch of the Extension established seven national war goals. Three of the goals concentrated on food production while the others "aimed at helping young people define their responsibilities in the community" (Rasmussen, 1989, p. 113). 4-H participated in numerous homefront campaigns supporting American troops. One example of an activity that 4-Hers and home demonstration workers participated in was the baking of homemade candy and cookies for hospitalized soldiers (Bliss et al., 1952). The Extension had again proven its worth during an emergency state.

The later part of the 20th century brought many changes to the society of the United States. The number of farms declined considerably; however, the amount of farmland per farms was on average larger than early 20th century farms. Another trend that had an impact on the focus of the Extension was families moving into urbanized areas. The major challenge of the Extension was to continue meeting the needs of the people. The Extension continued to help farms by being influential in the development of new technologies and machinery, commercial fertilizers and hybrid seeds research (Cooperative State Research, 2006b). It also continued its commitment to 4-H clubs and urban gardening.

The Cooperative Extension in the 21st Century

Over the past two hundred years, American society has evolved from an agrarian culture to an industrial based society to a service-oriented one fueled by technological advancements. As these changes have occurred, the needs of the community have shifted dramatically from a rural society to an urbanized nation. According to the 2000 U.S. Census, seventy nine percent of the population lives in an urban area (U.S. Census Bureau, 2000). The result of the change from a framing society to a technological advanced society on the go is the modern embodiment of the federal branch of the Cooperative Extension Service: the Cooperative State Research, Education and Extension Service (CSREES).

In 1994, the Department of Agriculture reorganized two agencies by combining the efforts of the Cooperative Extension Service and the Cooperative State Research Service. The combination of the two units was to "achieve greater efficiency, effectiveness, and economies in the organization and management of the programs and activities carried out by the Department" (Cooperative State Research, 2006c). The two agencies brought forth a diversified mission for the CSREES: "to advance knowledge for agriculture, the environment, human health and well-being, and communities by supporting research, education, and extension programs in the Land-Grant University System and other partner organizations" (Cooperative State Research, 2006c). Through this mission, the CSREES is a supporting bureau providing leadership and economic funding for national created programs at the state and county government levels. The implementation and execution of the research, education and extension programs is performed at the state and local level as well as at land-grant institutions.

Eleven emphasis areas for research and education have been identified by the CSREES. These eleven emphasis areas focus on the educating of our society about emerging issues and developments that promote an informed and knowledgeable population. Each area is centered on improving quality of life. These National Emphasis Areas are:

- Agricultural and Food Biosecurity
- Agricultural Systems
- Animals and Animal Products
- Biotechnology and Genomics
- Economics and Commerce
- Families, Youth and Communities
- Food, Nutrition and Health
- Natural Resources and Environment
- Pest Management
- Plants and Plant Products
- Technology and Engineering

The concentration of these areas is fulfilled through cooperation with the Land-Grant institutional system, and public and private partners (Cooperative State Research, 2006c).

The CSREES provides leadership and funding to support the research and educational endeavors of these partners to develop and implement programs that help individuals with improving the above quality of life issues. By providing support, the programs enable communities and individuals to better understand how to solve problems affecting daily life and improve the quality of life at the community level. The CSREES assists with problems such as improving agricultural productivity; creating new animal and plant products as well as protecting the health of the animals and plants; strengthening children, youth and families; and revitalizing rural American communities (Cooperative State Research, 2006c).

County and Local Extension

Extension is carried out in county and local regions across the country. The organization and funding allocation of most extension programs is organized by the land-grant institution of that state. The third arm of the land-grant institutions, extension, is achieved through the development and/or support of programs administered by the county and local offices as well as the institution.

The extension office is often viewed as the closest channel to understanding the needs of the people it serves and subsequently delivering programs and information that will aid in the fulfillment of these needs (McDowell, 2001). Therefore, the local extension seeks to provide useful information and programs to the local community based on needs that are relevant to each particular community. The offices focus on programs and information regarding six major areas:

- 4-H Youth Development
- Agriculture
- Leadership Development of extension personnel and volunteers
- Natural Resources
- Family and Consumer Sciences
- Community and Economic Development (Cooperative State Research, 2006b)

Each emphasis area is directed towards educating the community population on issues that go beyond the historical agricultural mission of the extension service. Many of the areas look at developing skills for an urbanized society.

When the extension system was first developed, regional agents with general knowledge of farming techniques were employed to educate farmers in a portion of a state. As present day funding of the cooperative extension and demand for generalist extension agents decreases, many extension systems are revisiting the strategy of employing regional agents. However, this revitalized strategy places new educational demands on the regional agents. Since information has become more readily available, many farmers have discovered that basic principles of farming can be found quickly over the internet. With the ease of gathering basic information, many farmers are looking towards extension agents as specialists in a certain field of study that is not easy understood via the internet.

In October 2002, the Alabama Cooperative Extension System reorganized its system from a county based system that delivered general information to a regional one offering experts with specialized knowledge in areas of agriculture and various subject areas as needed. The reason for this change in structure is the decreasing number of farmers with an increasing expectation of agents to have specific information about complicated and detailed subjects (Langcuster, 2004).

As technology advances and the trend of urbanization continues, the extension system no longer serves just farmers. The Cooperative Extension is seen as the "People's

Department" (Conner, 2005). Cornell Cooperative Extension's mission has expanded to include programs and support services such as horticulture, energy efficiency, and budgeting that reflect the changing and diverse populations of the counties it serves (Cornell Cooperative Extension, 2007). Many of the cooperative extension systems are recognizing the changing demographics of the population now served and in turn are developing resources geared towards this diverse group.

As funding for cooperative extension programs is cut and the technology age continues, the cooperative extension system is faced with the challenge of keeping up to date on trends and information in urbanization, agriculture, human ecology and economic development. One of the resources it has utilized to keep up with the demand of current information in the 21st Century is the internet. The Cooperative Extension Service, Land-Grant institutions and CSREES have developed a website called eXtension. The website is a collaborative effort to build a national extension system dedicated to providing accurate and up-to-date information on topics that will help with decision making and improving the quality of life. The slogan attached to the website is "Bringing the learning, discovery, and engagement resources of your university to you" (eXtension, 2006).

One advantage of the eXtension website is it brings together each separate cooperative extension system. This newly formed relationship allows each system the ability to communicate more effectively and efficiently about current research, trends and issues concerning the population served. Through the collaborative website, agents and volunteers will have access at all times to information on numerous topics related to the services offered by the Extension. Cooperative Extension employees will be able to ensure quality information to their clients.

The population of the United States is continuously changing as well as the needs of each ethnic and/or cultural group. The Cooperative Extension is confronted with the development of diverse programs to fit the needs of each population. One growing group in the United States is the Hispanic population which has mainly migrated into the southern half of the United States. Many of these immigrants are working within the construction, textiles, and agricultural industries. To better serve this population, the Extension system commissioned a committee of extension professionals focused on developing resources and programs for the Hispanic population.

Through a website called Extension en Espanol, Extension personnel across the states are sharing their knowledge and materials on how to accommodate this growing population. The committee involved with this project is committed to maintaining free web documents on a variety of relevant topics; furnishing links to Spanish-language materials of interest; providing materials to aid in the learning about the language, communities and cultures of the Hispanic population; and supplying a continuous updated reference section and contact list (Watson, n.d.). The website aids in helping extension workers with learning and understanding the unique cultures and values the Hispanic population brings to America.

Another valuable service that the Cooperative Extension system has developed to aid in the continual education of its personnel is a network of state cooperative extension delegates with specialized knowledge associated with disasters and disaster response techniques. The Extension Disaster Education Network (EDEN) provides collaborative expertise of extension professionals on "disaster mitigation, preparedness, response, and recovery that will enhance their short- and long-term programming efforts" (Extension Disaster, 2005, ¶ 2).

The mission of EDEN is "to share education resources to reduce the impact of natural and man-made disasters" (Extension Disaster, 2005, ¶ 3). The mission is fulfilled through a five point plan of action that includes "interdisciplinary and multi-state research and education programs addressing disaster mitigation, preparation, response and recovery; link[ing] federal, state and local agencies and organizations; anticipat[ing] future disaster education needs and actions; credible and reliable information;" and delivering prompt and timely information and communications that meet audiences needs (Extension Disaster, 2005, ¶ 4). This resource is another means of accomplishing the "reaching out" objective of the cooperative extension system.

As the Cooperative Extension Service moves into the 21st century, the topics and issues that face the United States will change. In order to continue being an important and valuable provider of information and services, the Cooperative Extension Service will need to continue developing programs that address the changing issues confronting the population. The continual collaboration of resources and knowledge of local, state and federal experts will aid in keeping up-to-date on current and future agricultural and domestic trends.

Conclusion

The Cooperative Extension Service has proven over the last century to be an important part of the United States governmental system by reaching out to the general population. Education has and continues to be the main purpose for the Extension Service. However, when more than educational methods were needed to carry out an objective of the federal government, the Extension would step up to help with the new initiatives. In times of crisis, the Cooperative Extension came through not only for the government but also for the American people. It truly lives up to its nickname, "the People's Department."

References

Applebee, G. (2000). Cooperative extension. In A. Wilson & E. Hayes (Eds.), *Handbook of Adult and Continuing Education* (pp. 408-422). San Francisco: Jossey-Bass.

Bailey, J. C. (1945). *Seaman A. Knapp: Schoolmaster of American agriculture.* New York: Columbia University Press.

Bliss, R. K., Symons, T. B., Wilson, M. L., Gallup, G., Reese, M. J., & Schruben, L. M. (Eds.). (1952). *The spirit and philosophy of extension work.* Washington, D.C.: Graduate School, United States Department of Agriculture and the Epsilon Sigma Phi, National Honorary Extension Fraternity.

Brunner, E. D., & Yang, E. H. (1949). *Rural America and the extension service.* Menasha, WI: George Banta Publishing Company.

Conner, C. (2005). About USDA: Welcome From the Secretary. Retrieved December 29, 2007 from http://www.usda.gov/wps/portal/usdahome

Cooperative State Research, Education, and Extension Service. (2002a). Hatch Act of 1887. Retrieved December 29, 2007 from http://www.csrees.usda.gov/about/offices/legis/pdfs/hatch.pdf

Cooperative State Research, Education, and Extension Service. (2002b). Smith-Lever Act. Retrieved December 29, 2007 from http://www.csrees.usda.gov/about/offices/legis/pdfs/smithlev.pdf

Cooperative State Research, Education, and Extension Service. (2004). About Us: First Morrill Act. Retrieved December 29, 2007 from http://www.csrees.usda.gov/about/offices/legis/morrill.html

Cooperative State Research, Education, and Extension Service. (2006a). About Us: Federal Assistance. Retrieved July 28, 2006 from http://www.csrees.usda.gov/about/fed_asst.html

Cooperative State Research, Education, and Extension Service. (2006b). About Us: Extension. Retrieved December 29, 2007 from http://www.csrees.usda.gov/qlinks/extension.html

Cooperative State Research, Education, and Extension Service. (2006c). About Us: CSREES Background. Retrieved December 29, 2007 from http://www.csrees.usda.gov/about/background.html

Cornell Cooperative Extension (CCE). (2007). CEE Diversity Initiatives and Resources. Retrieved December 30, 2007 from http://www.cce.cornell.edu/

eXtension. (2006). eXtension: About. Retrieved December 29, 2007 from http://about.extension.org/wiki/eXtension:About

Extension Disaster Education Network. (2005). About EDEN and this website. Retrieved December 29, 2007 from http://www.eden.lsu.edu/abouteden/default.aspx

Gee, W., & Terry, E. A. (1933). *The cotton cooperatives in the southeast.* New York: D. Appleton-Century Company Inc.

Langcuster, J. (2004, August 18). Alabama Extension changing with times. *Southeast Farm Press*, p. 13.

McDowell, G. R. (2001). *Land-Grant universities and extension into the 21st century: Renegotiating or abandoning a social contract.* Ames, IA: Iowa State University Press.

Rasmussen, W. D. (1989). *Taking the university to the people: Seventy-five years of Cooperative Extension.* Ames, IA: Iowa State University Press.

Sanders, H. C. (Ed.). (1966). *The Cooperative Extension service.* Englewood Cliffs, NJ: Prentice-Hall, Inc.

Schwieder, D. (1993). *75 years of service: Cooperative Extension in Iowa.* Ames, IA: Iowa State University Press.

Simons, L. R. (1962). *Early development of Cooperative Extension work in agriculture and home economics in the United States.* New York: New York State College of Agriculture.

Smith, C. B., & Wilson, M. C. (1930). *The agricultural extension system of the United States.* New York: John Wiley & Sons, Inc.

U.S. Census Bureau. (2000). American fact finder. Retrieved December 29, 2007 from http://factfinder.census.gov/

Warner, P. D., & Christenson, J. A. (1984). *The Cooperative Extension Service: A national assessment.* Boulder, CO: Westview Press, Inc.

Watson, B. (n.d.). About Extension en Espanol. Retrieved December 29, 2007 from http://extensionenespanol.net/about.cfm

Woodward, C. V. (1951). *A history of the South: Origins of the new South 1877-1913*. In W. Stephenson & E. Coulter, M. (Vol Eds.), Volume 9. Louisiana State University Press and the Littlefield Fund for Southern History of the University of Texas.

Chapter 11

Distance Education

Cynthia D. Borel

Introduction

The United States Distance Learning Association (USDLA) defines distance learning as the acquisition of knowledge and skills through mediated information and instruction. Distance learning encompasses all technologies and supports the pursuit of life long learning for all. Distance learning is used in all areas of education including Pre-K through grade 12, higher education, home school education, continuing education, corporate training, military and government training, and telemedicine. Research studies comparing distance learning classrooms quite consistently found them to be similar in effectiveness as those using traditional face-to-face instructional methods. In addition, studies often point out that student attitudes about distance learning are generally positive (United States Distance Learning Association, 2007).

The concepts that form the basis of contemporary distance education are more than a century old. Certainly, there has been a growth and change in distance education recently, but it is the long traditions of the field that continue to give it direction for the future (Simonson, Smaldino, Albright & Zvacek, 2000). Rapid advances in communications technologies are causing a dramatic increase in the application of distance learning to all levels of education.

According to the Educational Fair Use Guidelines for Distance Learning (2001), distance learning is broadly viewed as an educational process that occurs when instruction is delivered to students physically remote from the location or campus of program origin, the main campus, or the primary resources that support instruction. In this process, the requirements for a course or program may be completed through remote communications with instructional and support staff including either one-way or two-way written, electronic or other media forms. Distance learning on the internet usually takes one of the following forms:

- electronic mail (delivery of course materials, sending and receiving assignments, getting/giving feedback, using a course listserv and electronic discussion groups;
- bulletin boards and newsgroups for threaded discussion of special topics;
- downloading of course materials or tutorials;
- interactive tutorials on the Web;

- real-time, interactive conferencing using MOO (Multiuser Object Oriented) systems or Internet Relay Chat;
- intranets, such as corporate websites protected from outside access that distribute training for employees; and
- informatics, the use of online databases, library catalogs, and gopher and websites to acquire information and pursue research related to study (Kerka, 1996; Wulf, 1996).

The U.S. Department of Education's Office of Educational Research and Improvement defines distance education as "the application of telecommunications and electronic devices which enable students and learners to receive instruction that originates from some distant location" (Simonson, Smaldino, Albright & Zvacek, 2000, p. 20). Typically, the learner is given the ability to interact with the instructor or program directly and may be given the opportunity to meet with the instructor on a periodic basis.

Distance education involves teaching through the use of telecommunications technologies to transmit and receive various materials through voice, video and data. These avenues of teaching often constitute instruction on a closed system limited to students who are pursuing educational opportunities as part of a systematic teaching activity or curriculum and are officially enrolled in the course (The Conference on Fair Use, 1996).

Faced with the challenge of retraining 50 million American workers, corporate America is using distance learning, both internally and externally, for all aspects of training. Distance learning allows major corporations to train employees more effectively and efficiently than with conventional methods, which can save millions of dollars. Programming for distance learning provides the receiver many options both in technical configurations and content design. Educational materials are delivered primarily through live and interactive classes. The intent of these programs is not necessarily to replicate face-to-face instruction. Interactivity is accomplished via telephone (one-way video and two-way audio), two-way video or graphics interactivity, two-way computer hookups, or response terminals (USDLA, 2007).

Distance learning is also used to support rural and inner city classes with student enrichment, student courses, staff development and in-service training for instructors and administrators. In higher education, distance learning is providing undergraduate and advanced degrees to students in offices, at community colleges and at various sites. Students for whom convenience may be a crucial factor in receiving college credit are earning degrees by satellite, audio, and over the Internet (USDLA, 2007). In July 2003, the U.S. Department of Education released a study revealing that almost 90% of American public colleges and universities offered electronic distance learning in the 2000-2001 academic year (Epper & Garn, 2003).

Although the label distance learning could be applied to any situation where students are learning at far-off sites, the term is normally limited to teaching via satellite or other long-distance telecommunication technology. Distance learning is defined as "an educational process in which a significant proportion of the teaching is conducted by someone removed in space and/or time from the learner" (Clifford, 1990, p. 1).

Distance education first appeared as a concept in the 19th century consisting of correspondence courses. It resurfaced as the open universities of the 1970s, and then as the videotape, broadcast, satellite, and cable productions of the 1980s (Majdalany & Guiney, 1999). Today, distance education refers to the use of audio, video, and computer videoconferencing technologies as delivery modes (White & Bridwell, 2004).

In the past, distance education was seen as a convenient but somewhat inferior method of delivering educational content. Developed from the traditional mail-order correspondence courses of the early 1900s, the inventions of the radio and television brought sound and video into the distance education arena. Distance education has since emerged as one of the primary methods of delivering instruction. With the development of new technologies and an effort to reach more students at a lower cost than traditional delivery methods, more businesses are participating in distance education and learning activities.

Distance education has traditionally served as an alternative method for delivering academic course work to students unable to attend traditional campus based classes for over 100 years. The design of distance education varies from correspondence courses to technologically based courses using the internet and the World Wide Web. Distance education offers students considerable benefits, including increased access to learning, lifelong learning opportunities, and convenience of time and place (Mielke, 1999).

Following the Second World War, there were hundreds of proposals for world universities or other forms of international higher education for intellectual inquiry and exchange among scholars from all countries and all fields of knowledge (Rossman, 1992). When online education gained widespread attention in the 1990s, some authorities predicted that it would be short lived and never compete successfully with traditional face-to-face education (Carnevale & Olsen, 2003). However, this prediction has not proven true. Distance education has taken a strong hold on the education community and continues to grow. Many institutions are being developed daily to meet the growing demands of our society. Although online education has experienced the most dramatic growth, other types of distance learning have also expanded, including television-based programs (Carnevale & Olsen, 2003).

Since the mid-1990s, there has been an explosion in the number of U.S. colleges and universities providing courses and degree programs via distance education (Wood, 2001). According to Lewis, Snow, Farris and Levin (1999):

> Distance education has become a common feature at many post secondary institutions and many institutions expect it will become even more common in the future providing courses and degree programs via distance education--off-campus locations via audio, live or prerecorded video, or computer technologies, including both synchronous and asynchronous instruction. (p. 6)

According to the U.S. Department of Education National Center for Education Statistics, higher education institutions offering distance education courses increased from 33% in 1995 to 44% in 1998. Of the four-year public institutions, 79% offered distance education classes in 1997-1998. Distance education course offering doubled between 1994-1995 and 1997-1998. The Institute for Higher Education estimates that distance courses have an enrollment of 1.6 million students and that online education is rapidly expanding (Askov, Johnston, Petty, & Young, 2003). Despite initial misgivings that distance learning might lower the quality of education, studies show that its benefits are clear and demonstrable, and many forms of distance learning are quickly gaining acceptance (Belanger & Jordan, 2000; Grubbs & Lockey, 2000; Schoech, 2000). Distance education has begun to move from being a less-desirable, second-rate method of providing education to being an alternative that has the potential to provide students with more interactivity, flexibility, and variety in their education than ever before. This potential is gradually being recognized, in university and corporate environments, where various pressures have forced leaders in those environments to explore alternatives to existing teaching traditions (Geisler, 1999).

In today's learning environment, technology has drastically changed the features of distance education. As telecommunications systems become more advanced distance education increasingly has the ability to extend education beyond the walls of the traditional classroom levels. The need to maintain a balance between being learner centered (placing learners at the center of a learning activity) and learner positive (providing positive experiences for the learner) is an important issue in inclusive learning environments (Imel, 1995).

A Historical Perspective

In the 1800's, distance learning was made popular by the postal service and was originally known as correspondence study. Correspondence study was conducted through the mail by a school or other qualified institution that kept students and instructors in touch through writing. The United States was not the only country involved with correspondence courses however (Public Broadcasting System [PBS], 2005).

The military's use of distance learning is also nothing new. Long before the introduction of online courses, CD-ROMs, and satellite feeds, the military was using correspondence courses to educate its service members in every corner of the globe. But now, internet technology is allowing the military to bring educational opportunities to its troops more quickly, efficiently, and completely than ever before.

The roots of distance education are at least 160 years old, starting in 1833, a Swedish newspaper offered the opportunity to study "composition through the medium of the post". In 1837, due to the penny post, English phonographer Isaac Pitman taught correspondence courses by shorthand in Great Britain, the system was based on phonetic rather than orthographic principles. European countries offered courses in shorthand and languages as early as the 1840's (Simonson, Smaldino, Albright & Zvacek, 2000).

In 1844, Samuel Morse invented the electric telegraph. The first telegraph line was laid in the United States from Baltimore to Washington and he sent the first message, "What hath God wrought!" Due to legal claims by his partners and rival inventors, he did not receive a patent until 1854 (PBS, 2005). Pitman's shorthand system was introduced to the U.S. in 1852 by his brother, Benn Pitman, who founded the Phonographic Institute in Cincinnati, Ohio. Pitman's shorthand has been adapted into 15 languages and is still one of the most used shorthand systems in the world (PBS, 2005).

In 1873, Anna Eliot Ticknor founded a Boston-based society that encouraged studying at home. The Society to Encourage Studies at Home attracted more than 10,000 students in 24 years. Students of the classical curriculum (mostly women) corresponded monthly with instructors, who offered guided readings and frequent tests (Simonson, Smaldino, Albright & Zvacek, 2000).

In 1876, Alexander Graham Bell patented the telephone (PBS, 2005). From 1883 to 1891, academic degrees were authorized by the state of New York through the Chautauqua College of Liberal Arts to students who completed the required summer institutes and correspondence courses. In 1886, H.S. Hermond of Sweden began teaching English by correspondence and in 1898 he founded Hermod's, which would become one of the world's largest and most influential distance teaching organizations (Simonson, Smaldino, Albright & Zvacek, 2000).

In 1891, Thomas J. Foster editor of the Mining Herald, a daily newspaper in eastern Pennsylvania, began offering a correspondence course in mining and the prevention of mine accidents. His business developed into the International Correspondence Schools, a commercial school whose enrollments exploded in the first two decades of the 20th century, from 225,000 in 1900 to more than 2 million in 1920 (Simonson, Smaldino, Albright & Zvacek, 2000). In 1892, William Rainey Harper established the first college-level courses by mail at the University of Chicago creating the world's first university distance education program (PBS, 2005).

In 1895, while experimenting with a homemade apparatus that sent long-wave signals over a few kilometers, Italian physicist Marchese Guglielmo Marconi invented the wireless telegraph (radio). The system was patented in 1896 and Marconi's Wireless Telegraph Company, Ltd., was founded a year later in London to develop its commercial application. In 1899, Marconi established communication across the English Channel between England and France, and in 1901 he communicated signals across the Atlantic Ocean between Cornwall, England, and St. John's in Newfoundland (PBS, 2005).

In 1906, The Calvert School of Baltimore becomes the first elementary school in the United States to offer correspondence study. In 1915, The National University Continuing Education Association (NUCEA) formed at the University of Wisconsin at Madison to coordinate the correspondence and extension courses of its member schools. The creation of this association broadened the focus of distance education to other issues, such as the necessity of new pedagogical models and new national-level guidelines, university policies regarding acceptance of credit from correspondence courses, credit transferal, and standard quality for correspondence educators. Renamed the University Continuing Education Association, it helped institutions expand access to higher education while providing national leadership in support of policies that advanced workforce and professional development (PBS, 2005).

Between 1918 and 1946, the Federal Communications Commission granted educational radio broadcasting licenses to 202 colleges, universities, and school boards (PBS, 2005). During the 1920s, distance education began to enrich the secondary school curriculum (Simonson, Smaldino, Albright & Zvacek, 2000). The United States Marine Corps begins enrolling troops in correspondence courses through the Marine Corps Institute, originally known as the Vocational Schools Detachment, Marine Barracks, Quantico, Virginia. The Marine Corps Institute continues to thrive with approximately 150 courses at both vocational and baccalaureate levels. Also during this time, the first educational radio licenses were granted to the University of Salt Lake City, the University of Wisconsin and the University of Minnesota. Pennsylvania State College broadcasted courses over the radio. By 1923 over ten percent of all broadcast radio stations were owned by educational institutions that delivered educational programming. Despite the popularity of instructional radio, there was only one college-level credit course offered by radio by the year 1940 (PBS, 2005).

In 1923, students in Benton Harbor, Michigan were offered vocational courses (Simonson, Smaldino, Albright & Zvacek, 2000). Also in 1923, Russian immigrant Vladimir Zworykin patented the first practical television camera tube, the iconoscope. His development of the kinescope cathode ray picture tube formed the basis for subsequent advances in the field. Most historians credit Zworykin as "the father of television" (PBS, 2005).

In 1926, under the sponsorship of the National Better Business Bureau and the Carnegie Corporation, sixteen institutions helped form the National Home Study Council. The Council was established to improve the standards of private and federal correspondence schools. Within its first year, the Council prevailed upon the Fair (later Federal) Trade Commission to develop the Fair Trade Practice Rules for the Private Home Schools. With the council's cooperation, the rules were first issued in 1927 and later revised in 1936. For the next 40 years, the rules were the primary enforcement codes used by the federal government to prosecute unethical home study school operators (Simonson, Smaldino, Albright & Zvacek, 2000).

In the early 1930s, experimental television teaching programs were produced at the University of Iowa, Purdue University and Kansas State College (Simonson, Smaldino, Albright & Zvacek, 2000). As early as 1933, radio broadcast of college courses existed in Iowa. Open universities in many countries provided college courses to millions of students (Rossman, 1992). In 1934, the State University of Iowa becomes the first educational institution to broadcast courses via television (PBS, 2005).

However, it was not until the 1950s that college credit courses were offered via broadcast television: Western Reserve University was the first to offer a continuous series of such courses. Beginning in 1951, Sunrise Semester was a well-known televised series of college courses offered by New York University on CBS from 1957 to 1982 (Simonson, Smaldino, Albright & Zvacek, 2000).

In 1955, the Distance Education and Training Council (DETC) was established. Shortly thereafter it gained the approval of the Department of Health, Education and Welfare as a nationally recognized accrediting agency under the terms of Public Law. Today, more than 2.5 million Americans are enrolled in DETC-accredited institutions (PBS, 2005).

The Internet began in the 1960s at the height of the cold war when the United States Department of Defense was trying to figure out how U.S. authorities could communicate with each other in the aftermath of a nuclear attack. The foremost military think tank at the time, the Rand Corporation, worked on the first communication network that evolved into today's internet. In 1962, the Rand Corporation began work on an instrument to facilitate the transfer of data over a network (Leshin, 1998).

In 1963, the Instructional Television Fixed Service (ITFS) was created as a result of a Federal Communications Commission (FCC) resolution, which reserved selected licensed transmission frequencies to local credit-granting institutions for educational purposes. The channels were used solely to deliver instruction or in partnership with companies that delivered a subscriber-based video service that competed with land-based cable television systems to deliver entertainment programming. ITFS provided low-cost, limited (20-35 mile range) distribution of broadcast courses. The full allocation of 20 channels is usually available to school systems, colleges and universities in most communities. The first university to apply for ITFS licensing was the California State University (CSU) System (PBS, 2005).

In 1964, television provided the impetus for the next generation in distance education courses. Funded by the Carnegie Corporation and directed by Dr. Charles Wedmeyer, the University of Wisconsin's Articulated Instructional Media (AIM) Project sought ways to incorporate various communications media into instructional curricula so that the self-directed learners could benefit from the strengths of multiple modes of content presentation and interaction alternatives when compared to the more traditional correspondence format (PBS, 2005).

The AIM program utilized correspondence materials, study guides, radio and television broadcasts, audiotapes and telephone conferencing to provide instruction for off-campus students. The project demanded a systems approach to program development, and it demonstrated that the functions of a instructor could be integrated to provide a total distance-learning program. Although AIM represented a significant milestone in the history of distance learning, it suffered from three fatal flaws: (1) no control over its faculty and the curriculum; (2) no control over its funds and; (3) no control over academic credits and degrees for its students (PBS, 2005).

In 1967, the British government established a committee that examined the successes and flaws of the AIM project to create a new educational institution. Their findings were instrumental to the advent of the British Open University (PBS, 2005). Also, in 1967, President Lyndon Johnson signed the Public Broadcasting Act authorizing the creation of the Corporation for Public Broadcasting (CPB) to promote non-commercial use of television and radio. CPB's primary purposes included developing high quality programs, establishing a system of national interconnection to distribute the programs, and strengthening and supporting local public TV and radio stations. In January of 1969, CPB negotiated with AT&T to interconnect 140 stations, creating the first true national public television system. This system became permanent in November 1969 with the establishment of the Public Broadcasting Service (PBS, 2005).

In 1969, ARPANET was created connecting four U.S. campuses: Stanford Research Institute, the University of Utah, UCLA, and UC Santa Barbara. ARPANET became an immediate success allowing military institutions and universities to share their research (Leshin, 1998). The British Open University was established as a fully autonomous, degree-granting institution. Open University units were not founded within conventional universities, thus made it able to overcome the flaws of AIM and allowed it to hold complete control of its faculty, curriculum and students. The British Open University broke traditional barriers to education by allowing any student to enroll regardless of previous educational background or experience. It currently has more than 200,000 students and has enrolled more than 2 million people. The British Open University is recognized throughout the world as a prototype for current day non-traditional learning (PBS, 2005).

The basic Open University system utilizes television courses rigorously developed by a team of content specialists and instructional designers. The British Open University stresses the comprehensiveness of a delivery system more than the use of television. Courses are supplemented by study guides, textbooks, other learning resources and various interactive opportunities (PBS, 2005).

In 1970, National Public Radio (NPR) was established to ensure equal interconnection between public radio stations. The state of California funded a two-year task force under the leadership of Coast Community College vice chancellor, Dr. Bernard Luskin, to design the television course or telecourse of the future. The task force defined a telecourse as a complete course of study in a given subject, not a visual aid like a single movie, filmstrip, slide show, audiotape, or vinyl record. Students are separated from the instructor, standing or sitting before a camera in a classroom or studio somewhere else. The interaction may occur in real time or asynchronously. Provisions were made for such teaching functions as answering student questions, giving and grading tests, and reporting student progress to the school. All curricula must meet established academic standards (PBS, 2005). Also, in the 1970s, government and university networks continued to develop as many organizations and companies began to build private computer networks.

Distribution and licensing of Luskin's telecourses was assigned to Coastline Community College. Coastline arranged for classes to be broadcast by a public television station KOCE-TV to colleges, universities and libraries in Orange County. Having no physical campus, Coastline became the first virtual college in the United States. In 1971, the microprocessor was invented by Intel and the first email messages were sent. By 1972, three community college districts: Miami-Dade Community College District (FL), Coast Community College District in Costa Mesa (CA), and Dallas County Community College District (TX) – were producing and offering telecourses. In 1978, the first computer bulletin board systems (BBS) was established (PBS, 2005).

In the 1980s, with the advent of satellite and cable programming services, broadcast television began to change. In 1981, the Annenberg Foundation and the Corporation for Public Broadcasting (CPB) began funding the development of television courses and the Public Broadcasting Service (PBS) established a programming service devoted to national delivery of educational programs known as the Adult Learning

Service (ALS). In 1982, the National University Teleconferencing Network (NUTN) used satellite broadcasting among 40 of its members (PBS, 2005).

In 1984, the first online undergraduate courses were delivered by the New Jersey Institute of Technology. In 1985, the National Technological University (NTU) opened as an accredited university offering graduate and continuing education courses in engineering and awarding its own degrees. Courses were uplinked to NTU by satellite. This development illustrated a more market-driven approach to distance education. In 1987, Mind Extension University, a cable network broadcasting courses and full-degree programs developed by community colleges and universities, was founded. In 1989, the first online degree programs were offered by the University of Phoenix and Connect-Ed (PBS, 2005).

In the late 1980s and early 1990s, the development of fiber optic communication systems allowed for the expansion of live, two-way, high-quality audio and video systems in education (Simonson, Smaldino, Albright & Zvacek, 2000). In 1991, Tim Berners-Lee developed the World Wide Web. In 1997, The California Virtual University, a consortium of nearly 100 California colleges and universities, opened with over 1500 online courses. In 1998, Western Governors University and the British Open University announced the creation of a distance education consortium called the Governors Open University System (PBS, 2005).

In 1999, The British Open University opened a new sister institution--The United States Open University. Jones International University receives North Central Accreditation, which was a significant milestone in the acceptance of virtual universities. Also in 1999, The US Department of Education established the Distance Learning Education Demonstration Program which served as a pilot program of 15 post-secondary schools, systems and consortia permitted to offer federal financial aid for distance learning programs. Learning portals, like HungryMinds, Click2Learn, eCollege, and Blackboard emerged on the education landscape (PBS, 2005).

Print materials, audio/video programs and satellite broadcast were well established on the educational landscape, but now internet and CD-ROM delivery were poised to become the largest medium for distance learning. Postsecondary institutions planned to increase their delivery of distance education. A variety of media were used and it is no surprise that the internet, interactive video, and pre-recorded video delivery are among the chosen favorites (National Center for Education Statistics, 2003).

By providing instruction via the World Wide Web or on a CD-ROM/Internet hybrid, even business travelers or students in isolated areas can enjoy interactive, virtual classrooms no matter where they are or what time zone they may be in. With the introduction of affordable digital communications and cellular handheld devices, the world now has an abundance of distance learning opportunities for anyone, at anytime, any anywhere (PBS, 2005).

Combining new technologies like animations and streaming video with older (relatively speaking) online media such as e-mail, listservs, and chat rooms, a distance education instructor can build a successfully interactive course. A student in such a course would have options for both synchronous (at the same time) and asynchronous (not simultaneous) learning environments (PBS, 2005).

The original target groups of distance education efforts were adults with occupational, social, and family commitments and this remains the primary target today. Distance education provides the opportunity to widen intellectual horizons, as well as the chance to improve and update professional knowledge. Further, it stresses individuality in learning and flexibility in both the time and place of study (Simonson, Smaldino, Albright & Zvacek, 2000).

Types of Distance Learning

There are two primary forms of communication utilized to deliver instruction — asynchronous and synchronous. The main difference between the two is whether instructors and learners are participating at the same time or not. Distance learning programs based on asynchronous methods are recorded instructional materials. These types of technologies (telecommunications system, such as broadcast television, including cable, or electronically stored media such as video, audio, and computer software) permit participants to be separated in time as well as by distance from the delivery of instruction (Simonson, Smaldino, Albright & Zvacek, 2000).

Categories of Technological Options

According to Gottschalk (2003), a wide range of technological options are available to the distance educator. They fall into four major categories:

(1) Voice - Instructional audio tools include the interactive technologies of telephone, audioconferencing, and short-wave radio. Passive (i.e., one-way) audio tools include tapes and radio.
(2) Video - Instructional tools include still images such as slides, pre-produced moving images (e.g., film, videotape), and real-time moving images combined with audioconferencing (one-way or two-way video with two-way audio).
(3) Data - Computers send and receive information electronically. The term data is used to describe this broad category of instructional tools. Computer applications for distance education are varied and include:

- Computer-assisted instruction (CAI) - uses the computer as a self-contained teaching machine to present individual lessons.
- Computer-managed instruction (CMI) - uses the computer to organize instruction and track student records and progress. The instruction itself need not be delivered via a computer, although CAI is often combined with CMI.
- Computer-mediated education (CME) - describes computer applications that facilitate the delivery of instruction. Examples include: electronic mail, fax, real-time computer conferencing, and World Wide Web applications.

(4) Print - is a foundational element of distance education programs and the basis from which all other delivery systems have evolved. Various print formats are available including: textbooks, study guides, workbooks, course syllabi, and case studies (Gottschalk, 2003).

Key Players in Distance Learning

The following briefly describes the roles of each key player in the distance education enterprise and the challenges they face:

Students – the characteristics required of distance learners differ from those of the traditional learner (Imel, 1998). The primary role of the student is to learn. Under the best of circumstances, this demanding task requires motivation, planning, and the ability to analyze and apply the information being taught. In a distance education setting, the process of student learning is more complex for several reasons (Willis, 1995a):

- Many distance-education students are older, employed, and have families.
- Distance students have a variety of reasons for taking courses. Some students are interested in obtaining a degree to qualify for a better job. Many take courses to broaden their education and are not really interested in completing a degree.
- The learner is usually isolated; without face-to-face contact distance students may feel ill at ease with their instructor as an individual and uncomfortable with their learning situation.
- Technology is typically the conduit through which information and communication flow. Until the instructor and students become comfortable with the technical delivery system, communication may be inhibited.

Faculty - The success of any distance education effort rests squarely on the shoulders of the faculty. In a traditional classroom setting, the instructor's responsibility includes assembling course content and developing an understanding of student needs. Special challenges confront those teaching at a distance (Gottschalk, 2003). If instructors are to successfully incorporate distance learning on the internet into their classrooms, then instructors, administrators, and educators need to have a firm grasp of the phenomenon associated with being connected to the Internet. At the very minimum, instructors need to learn and understand how distance learning can become a part of their classrooms. The instructor must:

- Develop an understanding of the characteristics and needs of distance students with little first-hand experience and limited, if any, face-to-face contact.
- Adapt teaching styles to meet the needs and expectations of multiple, often diverse, audiences.
- Develop a working understanding of delivery technology, while remaining focused on their teaching role.
- Function effectively as a skilled facilitator as well as content provider (Gottschalk, 2003).

According to the Rochester Institute of Technology, there are several characteristics of successful distance learning educators and they include:

- Ability, willingness and time to learn new technology, material and methods.
- Ability to project their own personality, sense of humor, and genuine interest in the students.
- Willingness to use teaching techniques that may differ from those used for a traditional course.
- Adaptability as a team player and with distance learners.
- Ability to prepare comprehensive course plans, yet be flexible about modifications.
- Interested in and responsive to student queries and possess the ability to provide frequent student feedback.

Facilitators – facilitators act as a bridge between the students and the instructor, the instructor often finds this beneficial. To be effective, a facilitator must understand the students being served and the instructor's expectations. Most importantly, the facilitator must be willing to follow the directions established by the instructor (Gottschalk, 2003).

Support Staff – support staff are the silent heroes of the distance education enterprise and they ensure that the myriad details required for program success are dealt with effectively. Most successful distance education programs consolidate support service functions to include student registration, materials duplication and distribution, textbook ordering, securing of copyright clearances, facilities scheduling, processing grade reports, and managing technical resources. Support personnel are truly the glue that keeps the distance education effort together and on track (Gottschalk, 2003).

Administrators - effective distance education administrators are more than idea people. They are consensus builders, decision makers, and referees. They work closely with technical and support service personnel, ensuring that technological resources are effectively deployed to further the institution's academic mission. Most importantly, they maintain an academic focus, realizing that meeting the instructional needs of distance students is their ultimate responsibility (Gottschalk, 2003).

The Distance Learning Interaction

Many problems in distance education arise because of communication about concepts and practices. Distinguishing among the three types of interaction will refine conceptual terms and will also do much to clarify the misunderstandings between educators who use different media (Moore, 1989).

Learner-Content Interaction - is interaction between the learner and the content or subject of study. Without it there cannot be education, since it is the process of intellectually interacting with content that results in changes in the learner's understanding, the learner's perspective, or the cognitive structures of the learner's mind (Moore, 1989).

Learner-Instructor Interaction - is interaction between the learner and the expert who prepared the subject material, or some other expert acting as instructor, regarded as essential by many educators, and as highly desirable by many learners. In this interaction, distance instructors attempt to achieve goals held in common with all other educators (Moore, 1989).

Learner-Learner Interaction - is inter-learner interaction, between one learner and other learners, alone or in group settings, with or without the real-time presence of an instructor (Moore, 1989).

Barriers to the Adoption of Distance Education

Barriers to distance learning exist both inside and outside the higher education community. "Some obstacles serve to create standards and ensure high quality, while others serve as political, personal and institutional gatekeepers to bar any change" (Levine & Sun, 2003, p. 23). According to Berge (1998), impediments to online teaching and learning can be situational, epistemological, philosophical, psychological, pedagogical, technical, social, and/or cultural and include:

- faceless teaching
- fear of the imminent replacement of faculty by computers
- diffusion of value traditionally placed on getting a degree
- faculty culture
- lack of adequate time to implement online courses
- many distance learners lack independent learning skills and local library resources
- lack of formalized agreements to sustain program commitment though difficulties and problems
- high cost of materials
- taxpayer ignorance of the efficacy of distance education
- lack of a national agenda, funding priority, and policy leadership
- increased time required for both online contacts and preparation of materials/activities
- the more technologically advanced the learning system, the more can go wrong
- non-educational considerations take precedence over educational priorities
- resistance to change
- lack of technological assistance.

According to Moore (1994), barriers to the adoption of distance education, may lie in the procedures of the administrative systems, procedures that postpone changes in the way teaching is designed, delivered, and administered. These "administrative systems were originally built to meet the needs of traditional students in traditional classes taught by traditional professors" (p. 1). Now these administrative systems represent barriers to the adoption of distance education. These barriers exist at four levels: the federal level, the regional level, the state level, and the institutional level. Barriers that originate at the federal level include the decisive factors used to determine what programs are eligible for federal funding and the criteria used in monitoring and evaluating programs, both which are heavily biased toward traditional forms of provision (Moore, 1994).

According to the USDLA (2003), funding for both satellite and web-based distance education systems can be accomplished through various means:

- Issuing bonds to cover construction costs
- Legislation to install satellite dishes and other technology packages at schools and community buildings
- State and federal grant programs
- Various other options including taxes and levies

At the institutional level, barriers include administrative structures and procedures that are intended to serve students but are often unsuitable for distance learners. These barriers are found in rules and regulations concerning registration, tuition payment, student support, library services, examinations, and, most especially, in the scheduling and location of instruction (Moore, 1994).

Additional administrative barriers include the problems of territoriality and the need to devise ways of rewarding institutions for cooperating with each other instead of competing, the concern of intellectual property and the need to reform policies that take into account the different roles of faculty when working in design teams, collective bargaining and the need to promote experimentation and improvement in faculty hiring arrangements. There are many other administrative barriers. The barriers obstructing the development of distance education are not technological, nor even pedagogical. The major problems are associated with organizational change, change of faculty roles, and change in administrative structures (Moore, 1994).

Organizational Barriers in Distance Learning

"Student and instructor concerns represent the human aspects of distance programs" (Galusha, 1997, p. 8). Galusha (1997) identified other organizational barriers that present challenges:

- Infrastructure and technology problems
- Organizational and administrative support for faculty
- Availability of funds for institutions and students
- Competent computer technology staff
- Cost of program
- Inadequate telecommunication facilities
- Compatible communication systems
- Government regulations

Despite the challenges of distance education, education enrollments have increased significantly over the last decade, suggesting that distance education offers an alternative to the traditional classroom experience and accommodates many students' individual circumstances and educational needs (Parrott, 1995).

Faculty Barriers in Distance Learning

Almost certainly the greatest number of barriers concerns the management of faculty. Until, and unless, the conditions of appointment and the rewards of practicing instructors reflect the importance of distance teaching, restructuring the system will be difficult (Moore, 1994). "Faculty compensation concerns, the lack of developmental skills and maintenance time are the greatest barriers to distance education across all organizational stages of capabilities" (Berge & Muilenburg, 2001, p. 7). Other faculty barriers to distance learning include as identified by Galusha (1997) were:

- Lack of staff training in course development and technology
- Lack of support for distance learning in general
- Inadequate faculty selection for distance learning courses
- Adjustment of teaching styles to the roles of mentor, tutor and facilitator
- Threat to tenure and human resource staffing
- Lack of acceptance of distance learning programs

Student Barriers in Distance Learning

Problems and barriers encountered by the student fall into several discrete categories; costs and disincentives, lack of feedback and instructor contact, lack of student support and services, alienation and isolation, lack of experience, and lack of training. Distance learners are more likely to have insecurities about learning than traditional students. These insecurities are founded in personal and school related issues such as financial costs of study, interference of family life, perceived insignificance of their studies and lack of support from employers. These pressures often result in a higher dropout rate among distance learners than among traditional students (Galusha, 1997).

Elements of a High-Quality Online Course or Program

High-quality, interactive courses are not just possible but a reality. Elements of a high-quality online course or program reflect one that is learner-focused and comprises the following components: effective virtual students, course designs, online facilitation, and student support (Palloff & Pratt, 2003). In the center is a community built and branching out to support each of these components. The effective virtual student has access to technology, communicates effectively in text, is committed, reflective, flexible and a critical thinker. The effective online facilitator is open, honest, responsive, respectful, flexible, and empowering. The effective course design fits with the curriculum, is learner focused, accessible, has relevant content, is collaborative, interactive cohesive, and addresses learning styles and culture. The effective student support will consist of technical support and training, is learner-centered, and offers advising, library services, registration, bookstore and registrar assistance.

The effective classroom provides necessary tools to learners; creates expectations for an environment conducive to learning; brings together instructor and students to share information and exchange ideas; allows learners the freedom to experiment, test their knowledge, practice tasks and apply what they have learned; and provides the mechanisms necessary for evaluating performance.

According to Tomei (2001, 2006), some of the most important elements of the technological infrastructure are people, money and resources. Palloff and Pratt (2001) specify the individuals who should be considered while the infrastructure is being built: faculty, students, administrators, instructional designers, technology coordinators and support staff. Budgetary concerns should include hardware and software purchase and upgrades, technical support and assistance, and incentives for faculty to develop online courses. The resources component of the infrastructure includes the allocation of time and effort essential to making the use of technology viable (Palloff & Pratt, 2001).

Characteristics of the Adult Distance Learner

Knowles (1984) theory of andragogy (adult learning) is an attempt to differentiate the ways adults learn from the way children learn. Knowles emphasizes that adults are self-directed and expect to take responsibility for decisions. A number of assumptions are made based on this theory. This theory indicates that adults are:

- autonomous and self-directed
- goal oriented
- relevancy oriented (problem centered)--they need to know why they are learning something
- practical and problem-solvers, and
- have accumulated life experiences.

Adult students come to colleges with a distinct set of characteristics. They are more likely to attend part-time, take courses for self-improvement initially rather than for degree completion, and enroll intermittently. They often work full-time and support dependents, frequently as single parents. They are likely to take longer to complete their programs, but because they take their education seriously, they generally earn better grades than younger students do (Howell, 2001).

Adults typically, have different motivations for learning than children: to make or maintain social relationships, to meet external expectations, learn to better serve others, professional advancement, escape or stimulation, and/or pure interest. Adults also have different barriers than children on their way to learning. Some of these potential barriers might include many other responsibilities (families, careers, social commitments); lack of time; lack of money; lack of childcare; scheduling problems; transportation problems; insufficient confidence; having to learn, but not being interested or ready.

Adults bring realistic, practical goals for their education and valuable life experience to the learning environment. However, adult students attending colleges for the first time are sometimes inadequately prepared, both academically and psychologically, for expected college-level learning. Adult students generally enroll in college with already established lives, bringing far more experience and practical information than younger students. Adult learners are interested in knowing how new knowledge relates to what they already know so that they can create a framework within which they can make sense of the new information. This connectedness must show the adult learner the benefit of being able to associate new learning with their previous experiences and accomplishments (Howell, 2001).

Conclusion

All technologies in an education environment, whether old or new, should be judged on how they can be used to promote and enhance learning. The issue in distance learning is not the technology, but the goals for student learning, including how and where that learning should take place. The challenge is to use any technology or medium in ways that enhance and support learning and to respond to the needs of learners. When planning and implementing distance learning opportunities, the technology should be invisible and the emphasis should be placed on the learning (Imel, 1998).

The increasing power of the consumer in addition to technology's ability to transcend space, time, and political boundaries is causing a shift in the decision-making process away from public policy and toward market-driven mechanisms. Content and mode of delivery are increasingly defined by external groups: students as well as employers. Communications technologies will contribute to both the increase in the number of providers and the choices for consumers, resulting in a more open higher education marketplace. New developments in technologies and the explosive growth of networks will continue to erode the geographic control of higher education. Students will likely select educational institutions based more on offerings, convenience, and price than on geography. This competition will not be limited to the United States or North America; it will be global (Twigg, 1997).

Distance education is a core educational strategy. It holds great potential on a number of levels. Yet the potential for failure or for mediocre distance programs is high. Developing proactive, strategic plans requires the commitment of entire institutions, as have been described herein. Going that extra mile will ensure pedagogical integrity, student satisfaction, and ultimately, the success of distance education programs (Buchanan, 2000; Lei, 2007; Roblyer & Ekhaml, 2000).

Distance education has the potential to offer new learning opportunities unrestricted by time, distance, or individual differences among students. However, existing educational practices cannot accommodate distance education without corresponding shifts in the fundamental views of teaching and learning as well as in state, federal, and institutional policies (Chang, 1998).

Distance learning provides new opportunities that do not exist in the conventional classroom mode. The written and "faceless" interaction draws out shy students who might not participate as much in a classroom environment. The different methods accommodate different learning styles. These opportunities provide access to students who might not be able to get to campus (or get there on a regular basis). This learner-centered instruction encourages student self-sufficiency, self-motivation, problem solving, and responsibility for the student's own learning (Chou, 2004).

The public's need for reliable information about education programs is even greater in the distance learning environment. Accreditors should be empowered to think creatively and cooperatively, so their standards and processes remain relevant and foster the development of quality distance learning programs (Bobby & Capone, 2000). Distance learning cannot thrive without careful attention to the culture of the learning environment, champions who will lead distance learning efforts, communication of distance learning values and changing strategies to bring it all together (Rosenberg, 2001).

Even students who take classes on campus sometimes enroll in distance learning courses as a way to advance toward their degrees, while simultaneously working and/or taking care of their families. Willis (1995b) provided suggestions and responsibilities for distance learners' study skills, course organization information, and scheduling. Students should familiarize themselves with the course design; read the course syllabus; identify tools necessary to complete assignments; be realistic; set interim goals and deadlines, and stick to them; organize goals in a study schedule; avoid interruptions; know where to study; stay in touch with your instructor; prepare for assignments and tests; use good communication skills; evaluate progress regularly; time tests wisely; find some study-buddies; discuss progress; and use relaxation techniques to focus better.

The traditional school will never go away; however, distance learning is a significant player in today's educational community. The advances in technology of the 21st century have provided the educational arena with a variety of options in teaching and fulfilling the objective that learning is a life-long process. Distance education affords all students the opportunity to attend classes and earn a degree.

According to Bauer (n.d.), in the world of education, the roles of faculty and students are ever changing. While distance learning is not a new idea, it is finally coming into its own with the advancements in communications made possible through the use of technology. With recent advances in technology an opportunity exists to increase access to education.

References

Askov, E., Johnston, J., Petty, L., Young, S. (2003). *Expanding access to adult literacy with online distance education.* Retrieved December 30, 2007 from http://www.ncsall.net/fileadmin/resources/research/op_askov.pdf

Bauer, J. C. (n.d.). *Distance learning: A student's perspective.* Retrieved December 30, 2007 from http://www.ucclermont.edu/~bauerj/AURCOBauerPaperRevised.htm

Belanger, F., & Jordan, D. H. (2000). *Evaluation and implementation of distance learning: Technologies, tools and techniques.* Hershey, PA: Idea Group.

Berge, Z. L., (1998, Summer). Barriers to online teaching in post-secondary institutions: Can policy changes fix it? *Online Journal of Distance Learning Administration, 1*(2), Summer. Retrieved on December 30, 2007 from http://www.westga.edu/~distance/Berge12.html

Berge, Z., & Muilenburg, L. (2001). Obstacles faced at various stages of capability regarding distance education in institutions of higher education. *Tech Trends, 46*(4), 40-45.

Bobby, C., & Capone, L. III (2000). *Understanding the implications of distance learning for accreditation and licensure of counselor preparation programs.* Greensboro, NC: ERIC Counseling and Student Services Clearinghouse (ERIC Document Reproduction No. ED446329).

Buchanan, E. A. (2000). Going the extra mile: Serving distance education students. *Online Journal of Distance Learning Administration, 3*(1). Retrieved December 30, 2007, from http://www.westga.edu/~distance/buchanan31.html

Carnevale, D., & Olsen, F. (2003, June). How to succeed in distance education. *Chronicle of Higher Education, 49*(40), A31-A34

Chang, V. (1998). *Policy development for distance education.* (Order No. JC980402). East Lansing, MI: ERIC Digest (ERIC Document Reproduction Service No. ED423922)

Chou, C. (2004). A model of learner-centered computer-mediated interaction for collaborative distance learning. *International Journal of Educational Telecommunications, 3*(1), 11-19.

Clifford, R. (1990). *Foreign languages and distance education*: Washington, DC: ERIC Clearinghouse on Languages and Linguistics. (ERIC Document Reproduction Service No. ED327066).

The Conference on Fair Use (CONFU). (1996, November). *Educational fair use guidelines for distance learning.* Retrieved December 30, 2007 from http://www.utsystem.edu/ogc/intellectualProperty/confu.htm

Educational Fair Use Guidelines for Distance Learning (2001). *CONFU: The conference on fair use.* Retrieved December 30, 2007 from http://www.utsystem.edu/ogc/intellectualProperty/distguid.htm

Epper R. M., & Garn, M. (2003, August). *Virtual college and university consortia: A national study.* State Higher Education Executive Officers (SHEEO) and the Western Cooperative for Educational Telecommunications (WCET). Retrieved December 30, 2007 from http://wcet.info/services/publications/vcu.pdf

Galusha, J. M. (1997). Barriers to learning in distance education. *Interpersonal Computing and Technology: An Electronic Journal for the 21st Century, 5*(3-4), 6–14.

Geisler, G. (1999). *Distance education: A killer app?* In B. Dempsey & P. Jones (Eds.), Internet Issues and Applications, 1997-1998. Lanham, MD: Scarecrow Press.

Gottschalk, T. H. (2003). *Distance education: An overview of the University of Idaho.* Retrieved December 30, 2007 from http://www.uidaho.edu/eo/dist1.html#delivery

Grubbs, L., & Lockey, M. (2000). Get smart: The pluses and minuses of e-learning. *PC World Communications, Inc., 18*(11), 116-123.

Howell, C. L. (2001). *Facilitating responsibility for learning in adult community college students.* ERIC Clearinghouse for Community College, 1-4. [ERIC Document Reproduction Service No. ED451841]. Retrieved December 30, 2007 from http://www.eric.ed.gov/ERICDocs/data/ericdocs2sql/content_storage_01/0000019b/80/16/f2/e8.pdf

Imel, S. (1995). *Inclusive adult learning environments*. ERIC Digest no. 162. Columbus, Ohio: ERIC Clearinghouse on Adult, Career, and Vocational Education, 1995. [ERIC Document Reproduction Service No. ED385779]. Retrieved December 30, 2007 from http://www.eric.ed.gov/ERICDocs/data/ericdocs2sql/content_storage_01/000 0019b/80/14/1d/2e.pdf

Imel, S. (1998). *Distance learning: Myths and realities*. Columbus, OH: ERIC Clearinghouse on Adult, Career and Vocational Education. [ERIC Document Reproduction Service No. ED426213]. Retrieved December 30, 2007 from http://www.eric.ed.gov/ERICDocs/data/ericdocs2sql/content_storage_01/000 0019b/80/17/2f/9f.pdf

Kerka, S. (1996). *Distance Learning, the internet and the world wide web*. Columbus, OH: ERIC Clearinghouse on Adult Career and Vocational Education (ERIC Document Reproduction Service No. ED395214). Retrieved December 30, 2007 from http://www.eric.ed.gov/ERICDocs/data/ericdocs2sql/content_storage_01/000 0019b/80/14/84/59.pdf

Knowles, M. (1984). *Andragogy in action*. San Francisco: Jossey-Bass.

Lei, S. (2007). Teaching practices of instructors in two community colleges in a western state. *Education, 128*(1), 148-160.

Leshin, C. B. (1998). *Student resource guide to the internet: Student success online*. Upper Saddle River, NJ: Prentice Hall Inc.

Levine, A., & Sun, J. C. (2003). *Barriers to distance education. Distributed education: Summary of a six-part series*. American Council on Education Center for Policy Analysis. Retrived December 30, 2007 from http://www.acenet.edu/bookstore/pdf/distributed-learning/summary/dist-ed-ex-summ-06.pdf

Lewis, L., Snow, K., Farris, E., & Levin, D. (1999). Distance education at postsecondary education institutions: 1997-98. *Education Statistics Quarterly, National Center for Education Statistics, 2*(1). Retrieved December 30, 2007 from http://nces.ed.gov/programs/quarterly/vol_2/2_1/q5-7.asp

Majdalany, G., & Guiney, S. (1999). *Implementing distance learning in urban schools.* New York, NY: ERIC Clearinghouse on Urban Education, Institute for Urban and Minority Education, Instructor College. (ERIC Document Reproduction Service No. ED438338). Retrieved December 30, 2007 from http://www.eric.ed.gov/ERICDocs/data/ericdocs2sql/content_storage_01/0000019b/80/16/0f/37.pdf

Mielke, D. (1999). *Effective teaching in distance education.* New York, NY: ERIC Clearinghouse on Teaching and Instructor Education (ERIC Document Reproduction Service No. ED436528). Retrieved December 30, 2007 from http://www.eric.ed.gov/ERICDocs/data/ericdocs2sql/content_storage_01/0000019b/80/15/fa/6f.pdf

Moore, M. G. (1989). Three types of interaction. *The American Journal of Distance Education, 3*(2). [Editorial]. Retrieved December 30, 2007 from http://www.ajde.com/Contents/vol3_2.htm#editorial

Moore, M. G. (1994). Editorial: Administrative barriers to adoption of distance education. *The American Journal of Distance Education, 8*(3). Retrieved December 30, 2007 from http://www.ajde.com/Contents/vol8_3.htm

National Center for Educational Statistics (NCES). (2003). *Distance education at degree-granting postsecondary institutions: 2000-2001* (NCES 2003-017). Retrieved December 30, 2007 from http://nces.ed.gov/fastfacts/display.asp?id=80

Palloff, R. M. & Pratt, K. (2001). *Lessons from the cyberspace classroom: The realities of online teaching.* San Francisco: Jossey-Bass.

Palloff, R. M. & Pratt, K. (2003). *The virtual student: A profile and guide to working with online learners.* San Francisco: Jossey-Bass.

Parrott, S. (1995). *Future learning: Distance education in the community college.* Los Angeles, CA. ERIC Clearinghouse for Community Colleges. (ERIC Document Reproduction Service No. ED385311). Retrieved December 30, 2007 from http://www.eric.ed.gov/ERICDocs/data/ericdocs2sql/content_storage_01/0000019b/80/14/18/2a.pdf

Public Broadcasting System (PBS). (2005). *Distance learning: An overview: Glossary.* Retrieved September 1, 2005 from http://www.pbs.org/als/dlweek/abc/indexuw.html

172

Roblyer, M., & Ekhaml, L. (2000). How interactive are your distance courses? A rubric for assessing interaction in distance learning. *Online Journal of Dstance Learning Administration, 3*(2). Retrieved December 30, 2007 from http://www.westga.edu/~distance/roblyer32.html

Rosenberg, M. J. (2001). *Building successful online learning in your organization: Strategies for delivering knowledge in the digital age.* New York: McGraw-Hill

Rossman, P. (1992). *The emerging world electronic university: Information age global higher education.* New York: Greenwood Press

Schoech, D. (2000). Teaching over the internet: results of one doctoral course. *Research on Social Work Practice, 10*(4), 467-487.

Simonson, M., Smaldino, S., Albright, M., & Zvacek, S. (2000). *Teaching and learning at a distance: Foundations of education.* Upper Saddle River, NJ: Prentice-Hall, Inc.

Tomei, L. (2001). *Teaching digitally: A guide for integrating technology into the classroom curriculum.* Norwood, MA: Christopher-Gordon Publishers.

Tomei, L. (2006). The impact of online teaching on faculty load: Computing the ideal class size for online courses. *Journal of Technology and Teacher Education, 14*(3), 531-541.

Twigg, C. A. (1997). Putting learning on track. *Educom Review, 32*(5), 60-61.

U.S. Distance Learning Association (USDLA). (2007). *Research info and statistics.* Retrieved December 30, 2007 from http://www.usdla.org/html/aboutUs/researchInfo.htm

White, B., & Bridwell, C. (2004). Distance learning techniques. In M. Galbraith (Ed.), *Adult Learning Methods: A Guide for Effective Instruction* (3rd ed.), Malabar, FL: Krieger Publishing.

Willis, B. (1995a, October). *Guide #2: Strategies for teaching at a distance: Distance education at a glance.* University of Idaho, College of Engineering, Engineering Outreach. Retrieved December 30, 2007 from http://www.uidaho.edu/eo/dist2.html

Willis, B. (1995b, October). *Guide #8: Strategies for learning at a distance: Distance education at a glance.* University of Idaho, College of Engineering, Engineering Outreach. Retrieved December 30, 2007 from http://www.uidaho.edu/eo/dist8.html

Wood, P. A. (2001). *The U.S. department of education and student financial aid for distance education: An update.* Washington, DC: ERIC Clearinghouse on Higher Education. (ERIC Document Reproduction Service No. ED457762). Retrieved December 30, 2007 from http://www.eric.ed.gov/ERICDocs/data/ericdocs2sql/content_storage_01/000 0019b/80/19/4e/f8.pdf

Wulf, K. (1996). Training via the internet: Where are we? *Training and Development, 50*(5). 50-53.

Chapter 12

Military and Armed Forces

Eli M. Perez Rivera

Introduction

Advances in technology and the war on terrorism have created a greater need for a more educated military force than in any preceding period in the history of the United States. Contemporary Armed Forces must be capable of using new technology and understand the impact on the country and the world. New approaches to education, training and fostering understanding are challenging the established educational programs to offer service members a more self-regulated, learning centered instructional service to military members. The Department of Defense (DoD) has demonstrated an ever increasing focus on distance learning technology to promote and continue service related educational goals (Pentagon Issues, 2006).

The Pentagon continues to examine and fund a networked centered education at military installations in an effort to transform the armed services to fight in the information age. This effort is actively transforming the system by offering a more learner-centered delivery system which brings greater expectations of service members who should assume an increased responsibility for the acquisition of knowledge and the development of their own skills. Breakthroughs in education have come from technologies that are derived from today's distance learning, multimedia, virtual reality, tele-presence concepts, and satellite feeds (Military Transformation, 2007).

The Department of Defense goals for adult education programs are to transform educational instruction by relying more on the use of web-based training and the significant use of innovation in instructional programs (Military Education, 2004). These initiatives also have multiple purposes. One is to serve as an enlistment incentive. The Department of Defense desires to bring in potential military recruits by providing enticing recruitment programs. Another educational incentive occurs after enlistment and is used as a tool to retain soldiers in the service.

Background

"Education as a lifelong process is an accepted objective of the armed services of the United States. Therefore, the policy of the Army, Navy, Air Force and Marine Corps is to look upon education not merely as an extension of schooling, but as a continuing necessity for service personnel" (Brodsky, 1970, p. 283). Educational opportunities for Armed Forces personnel are provided to improve job performance, develop individual's capacity for increased responsibility, and to create a more balanced life during and after service obligations (Brodsky, 1970).

The Armed Forces role in education can be traced to the Revolutionary War. President George Washington emphasized the need for promotion and distribution of knowledge and had proposed a national university. Although the national university was not established, other statesmen and founding fathers supported the idea. In 1795 there were plans to provide a complete educational system for the new nation; however they were rejected by Congress (Pulliam, 1968). Today, the United States has the most comprehensive system of educational assistance for service members of any nation in the world. However, it was not until the 20th century that education benefits became more widely available to both veteran and active duty personnel (Yaeger, 2005).

By the 1900s, Congress recognized that military service prevented individuals from receiving training for employment and passed the Rehabilitation Act of 1919. This act provided veterans disabled in World War I a monthly education assistance allowance. At the end of World War II, educational benefits were offered to all veterans by the Servicemen's Readjustment Act of 1944, known as the G. I. Bill. Further expansion of benefits for Vietnam Era veterans, passed by Congress in 1966, offered educational assistance to active duty service members (History of Education, 2007).

With the advent of the all volunteer force in 1973, the military services and Department of Defense (DoD) increased educational benefits as an incentive for recruitment and to encourage recruits to select critical career fields. The current Montgomery G.I. Bill (MGIB), enacted in 1985, provides up to 36 months of education assistance that can be used by both veterans and active duty members. In the late 1990s the military services embarked on initiatives to employ information technology in a host of ways that extended military capability on the battlefield, in intelligence, and in support activities. The services also implemented programs to certify member's expertise in information technology. The significant transformation of the military and breakthroughs in technologies and delivery systems continue to challenge the way the Armed Forces educate its members today (Active Duty GI Bill, 2007).

The United States military has been viewed as a form of national service, an occupation, a profession, a workplace, and an industry with approximately 26 million Americans living today having served in the military (Segal & Segal, 2005). The military continues to be a powerful engine of social progress and the most efficient part of the American melting pot because it continues to clearly define its mission and because of the necessity that at each level of responsibility individuals be qualified to carry their part of the assigned mission (Powell, 1991). However, today's military is not the military of half a century ago. The U.S. military no longer relies on the draft for personnel but rather is an all voluntary service. It is also better educated and represented by more females, minorities, and married personnel than the draft era military (Segal & Segal, 2005). The military of today is dealing more with social issues relating to the inclusion of gays, the role of females, the well being of the family members and the transition of the service members back to civilian life than at any time in the history of the services (Executive Summary, 2003).

The military services are one of the largest employers in the United States and enlist approximately 180,000 young men and women into the Armed Forces each year (U.S. Department of Defense, 2005). Recruiting a quality force is as important as ever given the decreasing number of men and women in the military and the increasing sophistication of weapons and methods for fighting modern wars. Service missions have changed from solely war fighting to include peacekeeping and humanitarian efforts. Although access to post-high school opportunities has expanded in recent years, it is suggested that service recruiting campaigns are having an impact on the youth of our country. Among today's youth, the military is perceived as providing opportunities, furthering education, helping individuals grow and mature, and contributing to the country (Sellman, 2004).

Active duty service recruits are typically high school graduates and the high school diploma is a predictor of successful adjustment in the military. "Recruits with a high school diploma have a 70-percent probability of completing a three-year term of enlistment, compared with a 50-percent likelihood for non-graduates" (U.S. Department of Defense, 2005, p. 1). In the late 1960s and early 1970s, the Services provided high school graduates, including those with alternative education credentials, higher priority for enlistment. In the mid- to late 1970s, the Army, Navy, and Air Force classified GED holders and high school graduates differently because evidence showed that persons with GED certification experienced higher first-term attrition.

In 1987, the DoD implemented a three-tier classification of education credentials. Tier 1 comprises regular high school diploma graduates, adult diploma holders and non-graduates with some college credit (at least 15 hours). Tier 2 includes alternative credential holders such as General Education Development (GED) diplomas or certificates of completion. Tier 3 refers to non-high school graduates. According to Sellman (2004), approximately 80% of high school diploma graduate (Tier 1) recruits complete their first 3 years of service, compared to only 50% of dropouts (Tier 3). The completion rates for enlistees holding a GED or alternative credential is between 50% and 80%. Therefore, recruits from Tiers 2 and 3 are required to achieve higher Armed Forces Qualification Test (AFQT) scores in order to qualify for enlistment.

Educational Programs

On-Site College Degree Programs

Educational programs through accredited universities and colleges of both regional and national reputation are available through military partnerships. These programs can lead to an associates, bachelors, masters, and doctoral degree which are available to service member on military installations around the world. This relationship between colleges and the military can be traced back to the end of World War II when colleges were invited to overseas installations for the purpose of offering college courses to service members and their families. In 1949, the Armed Forces invited the University of Maryland (UMUC) to offer off-duty classes for its military and civilian personnel stationed in Europe. Classes began in October of that year at six Education Centers in Germany, and the program steadily expanded. Today, the military has a network of more than 300 schools and over 10,000 courses, as certified by the American Council on Education (ACE), to train members in the skills necessary for 142 different career occupations (Credit Programs, 2007).

Distance Learning Programs

Advances in distance learning technology have allowed rapid expansion of distance education offerings. With the need for better educated members amid a competitive civilian labor market and salaries, the military finds itself confronted with a new set of challenges to recruit, retain, and train its members. While education in the military has made significant gains, it is the use of distance learning that has attracted the attention of students and educators alike. This form of education is improving the ability of service members to further their education regardless of where they are located in the world.

On December 24, 1941, the War Department authorized the establishment of a correspondence school for Army enlisted soldiers. The Army Institute began operations on April 1, 1942 at Madison, Wisconsin in facilities donated by the University of Wisconsin. By February 1943, the name was changed to the United States Armed Forces Institute (USAFI) to reflect the extension of services to the Navy, Marines, and Coast Guard. Literacy and high school level courses, as well as college and vocational courses, were developed and offered by correspondence using the U.S. Postal Service and the military postal systems overseas. This method of study was an attractive and efficient method of instruction for service members at permanent duty stations scattered throughout the world. As USAFI developed there was a need for self-teaching and testing materials; hence USAFI began producing adult basic education instructional materials. Participating colleges and universities provided college and vocational courses through their extension divisions under contract with the government (Kime & Anderson, 2000).

In the early 1970's service members were provided opportunities to obtain self-education through correspondence courses established with the creation of the Army Training and Support Center (ATSC) at Fort Eustis, Virginia. In addition to the correspondence courses, ATSC provided service members course video tapes and television programs to fulfill educational needs (ATSC History, 2007).

Brauchle (1998) argued that although the military culture valued education and encouraged service members to use the benefits allotted to them, a person's ability is greatly determined by opportunity. Opportunity to participate is not constant throughout one's military career but varies based on location, job, and military specialization. Service members participated whenever opportunity rose, since education represented higher education, promotion, pay, prestige, and a number of other factors which helped motivate them to continue their education.

The Armed Forces are embarking on a transformation from traditional to web-based delivery of instruction offering standardized individual, self-development, and small group training to service members through the application of web-based education. By providing adult education at these levels, the Department of Defense is providing professional training and education to the service men and women at any time and any location in the world. All services are actively replacing traditional classrooms with distance learning technologies for both active and reserve components (Bonk & Wisher, 2000).

Army. The Army approved a comprehensive plan for both the Regular Army and the Reserve Component. This plan calls for the preparation of 745 classrooms at home and abroad and mobile and deployable classrooms for specialized training. The plan calls for the conversion of 525 courses to a distance learning format. Fielding of the facilities is being timed to coincide with the availability of multimedia courseware and the infrastructure required to deliver video teletraining (VTT) courses and other training products. The delivery system combines fiber optics, asynchronous transfer mode (ATM) switching, and some satellite transmissions to link classrooms, field training, armories, and reserve centers. Implementing the Army's distance learning system is planned to continue through 2010 (Bonk & Wisher, 2000).

In July 2000, the Army announced a new Education Recruiting Initiative entitled Army University Access Online (AUAO), also referred to as EArmyU. The EArmyU program officially launched in 2001 and the purpose of the program was to offer eligible enlisted soldiers the opportunity to work towards a college degree or certificate at anytime or anywhere. Additionally, while the United States is engaged on the war on terrorism, the program continues to serve more than 46,000 soldiers around the world from Iraq to Afghanistan, from Europe to bases in the U.S. (Hickson, 2004).

EArmyU is one of the most innovative e-learning programs in the world today. EArmyU is a continuing education program that uses e-learning, computer-based programs that allow enlisted soldiers in the Army to earn college credits and degrees at no or low cost while they serve on active duty. This program assists soldiers in furthering their professional and personal goals while simultaneously providing the Army with the best educated force that this nation can provide. EArmyU supports the goal of transforming the military into an objective force capable of responding to the diverse and complex demands of the 21st century (GoArmyEd, 2007).

EArmyU emphasized the electronic, online aspect of the program and provides access to more than 145 degree plans at 28 regionally-accredited colleges and universities. The program provides up to 100 percent funding for tuition, books, fees, email, and an internet service provider (ISP). All participating schools must provide maximum credit for military training and experience and also for tests such as the CLEP (College Level Examination Program). EArmyU, now known as GoArmyU, provides an integrated online interface to all schools, with common application and registration forms; a degree map customized for the soldier to track his or her progress toward the degree of choice; an integrated searchable catalog from the schools; and library, tutoring, and academic advisement services (GoArmyEd, 2007).

Air Force. The Extension Course Institute (ECI) was established in 1950 as one of Air University's professional specialized schools. As the Air Force's only correspondence school, the institute's original mission was to provide voluntary nonresident courses for both active duty and reserve Air Force personnel. In 1963, the Institute became an essential and mandatory part of a on-the-job-training program when it started providing self-study materials for the specialty knowledge portion of the Air Force's official upgrade training program. In 1969, the Extension Course Institute was given the additional mission of providing study reference materials used in preparation for specialty knowledge testing under the weighted airman promotion system. Since 1977 the Institute has functioned as the registrar for Air University. The Air University Registrar maintains records and issues diplomas, not only for the institute's courses but also for all Air University schools except the Air Force Institute of Technology (Air University, 2007).

Beginning in February 2000, the Registrar became a part of the Air University Academic Office (AU/CF) but continues to provide registrar support to the Air Force Institute for Advanced Distributed Learning (AFIADL). Today, with a staff of both civilian and military members, the institute supports formal training and educational programs of the Air Force, Air National Guard, and Air Force Reserve. The Institute provides career broadening courses to people throughout the Department of Defense and to civil service employees in all federal agencies (Air University, 2007).

Navy. The Navy possesses its own distance educational learning tools capable of assisting the service members anytime and anywhere. The program is called Navy E-Learning and was implemented in May 2001. The Navy's distance learning program delivers, tracks, and manages more than 2,000 E-courses, at no cost to the user, for more than 1.2 million active duty sailors, marines, Department of the Navy civilian employees, reservists, retirees, and family members of active duty military (U.S. Department of Defense, 2004).

Through distance education, the Navy is able to take training to its own members and support their professional and personal goals. The Navy E-Learning educational programs allow the adult student to search education, training and professional development references and other computer links. Individuals can assess their level of competence in their job specialty and track their progress. Navy E-Learning provides on demand access to web-delivered courses, as well as libraries of schoolhouse courses. Navy E-Learning tracks and manages more than 3,966 E-Learning courses, at no cost to the user, for approximately 1.2 million active-duty sailors, marines, Department of the Navy civilians, reservists, retirees and family members enrolled in the Defense Enrollment Eligibility Reporting System (DEERS). As of May 2001 there have been approximately 450,000 registered users using this site (Persons, 2004).

In addition to the Navy E-learning system, the Marines have instituted a new Distance Learning Program (DLP) to assist Marines across the world to remain in a high state of readiness, regardless of their location. The DLP is accessed through MarineNet which is a network of video teleconferencing systems located on Marine Corps installations throughout the U.S. and Japan. Another distance learning program is the Sailor/Marine Online Academic Advisor (SMOLAA), which offers programs through the Navy College Program Distance Learning Partnership institutions. This program allows sailors and Marines to ensure their credits align with a degree program offered by 18 Navy distance learning partner colleges (Naval Education and Training Command Public Affairs, 2006).

The Montgomery GI Bill

On June 22, 1944 President Franklin D. Roosevelt signed the Servicemen's Readjustment Act of 1944, which is also known as the GI Bill of Rights. The term GI came into use during this time to affectionately refer to soldiers and was the acronym for the words Government Issue. This Bill of Rights was a subject of intense debate and parliamentary maneuvering; however, this legislation for World War II veterans has since been recognized as one of the most important acts of Congress. During the past five decades, the law has made possible the investment of billions of dollars in education and training for millions of veterans. The nation has in return earned many times its investment in increased taxes and a dramatically changed society (GI-Bill History, 2007).

Though the GI Bill became law, many in Congress and educators at colleges and universities had serious misgivings about the law. Some felt it was too expensive and would not be used advantageously by veterans. Others feared veterans would lower standards in education. But dismal economic predictions for the post-war years created pressure to pass offsetting legislation. Many saw a postwar America faced with the loss of millions of jobs, creating unprecedented unemployment. Many business and government leaders anticipated a widespread economic depression after the war. As early as 1942, plans were being made to handle the anticipated postwar problems. The National Resources Planning Board, a White House agency, had studied postwar manpower needs and in June 1943 recommended a series of programs for education and training (GI-Bill History, 2007).

The American Legion was credited with designing the main features of the GI Bill and getting the bill through Congress. The Legion overcame objections by other organizations that the proposed bill was too sweeping and could jeopardize veterans receiving any type of assistance. At the time Congress had already failed to act on 640 bills concerning veterans. The GI Bill was introduced in the Congress in January 1944, and after a nationwide campaign it passed on June 13 and President Roosevelt signed it into law on June 22. During 1947, veterans accounted for 49 percent of college admissions. By July 25, 1956, when the original GI Bill ended, there were 7.8 of 16 million World War II veterans who had participated in an education or training program (GI-Bill History, 2007).

Since that time there have been GI Bills, or other legislation for veterans, with adjusted benefits to adapt to the constant changes in America. Men and women in uniform still earn education benefits. In addition to being used to help veterans ease into civilian life, education benefits now are offered as an incentive to join the current all-volunteer military forces. Public Law 550, the Veterans Readjustment Assistance Act of 1952, was approved by President Truman on July 16, 1952. This Korean GI Bill provided education and training benefits as well as home, farm, and business loans. But unlike the federally funded unemployment allowance for World War II veterans, it made payment of unemployment compensation a state function. This program ended on January 31, 1965 and during the course of the program 2,391,000 of 5,509,000 eligible veterans received training, including: 1,213,000 in institutions of higher learning, 860,000 in other schools, 223,000 on the job, and 95,000 in institutional on-farm training. The total cost of the Korean Conflict GI Bill education and training program was $4.5 billion (History of the GI Bill, 2007).

Public Law 358, the Veterans Readjustment Benefits Act of 1966, was approved by President Lyndon B. Johnson on March 3, 1966. Home and farm loans, job counseling, and employment placement services were additional benefits. This education and training program went into effect June 1, 1966. It was retroactive, providing benefits to post-Korean veterans, who served between February 1, 1955, and August 4, 1964, as well as to Vietnam Era veterans, who served between August 5, 1964, and May 7, 1975. Service personnel were also eligible for GI Bill education and training while they were on active duty. Additionally, this bill enabled veterans to take cooperative farm, on-the-job, flight, and correspondence training. The disadvantaged veterans, those who did not finish high school before entering service, were provided full Veteran Assistance (VA) benefits while completing high school without losing any entitlement for college or other training. This program ended on December 31, 1989. During the years of the program, a total of 8.2 million veterans and service members received training: 5.1 million in colleges, 2.5 million in other schools, 591,000 on the job, and 56,000 in farm training. The VA spent more than $42 billion during this time to provide educational assistance (History of the GI Bill, 2007).

Another program, the Veterans' Educational Assistance Program (VEAP) was the program required service member contributions. This program was available to those who entered active duty between December 31, 1976 and July 1, 1985. Service members could contribute between $25 and $100 a month which would be matched on a 2-for-1 basis by the government. Total contribution by the service person could be no more than $2700, but the DOD could make additional contributions into the fund on behalf of individuals in critical military fields to encourage enlistment or reenlistment in the Armed Forces. In 1996, Public Law 104-275 provided that specific VEAP participants who were on active duty on October 9, 1996 could elect to make use of the Montgomery GI Bill. The deadline for this election was October 8, 1997 and 41,041 veterans and service members took advantage of this opportunity (History of the GI Bill, 2007).

The Montgomery GI Bill (MGIB) is an educational assistance program enacted by Congress to attract high quality men and women into the Armed Forces. The GI Bill is an education benefit earned by active duty, selected reserve and National Guard service members. The benefit is designed to help service members and eligible veterans cover the costs associated with obtaining an education or training. The GI Bill has several programs, and each is administered differently, depending on the person's eligibility and duty status. The program is administered by the Department of Veterans Affairs (VA) and provides educational assistance in the form of monthly payments for qualified soldiers enrolled in VA approved college level education and training. Generally, to qualify for the GI Bill individuals would have to contribute $100 a month for the first 12 months they are on active duty, or qualify under VEAP conversion; completed High School or have an equivalency certificate before they apply for benefits; and served at least 2 years on active duty (Active Duty GI Bill, 2007).

The MGIB is an educational program for individuals who entered active duty after June 30, 1985. The MGIB was enacted not only to help with the readjustment of discharged service members but also to support the concept of an all volunteer armed force. A provision was made to allow certain veterans with remaining entitlements under the Vietnam Era GI Bill, to qualify for MGIB benefits if they continued active duty (Active Duty GI Bill, 2007).

Tuition Assistance Program

The Tuition Assistance Program helps service members finance voluntary participation in off duty postsecondary educational programs. The Armed Forces Tuition Assistance (TA) Program is a benefit paid to eligible members of the Army, Navy, Marines, Air Force, and Coast Guard and is usually paid directly to the institution. Congress has provided each service the ability to pay up to 100% for the tuition expenses of its members. Each service has its own criteria for eligibility, obligated service, application process and restrictions. Additionally active duty members may elect to use the MGIB in addition to their service to provide tuition assistance to cover high cost courses. Tuition assistance is not a loan and is considered part of a service member's base pay (Your Top 5 Education Benefits, 2007).

The Air Force Tuition Assistance (TA) program provides 100% tuition and fees for college courses taken by active duty personnel during off duty hours. The program is one of the most frequent reasons given for enlisting and reenlisting in the Air Force. The Army Tuition Assistance (TA) Program provides financial assistance for voluntary off duty education programs in support of a soldier's professional and personal self-development goals. The program is open to all soldiers (officers, warrant officers, and enlisted) on active duty and Army National Guard and Army Reserve on active duty. The Navy Tuition Assistance program pays 100% of tuition and required fees charged by educational institutions for course enrollments. Marine Corps Tuition Assistance (TA) offers financial assistance to service members who elect to pursue off duty or voluntary education. The Coast Guard's TA program is designed to assist eligible personnel (active duty, enlisted and civilian employees) in their professional development by providing funding for off-duty voluntary education courses to broaden their academic or Coast Guard technical background (Tuition Assistance, 2007).

Military Education Academies

Military service academies are responsible for contributing to the development of our nation's leaders and are ideal opportunities for continuing adult education. The academies include the U.S. Military Academy (West Point, New York), the U.S. Naval Academy (Annapolis, Maryland), the U.S. Air Force Academy (Colorado Springs, Colorado), the U.S. Coast Guard Academy (New London, Connecticut) (Military Service Academies, 2007). These four educational institutions assist in improving students' minds but also develop character and leadership potential. All of the academies provide their students with tuition, books, board, medical and dental care for four years as well as a monthly stipend. Admission is competitive and graduates receive a Bachelor of Science degree and a leadership job as a junior officer in the Military—Army, Marine Corps, Navy, Air Force, or Coast Guard (Service Academies, 2007).

The Army U.S. Military Academy (USMA) at West Point, New York was founded March 16, 1802. The United States Military Academy, also known as West Point, graduates more than 900 or 25 percent of the new officers required by the United States Army each year. A favorite saying of this institution is that much of the history they teach was made by the people they taught. The student body, or corps of cadets, numbers 4,000, of whom approximately 15 percent are women. This institution has created noted leaders such as Pershing, MacArthur, Eisenhower, Patton and Schwarzkopf that are among the more than 50,000 graduates of the Military Academy and countless others have served in the fields of medicine, law, business, politics, and science following their careers in uniform (About the Academy, 2007).

The Navy/Marine Naval Academy in Annapolis, Maryland was founded in 1845 by the Secretary of the Navy, George Bancroft. Since 1845 more than 60,000 young men and women have successfully completed the four years and then served in the U.S. Navy. Many Naval Academy graduates have achieved greatness and earned a special place in our nation's history during its struggle to grow and preserve its freedom. Every summer a new class of 1,200 young men and women from all 50 states and beyond attend the Navy/Marine Naval Academy (About U.S. Naval Academy, 2007).

The Air Force Academy is located in Colorado Springs, Colorado. On April 1, 1954, President Eisenhower signed the Air Force Academy Act and on June 24, of that year, Secretary of the Air Force Harold Talbott announced that Colorado Springs would become the permanent home of the Academy. On August 29, 1958, 1,145 cadets moved from temporary quarters in Denver to the Colorado Springs site (U.S. Air Force Academy, 2007).

During its history, the Academy has become a leader among undergraduate institutions. Of the more than 35,009 cadets to have graduated in 44 classes, more than 51.2 percent are still on active duty. Thirty-two cadets have earned Rhodes Scholarships, five cadets have accepted Marshall Scholarships, ninety-two cadets have been accepted as Guggenheim Fellows, seventy-two cadets have been selected as National Science Foundation Fellows, thirty-one cadets have accepted Fulbright-Hays Scholarships, eighty-five cadets have accepted scholarships to attend Harvard University's John F. Kennedy School of Government, thirty-six cadets have been selected as Hertz Fellows, and, 593 cadets have entered medical school (U.S. Air Force Academy, 2007).

The Coast Guard Academy was developed with the 1915 merger of the Life Saving Service and Revenue Cutter Service. The academy was moved to its present location in New London in 1932. The *Barque Eagle* was acquired as war reparation from Germany in 1947 and continues to serve as an important sea-going training platform for cadets. More than 5,000 applicants interested in becoming Coast Guard officers seek appointments to the academy each year. Many of those applications come from the service's enlisted ranks. Acceptance to the academy is based on an annual nationwide competition. There are no Congressional appointments, state quotas or special categories. Approximately 275 men and women are admitted to the academy each July and each cadet undergoes a year-round regimen that ties together education, training and adjustment to military life. All cadets complete a core curriculum oriented toward engineering, the sciences and professional studies. The curriculum is partnered with training and experience in Coast Guard operations and leadership studies (U.S. Coast Guard Academy, 2007).

Earned College Credit

College credit can be obtained through a series of testing. The Defense Activity for Non-Traditional Education Support (DANTES) offers servicemembers free examinations to earn college credits without enrolling in classes. These exams include the CLEP (College Level Examination Program), DANTES Subject Standardized Test (DSST), and Excelsior College Exams (ECE). The examination program also includes the SAT, LSAT, ACT, GRE, PRAXIS, GED, and GMAT assessment tests. The DANTES Distance Learning Program provides a wide range of non-traditional education programs critical for all service members who need alternatives to fulfill degree requirements when classroom courses are unavailable or when work schedules and family commitments do not permit class attendance. DANTES provides courses ranging from high school to graduate level through nearly 100 regionally accredited institutions. Other courses are oriented toward a non-degree-seeking or technically oriented student. Courses are available to personnel in all Military Services (Higher Education Programs, 2007).

American Council on Education (ACE)

The American Council on Education (ACE), under Department of Defense contract, develops credit recommendations based on its evaluation of Service school courses, military training, and most enlisted occupations. Since 1945, this Council has provided colleges and universities with guidelines on how to award credits for extra-institutional learning. Today, more than 2,300 accredited colleges and universities use American Council on Education credit award recommendations. The recommendations are published in the Guide to the Evaluation of Educational Experiences in the Armed Forces, commonly referred to as the ACE Guide (Higher Education Programs, 2007).

Servicemembers Opportunity Colleges (SOC)

The Servicemembers Opportunity Colleges (SOC) was established in 1972 and began with a network of approximately 1,550 colleges and universities that subscribe to criteria designed to meet the higher education needs of members of a mobile military population. Member schools have minimum residency requirements, award credit for military training and experiences, readily award credit for learning demonstrated through nationally recognized testing programs, and accept credit transferred from other member institutions. At the request of the Services, SOC has designed and established degree networks, with titles such as SOCAD, SOCNAV, and SOCMAR to meet needs unique to each service. It operates under a contract that DOD maintains with SOC's primary sponsor, the American Association of State Colleges and Universities (AASCU). Today, SOC is a Consortium of national higher education associations and over 1800 colleges and Universities who pledge to support the higher education needs of the military service member (Higher Education Programs, 2007).

Conclusion

The Department of Defense recognizes and appreciates the value that education has had in assisting the all-volunteer force to operate on the job in a smarter, more effective, and efficient manner. Recruits have identified educational opportunities as one of the top reasons that they join the military. Many highly qualified service members also choose to remain in the military because of these educational opportunities. The continuing education programs described above contribute significantly to achieving the priorities that the Department of Defense and the different services has established for recruitment, job performance, readiness, and retention.

The 2003 *Population Representation Report* reveals that both the diversity and the quality of the total force. The men and women of the armed services are of various racial and ethnic groups. They come from divergent backgrounds, from every state in our country, serve as Active and Selected Reserve and as enlisted members and officers of the Army, Navy, Marine Corps, Air Force, and Coast Guard. The mean cognitive ability and educational level of these soldiers, sailors, marines, and airmen are above the average of comparably-aged U.S. citizens (Executive Summary, 2003).

Although the force is diverse, it is not an exact replica of society as a whole. The military way of life is more attractive to some members of society than to others. Among the enlisted ranks, the proportion of African Americans continues to exceed population counts of the civilian labor force. Hispanics are underrepresented in the military, but their percentages have increased over the years. Minorities comprise proportionally less of the officer corps; however, their representation levels are in keeping with minority statistics among the pool of college graduates from which second lieutenants and ensigns are drawn. Women continue to be underrepresented in the military, disproportional to civilian society. However, statistics indicate that women continue to make gains in both numbers and proportionally (Executive Summary, 2003).

The all volunteer force is now facing increased recruiting challenges as a result of the Armed Forces' expanding roles and greater competition from colleges, universities, and private employers as compared to the early 1990s. Attention to human resource issues beyond numerical representation is necessary to manage recruiting and to promote readiness.

References

About the Academy (2007). *United States Military Academy: WestPoint.* Retrieved May 28, 2007, from http://www.usma.edu/about.asp

About U.S. Naval Academy (2007). *United States Naval Academy.* Retrieve May 28, 2007, from http://www.usna.edu/about.htm

Active Duty GI Bill User's Guide (2007). *Military.com: Education.* Retrieved May 28, 2007, from http://education.military.com/money-for-school/active-duty/gi-bill/active-duty-gi-bill-users-guide

Air University (2007). *The intellectual and leadership center of the Air Force.* Retrieved May 27, 2007, from http://www.maxwell.af.mil/au/index.asp

ATSC History (2007). *Army Training Support Center: History.* Retrieved on May 28, 2007, from http://www.atsc.army.mil/atsc/History.asp

Bonk, C., & Wisher, R. (2000, September). *Applying collaborative and e-learning tools to military distance learning: A research framework.* Alexandria, VA: US Army Research Institute for the Behavorial and Social Sciences.

Brauchle, K.C. (1998). *United States Armed Forces voluntary education program: The effect on enlisted servicemember retention.* Paper presented at the Annual Meeting of the American Association for Adult and Continuing Education, Phoenix, AZ.

Credit Programs (2007). *Today's Military: Credit Programs.* Retrieved on May 28, 2007, from http://www.todaysmilitary.com/app/tm/get/collegehelp/credit

Executive Summary (2003). *Office of the Under Secretary of Defense, Personnel and Readiness: Executive summary of the 2003 population representation in the military services.* Retrieved on May 28, 2007, from http://www.defenselink.mil/prhome/poprep2003

GI-Bill History (2007). *Born of controversy: The GI bill of rights.* Retrieved on May 27, 2007, from http://www.gibill.va.gov/GI_Bill_Info/history.htm

GoArmyEd (2007). *eArmyU mission statement.* Retrieved on May 27, 2007, from https://www.earmyu.com/public/public_earmyu-earmyu_mission_statement.aspx

Hickson, C. (2004). 46,000 take eArmyU courses online. *Military Connections.* Retrieved on May 27, 2007 from http://www.militaryconnections.com/news_story.cfm?textnewsid=1074

Higher Education Programs (2007). *Defense Activity for Non-Traditional Education Support (DANTES): Education Support to the DoD – Worldwide.* Retrieved May 28, 2007, from http://www.dantes.doded.mil/dantes_web/danteshome.asp?Flag=True

History of Education (2007). *History of Education: Selected moments of the 20ᵗʰ century, 1944 GI Bill of Rights.* Retrieved on May 28, 2007 from, http://fcis.oise.utoronto.ca/~daniel_sc/assignment1/1944gibill.html

History of the GI Bill (2007). *Congressional medal of honor: History of the GI bill.* Retrieved May 27, 2007, from http://www.medalofhonor.com/GIBill.htm

Kime, S., & Anderson, C. (2000). Contributions of the military to adult and continuing education. In A. Wilson & E. Hayes (Eds.), *Handbook of adult and continuing education* (pp. 464-479). San Francisco: Jossey-Bass.

Military Education. (2004, July). *DOD needs to develop performance goals and metrics for advanced distributed learning in professional military education: Report to the ranking minority member, committee on Armed Services, House of Representatives* (GAO-04-873). Washington, DC: U.S. Government Accountability Office.

Military Services Academies (2007). *U.S. Department of Defense.* Retrieved May 28, 2007, from http://www.defenselink.mil/faq/pis/20.html

Military Transformation: A Strategic Approach (2007). *Force Transformation: Department of Defense.* Retrieved on May 28, 2007 from http://www.oft.osd.mil/index.cfm

Naval Education and Training Command Public Affairs (2006). *Sailors jumpstart college degree with virtual counseling, SMART.* Retrieved May 27, 2007, from http://www.news.navy.mil/search/display.asp?story_id=24059

Pentagon Issues Guidelines for Distance Education. (2006, Sep/Oct). *Educause Review, 41*(5), p. 6.

Persons, D. (2004). *Navy e-learning migrates to Navy knowledge online.* Retrieved May 27, 2007, from http://www.news.navy.mil/search/display.asp?story_id=15816

Powell, C. (1991). America's military: A melting pot that works. *NPQ: New Perspectives Quarterly, 8*(3), 17-19.

Pulliam, J. (1968). *History of education in America.* Columbus, OH: Charles E. Merrill Publishing.

Segal, D., & Segal, M. (2005). America's military population. *Diversity Factor, 13*(2), 18-23.

Sellman, W. S. (2004, September 30). Predicting readiness for military services: How enlistment standards are established. *National Assessment Governing Board Report.* Retrieved May 27, 2007, from http://www.nagb.org/release/sellman.doc

Service Academies (2007). *Today's Military: Service Academies.* Retrieved May 28, 2007, from, http://www.todaysmilitary.com/app/tm/get/collegehelp/academies

Tuition Assistance (TA) Program Overview (2007). *Military.com: Education.* Retrieved May 28, 2007, from http://education.military.com/money-for-school/tuition-assistance/tuition-assistance-ta-program-overview

U.S. Air Force Academy (2007). *United States Air Force Academy: About the Academy.* Retrieved May 28, 2007, from http://www.usafa.af.mil/index.cfm?catname=Academy%20Info

U.S. Coast Guard Academy (2007). United States Coast Guard Academy: About the Academy. Retrieved May 28, 2007, from http://www.uscga.edu/display.aspx?id=333

U.S. Department of Defense (2004). Navy e-learning recognized by e-gov conference. *Navy News Release* (No. 346-02). Retrieved May 27, 2007 from http://www.defenselink.mil/releases/2002/b07032002_bt346-02.html

U.S. Department of Defense (2005). *Who is volunteering for today's military?* Retrieved May 27, 2007, from http://www.defenselink.mil/news/Dec2005/d20051213mythfact.pdf

Yaeger, J. (2005). The origins of joint professional military education. *Joint Force Quarterly, 37*(2), 74-82.

Your Top 5 Education Benefits (2007). *Military.com: Education.* Retrieved May 28, 2007, from http://www.education.military.com/money-for-school/your-top-5-education-benefits

Chapter 13

Labor and Workforce Education: A Union Training Perspective

Kristi D. Mathews

Introduction

The Labor Movement strives toward a new life. It dreams of a world where economic and social justice prevail...where society will be organized as a cooperative commonwealth...To attain this end it is necessary to develop a social conscience and a sense of responsibility in the labor movement. With this end in view, we set out to organize our educational work.
~Union Educator Fannia Cohn (1921)

The first decades of the 20th century marked a period of rapid change toward an industrialized America. One defining characteristic of this time period was the increasing attention toward worker education within the labor movement. In the 1930s, awareness of the need for worker education came to the forefront as a critical component for survival and progression. Trade unions and their management counterparts were at the heart of such growing social movements. An industrializing society was pleading for more skilled workers. Education and training were paving the way for the success of labor in the United States, and pioneering labor leaders began promoting and bargaining for these efforts with the real hope of improving the struggle of the working class and its circumstances (Beard, 1927).

Since the beginning of such movements, the education and training of workers in labor unions has been filled with opposition and controversy from inside and outside forces. Labor has seen increases in support for continuing education followed by periods of dramatic decrease. Today, the advances in technology and the demand for more formal and informal learning experiences for labor are increasing the pressure for more training and education for members. The development of Attitudes, Skills, and Knowledge (ASK) within labor organizations has been and continues to be the life-blood that causes manpower organizations to thrive where developed or to wither in situations where these components are not embraced. Education is no longer an option for union membership; it is a necessity for survival in today's workforce.

The Call of Labor to Adult Education

Workforce training has no greater mission than to develop the union membership into productive individuals equipped with the attitudes, skills, and knowledge that will make them an asset to their organizations and to society at large. Since adult education began to emerge as a field of practice, educators have been inundated with theories and models of adult learning. Despite differences in theory, one idea is nearly unanimously accepted. Training adults is a two-purpose process in which short-time goals of self-improvement can be made compatible with long-time policies of changing society (Merriam & Brockett, 1997). According to Malcolm Knowles (1968) it is ultimately the responsibility of those training adults to satisfy the needs of learners and help them achieve their goals both for themselves and for the workforce at large.

Adult education is no longer limited to the confines of the traditional education offered by colleges and universities. It is widely recognized that education, especially for adult learners, takes place outside of the conventional classroom. Labor forces are consistently seeking to upgrade the education and training of their membership. Never has there been a greater demand for programs designed for adult learners in fields that require technical expertise. Labor education in industrial fields is now viewed as a necessity for upgrading skills, staying on the cutting edge of new technologies, and advancing in careers through training, development, and certification. The speed at which the workforce is changing is forcing employers to consider such training more than ever before. Training is a critical component to workers due to the rapidly changing world in which work is becoming more sophisticated and complex. This call for change requires a clear definition of education and meaningful training.

Labor unions are far from a new concept in American culture. Unions are nearly as old as the Declaration of Independence. Unions first materialized as a means to a better life – improved wages and benefits, more acceptable working conditions, attaining a better education, having more job security and doing more dignified work. Through years of negotiating, collective bargaining and combating workplace injustice, unions have helped raise the standard of living for American workers. Training workforce labor is more than simply fulfilling a need for skilled manpower. It equips future leaders with the knowledge to carry on traditions for unions of the future. The fundamental focus of labor education is to inform the membership of their societal role and responsibility, while turning out the most highly skilled workforce possible.

Trade-union training is often mistaken for technical training. Without the aforementioned fundamental training of labor responsibilities, unions are in danger of losing focus and failing to equip future labor with the abilities to assert their economic rights to livable wages, lower hours, better working conditions, and protection against the arbitrary actions of employers (Zack, 1964). In 2006, 12% of employed wage and salary workers were union members (Bureau of Labor Statistics, 2007). Unions provide formal and informal opportunities for members to learn about worker rights, as well as public and political issues. Union settings generally encourage informal, collaborative learning about human rights and tend to encourage training that promotes human capital (Livingstone & Raykov, 2005). By providing a framework of labor union history, policy and procedures, unions can provide laborers that have quality training while continuing to improve economic position and quality of life for their membership.

Labor Training through the Apprenticeship System

Apprenticeship is likely the oldest form of training in recorded history. European apprenticeships can be traced back as far as the Middle Ages (U.S. Department of Labor, 1987). This ancient learning process allowed a newcomer to a trade to simultaneously gain knowledge and experience. An apprenticeship is the comprehensive training of a beginner, to learn a craft under the supervision of a skilled worker. The Division of Workforce Development (2005) defines apprenticeship as a voluntary, industry-driven program, which is sponsored by employers, employer associations, or jointly by management and labor. An apprentice, as an employee, receives supervised, structured, on-the-job training combined with related technical instruction regarding a specific occupation. An apprenticeship program is comprised of a combination of on-the-job training and classroom instruction. Exposure to skilled workers combined with the theoretical aspects of an occupation provides the scaffolding for a competent worker.

Apprenticeships are valuable for many career-training programs, specifically the construction trades. While the apprenticeship method is used more sparingly in other occupations and industries, the construction industry particularly relies upon apprenticeship programs for the development of skilled workers. These programs require cooperative efforts from many entities. Labor, management, and government must be cooperatively invested in this purposeful pursuit of excellence. To meet the needs of industry, apprenticeship programs are charged with the responsibility to produce the best skilled craftsman, which means recruiting, training and retaining the best while encouraging life-long learning of additional technical competencies.

The organized trade union is constantly competing with other training forces as well as with colleges, universities, and private (for-profit) training entities for the acquisition of talent. Some individuals have been taught to believe that college is the best educational choice regardless of what career path is chosen. However, in light of the ever advancing and emerging new technologies combined with fierce inner-industry competition both at home and globally, the United States workforce must be the most highly trained and skilled in their selected crafts.

The 1937 Fitzgerald Act, also referred to as the National Apprenticeship Act, enables the United States Department of Labor to establish guidelines to promote standards for apprenticeship sponsors while keeping the best interest of apprentices in the forefront of decision-making and policy. Under this 1937 Act, union apprenticeships conduct operations jointly through committees staffed with both labor and management that adopt standards and policies, which are approved by the United States Department of Labor's Bureau of Apprenticeship and Training (BAT) now known as the Office of Apprenticeship Training, Employer and Labor Services (OATELS).

Whether union or non-union, the Department of Labor sets national guidelines for the development of standards and registers all nationally recognized apprenticeship programs. The Fitzgerald Act of 1937 remains the basic legislation regarding the establishment of training through apprenticeship programs. Nationally recognized apprenticeships are registered with the United States Department of Labor. Through the Labor Department's registration, an apprenticeship meets government regulations (29CFR Part 29 and 29CFR Part 30) to ensure adequate training, in a safe work environment, with proper supervision guaranteed to occur without discrimination. Upon completion of any nationally registered apprenticeship, graduates receive certificates and diplomas, which are accepted by employers nationwide (Crosby, 2002).

Union Apprenticeship Selection

Labor has undergone a profound transformation since the initial industrialization of America. No longer does labor consist of mundane jobs divided into simple, easily-manageable job tasks. In contrast, the jobs of today are demanding higher levels of comprehension in virtually all skill sets including verbal, mathematical, and interpersonal. Despite this demand for a variety of skills, the American Management Association (Bureau of National Affairs, 1995) found that 36 percent of job applicants lack basic math and reading competencies for the jobs for which they apply. An awareness of such statistics is essential for training union workers.

Technology is unrelenting in its demand for trained intelligence (McKernan, 1994) because technology is changing as quickly as it is implemented. It is imperative that selection procedures for candidates ensure that training programs have qualified individuals with aptitudes appropriate for their chosen fields. The United States Department of Labor (1984) 29 CFR 29.5 – Standards of Apprenticeship (1977) makes provisions concerning the minimum qualifications required by a sponsor for persons entering an apprenticeship program.

Unions have dedicated time and research to develop some the most highly efficient training programs in the world. One way that unions ensure the fair and proper selection of apprentices to a trade is by the Apprenticeship Selection Procedures.

Selection procedures ensure the equality of access to all interested individuals while upholding the standard of excellence for those entering a trade. Selection procedures are in accordance with industry policy and collective bargaining agreement language and carefully lay out all requirements for entry into any program. Before beginning most training or apprenticeships, one must obtain a qualifying score on an aptitude test and complete an oral interview before a selection committee. Applicants desiring entry into training programs are ranked among a list of other applicants and offered entry according to their ranking. Entry into most union programs is highly competitive with the intention of taking only the upper echelon of applicants in order to establish and maintain the most highly skilled workforce possible.

Union Training

The age-old methodology of guiding the evolution of craftsmen from apprentices to journeymen is considered the keystone of training in trade-related occupations. Despite the numbers of individuals who believe that a college degree is the only door to career success, no other form of education for trades has been as successful, nor is there any form of education more honorable to the trades. Few would argue that what is required to have a successful learning experience in a technical field is dramatically different from traditional higher education. Trade unions tend to focus on training that offers the membership intellectual skills that provide trade-specific knowledge, often overlooked in traditional schooling (Zack, 1964).

In union programs, labor and management co-create training opportunities and share in the administration of the endeavor. Labor and management recognize a need for standardized and extensive training that covers all facets of a trade. Union training requires rigorous preparation of an individual studying a craft in its entirety, whereas non-union training is far less structured and appears to focus less on the needs of the individual worker. Londrigan and Wise (1997) concluded in a recent study that union apprentice training programs consistently outperform non-union training programs in every critical measure of success from diversity to completion rates.

A critical difference between the structure of joint labor-management apprenticeship programs versus training conducted by unilateral sponsors is that non-joint training generally makes greater use of specified task training. Training of non-union workers is often geared toward a trainee's ability to accomplish specialized tasks in lieu of broader training offered by traditional apprenticeship programs embraced by the union (The Business Roundtable, 1988). Though training on specified tasks is less economical and can be expedited more quickly, the overall broad knowledge of the traditionally trained union workforce learned slowly over time makes union workers more difficult to replace giving them more job stability and greater satisfaction.

National Joint Apprenticeship and Training Committee

Perhaps the best way to understand the intricacies of joint labor-management training is to see it in action at its very best. The National Joint Apprenticeship and Training Committee (NJATC) for the International Brotherhood of Electrical Workers (IBEW) and the National Electrical Contractor's Association (NECA) was founded in 1941 and has developed into what is perhaps the world's largest apprenticeship program. The NJATC came into existence when both labor and management discerned a need for employing the most highly skilled workforce possible. The IBEW, the world's largest electrical union, and NECA, the management association for the electrical contractors joined forces and determined to be unsurpassed in the training of skilled workers. The result was the National Joint Apprenticeship and Training Committee for the Electrical Industry, which has greatly enhanced training efforts through hundreds of local training programs across the United States.

This partnership between the IBEW and NECA remedied many of the problems that the electrical industry was facing. Both organizations realized that the industry was constantly changing and expanding at a rate that made it difficult to keep pace with the ever-changing technology. A little over two decades ago, the face of training definitively changed for the IBEW. Technological advancement made it necessary to enthusiastically pursue vast changes in education and training. For an occupation so demanding and complex, it became necessary to boost training and education to a new level.

The occupations of the electrical construction industry require top-notch individuals with exemplary training. The introduction of the NJATC to the electrical industry provided a program to train the finest and best-equipped electrical workers in the country, across the board from apprentice to journeyman status. The goal of the program was, and still is, to provide proficient and highly skilled electrical workers. The NJATC, the IBEW, and NECA have dedicated time to develop an efficient training program in order that an apprentice in training can become a well-qualified electrical worker through a systematic program of schooling coupled with on-the-job training. The electrical construction industry relies on the NJATC to meet their training needs.

The foundation of the NJATC philosophy lies in a belief that training, and training alone, will determine the degree of employability for members of the IBEW and NECA and provide a high standard of living for those members (US Department of Labor Bureau of Apprenticeship and Training, 2000). The NJATC provides extensive training to all apprentices and journeyman recognizing that there are no short cuts to competency in the electrical construction industry. Therefore, the NJATC provides a uniform, national training program that produces the most highly skilled workers and craftsman that the electrical construction industry has to offer. Through the NJATC, industry-driven apprenticeship provides union workers with meaningful occupations and equips society with a highly skilled workforce at virtually no cost to the taxpayers (US Department of Labor Bureau of Apprenticeship and Training, 2000). Superior workforce training is the cornerstone that supports the electrical construction industry. "It is what enables us to promote the NECA-IBEW team as the best choice for demanding customers and make good on our promises of quality, professionalism and reliability" (Ben Cook, NECA President, personal communication, 2003.)

Training Standards

Training standards ensure that all Joint Apprenticeship Training Committees nationwide follow specific policies and processes. Local apprenticeship programs across the country conform to the National Apprenticeship and Training Standards for the Electrical Industry to guarantee equality in the qualifications, selection, education and training of all apprentices. NJATC standards provide a thorough, scientifically determined job description for all apprenticeship programs. Following are examples of the basic standards specified under the U.S. Department of Labor Employment and Training Administration (2005) Title 29, Code of Federal Regulations, Part 29.5:

- full and fair opportunity to apply for apprenticeship;
- a schedule of work processes in which an apprentice is to receive training and experience on the job;
- organized instruction designed to provide apprentices with the knowledge in technical subjects related to their occupation;
- progressively increasing schedule of wages;
- supervision of on the job training with facilities appropriate for training; and
- evaluation of job performance and related instruction with appropriate documentation and periodic review.

Selection procedures for union apprentices carefully lay out all requirements for entry into any program. The NJATC has specific methods for applicant selection. Procedures are consistently applied to all parties interested in the apprenticeship. For example, the IBEW-NECA segment of the electrical construction industry accepts applications regardless of race, color, religion, national origin, or sex. Recognizing the need for apprenticeship diversity, the NJATC, IBEW and NECA are actively recruiting various ethnic and racial groups as well as women.

The Building and Construction Trades Department (BCTD), a department of the American Federation of Labor/Congress of Industrial Organizations (AFL-CIO), reported that the enrollment of minorities in union programs is about three times as high as non-union enrollment. In union apprenticeship programs, African Americans comprise about thirty percent of apprentices compared to fifteen percent for the non-union sector.

Work Process and On-the-Job Training (OJT)

The NJATC holds fast to an age-old philosophy that the best place to learn a job is on the job. What makes union apprentices and journeymen the most thoroughly trained with the most concise and contemporary knowledge is the fact that they are exposed to their careers first hand for a minimum 8,000 mandatory OJT hours prior to graduating the apprenticeship. Non-union competitors may require far less OJT and classroom hours; therefore, they have less expert guidance from those involved in the field. To produce an elite labor union, apprenticeships provide novices in a trade exposure to experts both in the classroom and on the job. On-the-job training is one of the fundamental aspects of apprenticeship where an apprentice practices virtually every aspect of the occupation for which they are training.

Every apprentice accepted into a registered apprenticeship program enters into an apprenticeship agreement. Apprenticeship agreements define the terms by which the training will occur. Under the supervision of a journeyman or other expert in their chosen field, the apprentice receives instruction, performs the job and receives feedback and evaluations from a supervisor. To complete training programs, apprentices must satisfactorily fulfill both on-the-job training and classroom requirements meeting the minimum standards for a specific trade as recognized and registered by the BAT or SAC. When combined with related instruction in the classroom, on-the-job training serves as the mechanism that gives life to the knowledge, thus reinforcing the skills needed in the workforce. The electrical union continues to set the standards by passing on attitudes, skills, and knowledge of the trade to present and future ambassadors of the IBEW and NECA.

Organized Instruction

The NJATC is constantly grooming the training arm of the industry. In 1990, the NJATC initiated the National Training Institute to expand the abilities of electrical apprenticeship instructors. The electrical industry sensed a need for quality instructors who had already proven they were skilled craftsmen. Though excellent in the trade, craftsmen were faced with a new challenge of becoming professional classroom instructors. The National Training Institute has graduated approximately 1,500 instructors from its four-year instructor-training program. It is yet another example of the electrical union's dedication to produce a paramount workforce, surpassing even their own expectations.

Each year, train-the-trainer courses are provided across the country in all aspects of the electrical trades. It is the responsibility and duty of union instructors and trainers on-the-job and in the classroom to pass on knowledge to the apprentices they seek to organize and train. At the 2003 NJATC National Training Institute Commencement, President Edwin D. Hill said, "Let the shoddy work, the slapdash and the shortcuts be associated with others, not with us. Our pride will not permit our great legacy of being the best to be compromised. It is up to you (the instructor) to pave the road that we travel with knowledge; to ensure that our members have the tools needed to fulfill their destiny as the future of this great union." The electrical union is setting the standard for other trades.

Union Wage Schedule

The organized electrical construction industry continues to provide successful, fulfilling careers that offer a high quality life for its membership. Through collective bargaining, unions have raised the standard of living for the majority of American workers. Though most workers in America do not belong to a union, most are enjoying the rights the union voice has established. However, there is still a distinct advantage to belonging to a union. According to the U.S. Department of Labor Statistics, union workers average about twenty-six percent more in earnings than non-union laborers. Apprentices who begin their program affiliated with the union earn at least half of the journeyman rate to start and increase incrementally throughout their program. The apprenticeship system provides a win-win situation for all parties.

Upon entry into an apprenticeship program, apprentices are paid a progressively increasing schedule of wages as they train as outlined in their specific registered apprenticeship standards. Union apprenticeship programs typically set higher first wage periods and continue to offer higher wages throughout the career of the worker compared to non-union counterparts (HRSDC, 2001; Union Apprenticeship, 2007).

Apprenticeship is different than other adult education programs. Apprentices have an uncommon economic and career advantage over most graduating students in traditional education programs. Apprentices graduate with modest burden, unlike most college university graduates who complete their schooling with substantial student loan debt and no job experience. In the apprenticeship program, contractors are allowed to employ apprentices on public work sites for less than the prevailing wage in exchange for providing training through a registered apprenticeship program. Apprentices have no school expense outside of textbooks and they are receiving a paycheck in the meantime. They are earning while they are learning and are productive members of society. Apprentices pay taxes and the training they are receiving is not, by design, a burden to society. These benefits coupled with superior training are cause for all to embrace quality apprenticeship as a legitimate, economical method of education and training.

Union Benefits

Non-union workers are less likely to receive health care and pension benefits. The Department of Labor Statistics reported in 1999 that seventy-three percent of union workers received medical care benefits compared to fifty-one percent of non-union workers. Many non-union workers pay all or a large portion of their benefits such as healthcare and retirement. The *Monthly Labor Review* revealed that benefit costs for union workers continued to rise sharply, with union employers paying 10.3 percent, compared with an increase of 6.2 percent paid for non-union worker's benefits in December of 2004 (Bureau of Labor Statistics, 2004).

Union workers also report much higher instances of pension and retirement benefits. Seventy-nine percent of union workers have defined-benefit retirement that will provide guaranteed monthly pension checks as opposed to only forty-four percent for the non-union sector. Among union workers, seventy-one percent have sickness and accident insurance whereas only thirty-six percent of non-union workers enjoy the same security for themselves and their family.

Thus, wage increases during training and benefits of union apprenticeship programs are far superior to non-union workers. All of this is an integral piece of what makes union training an ideal scenario. Benefits go far beyond the mentioned monetary and compensatory perks. There are many legal rights to which union members are privileged, whereas non-union workers remain unrepresented and vulnerable in unfair or harsh work situations. For example, jobs are more secure with the union which makes sure that no one is discriminated against and that everyone is treated fairly. Belonging to the union gives workers a voice on the job and the collective voice of the workers ensures that union member voices are heard.

Union leaders are mindful of the obligation to provide superior instruction by well-qualified instructors to their membership. The apprenticeship programs offered by the IBEW and NECA are intensive three to five year programs. Few other industries compare in intensity as apprentices engage in a rigorous, educational process of specified hours of relevant classroom instruction while having daily, hands-on exposure to the trade on an actual job site. Under the watchful supervision of skilled journeymen, apprentices are constantly exposed to their chosen trade for thousands of hours before entering the workforce as a journeyman. The NJATC currently has over 300 programs scattered across all states, as well as Canada and Puerto Rico.

Evaluations and Reviews

As with most adult education programs, the NJATC sets evaluation periods that occur throughout the apprenticeship. The local programs examine each apprentice's work and school records periodically to determine advancement. Those meeting the standards of the program in relevant instruction and on-the-job training receive pay increases. Those falling short of minimum standards will be delayed in pay raises and promotions. The joint committee, which is comprised of equal numbers of representatives from labor and management, can dismiss an apprentice for unsatisfactory performance.

The organized electrical construction industry is training more than 45,000 apprentices each year for jobs in the industrial, commercial, residential, and telecommunication sectors. Other organizations have attempted to mimic union-apprenticeship training programs while cutting corners and have fallen short of this goal. The AFL-CIO's Building and Construction Trades Department recently called upon the Labor Department to investigate claims of such flawed and failing apprenticeship training programs. Also, upon request from the AFL-CIO, the Government Accountability Office (GAO), the government's top investigative agency, confirmed the existence of serious problems in non-union apprenticeship training programs.

Among the findings of the Government Accountability Office were underlying issues that cause programs to only graduate a fraction of apprentices entering non-union programs. The all-trades graduation rate for union apprentice programs is approximately 82.2 percent, a staggering rate when compared with the 17.8 percent for non-union programs. The IBEW-NECA electrical apprenticeship graduates 69.5 percent as opposed to 30.5 percent for non-union electrical apprentices. The fact that the non-union sector is failing to make training a priority from start to finish is a shortcoming that the remainder of the industry is forced to bear.

The construction industry is facing the reality that a large number of skilled workers will be leaving the workforce in the next few years. Industry leaders are warning about these persisting labor shortages in the skilled trades (The Business Roundtable, 1997). The construction industry is facing this threat because of the aging labor force, high attrition rates, and the inability to recruit new and qualified apprentices. Mediocre programs that are failing to produce the next generation of journeymen cannot remedy this problem.

The statistics regarding union versus non-union training speak for themselves. Not only are graduation rates substantially lower for non-union, or open-shop training programs, there is also evidence to support a concern that open-shop training is much less stringent. For example, training for plumbing, carpentry and sheet metal union trades is substantially lengthier than for their non-union counterparts and practicing them requires a license in most states. Union sheet metal apprenticeship programs are one year longer and require 10,000 on-the-job training hours as opposed to the 7,200 in the open-shop programs (Byrd & Weinstein, 2005).

There are many reasons for the wide discrepancy between the performances of apprentices enrolled in programs that are sponsored jointly by unions and those that are non-union. Union apprentices are, as a rule, more skilled, more qualified and more committed to their trade than the open-shop program apprentice graduates. The National Labor-Management Cooperation Committee (2003) provided examples regarding the chasm between union versus non-union electrical industry training:

- Apprentices in the IBEW-NECA electrical union training programs have from 3-5 years of apprenticeship training depending upon their chosen career path. Others may never participate in any formal industry-based training.
- Telecommunication apprentices in the IBEW-NECA electrical union are required to complete 480 hours of classroom related instruction and 4,800 on-the-job hours. Others may receive as little as 40 hours of total training.
- Some 75,000 journeyman return to NJATC IBEW-NECA sponsored training classes each year for skill upgrades. Other programs may have no requirements for maintaining credentials and obtaining certifications.
- Instructors for the IBEW-NECA are offered an opportunity annually to attend a four-year instructor-training institute to become first-class instructors for the electrical industry. The training offered is basically the same curriculum used for teacher certification. Others may have no teaching experience or training.
- Safety training is mandatory for IBEW apprentices.
- Over $100 million is invested annually for training for union electricians. Non-union designates a very small fraction of contributions for training. In fact, approximately $5 million dollars is dedicated to training for all trades combined in the non-union world.
- Union and contractor representatives seek to upgrade and further the training and education of their apprentices by establishing partnerships with higher education institutions. Union apprentices are afforded opportunities for college credit, continuing education units and to obtain higher education degrees (Allen, 2002). In fact, the IBEW and NECA were the first to use American Council on Education (ACE) credits. ACE offers up to 55 college credit hours for completion of the apprenticeship. Programs across the country are encouraging their members to gain college credit.

Return on Investment

Given the effectiveness of union relationships between joint apprenticeship programs, many are attempting to mimic similar programs in the non-union realm of training. The problem at hand is that the ties between employee and employer are loose. There is no personal investment and therefore no real incentive for individual contractors to train employees since they have no guarantee that they will ever reap the rewards of the training (US Department of Labor, 1987). Union apprenticeships involve carefully managed programs in which the sponsor chooses apprentices, adheres to standards and pays apprentice wages while offering formal training and making every attempt to keep apprentices employed. In turn, an apprentice pledges loyalty to perform jobs and complete training classes (Crosby, 2002).

Through rigorous, extensive, and timely training, apprentices graduate well rounded in their fields and are skilled in the trade. They know how to perform the job and what purpose the job fulfills. Union apprentice graduates have pride in their work. These workers are much more likely to have a positive and productive attitude accompanied with a dynamic work ethic. The variety is an advantage to the job market.

Those in support of union training endeavors realize that there are no short cuts to meaningful education and training. "Attempts to shorten the terms of apprenticeship to meet skilled manpower needs are a joke. It prohibits training required to become a true craftsperson with skills required and knowledge needed to ensure a sense of pride and dignity" (Retired NJATC Executive Director A.J. Pearson, personal communication, October 25, 2005). Again, the IBEW and NECA are jointly refusing to put any product on the market that is substandard. Union apprenticeship programs are designed to increase the quality of the U.S. workforce while keeping the American living standard high. Quality training goes hand-in-hand with productivity, flexibility, attitude and performance (Eck, 1993). Investing whole-heartedly in the education and training of apprentices and labor forces is an investment into the future.

In times of economic pressure, other technical education programs have reacted to worker and financial shortage hastily and irresponsibly. Many make rash decisions and more often than not, training and education is the first item to be cut from the budget. Derek Bok, president of Harvard University is quoted as saying, "If you think education and training is expensive, try ignorance." By refusing to take the road frequently traveled by non-union competitors, which consistently erodes the value of the apprenticeship system, the combined initiative of the NJATC, IBEW and NECA are benefiting those involved by providing quality results from quality efforts and setting the pace for other trade unions to follow. The results of stern commitment to training are far reaching, not only to the customer, but also to union labor making them more marketable and versatile than competitors and providing them with a meaningful, life-long career.

Dedicated to excellence in providing exemplary adult education opportunities, the NJATC has become perhaps the world's largest and most successful construction training organization as well as one of the largest adult education programs in the United States. Each calendar year at 300 various training programs across the country, the NJATC trains more than 45,000 electrical apprentices and offers journeymen training to more than 76,000 individuals seeking to sharpen their skills and learn new technologies. Labor is striving for excellence in traditional areas while increasing its presence in new and emerging fields. The NJATC is a stellar performer in the area of training that is essential to increasing market-share, satisfying customers, and providing the best quality of life for membership.

Conclusion

Training, strengthening, and developing workers is indispensable to the attainment of a higher standard of living, growth, and maintenance of a dynamic nation (Zack, 1964). American labor is divided and facing issues never before seen in the history of this country. Whether union, non-union, joint, open-shop, for-profit, or not-for-profit, certain aspects of training skilled labor cannot be denied. Jobs are demanding well-trained, motivated workers with productive attitudes suited to face new challenges and reintroduce the United States to job security that outsourcing and globalization have claimed. America's workforce has seen its best days if workers are not marked by excellence in Attitude, Skills and Knowledge.

Adult education programs are charged with the task of developing the potential of adult learners. Regardless of the training program or the mission statement or politics surrounding the entity providing the training, losing sight of the individual learner is education's greatest error. Indeed, unions do an exemplary job of valuing the worker and providing the training that makes them excellent in the trades.

Education's mission to train, to educate, to provide society with productive workers, and most importantly to drive individuals to higher levels of self-efficacy, self-esteem, and self-sufficiency through encouraging life-long learning. John Dewey (1916), American philosopher, psychologist, and educational reformer believed that it is of the utmost importance that "a human being acquires the habit of learning" (p. 45) and that society respects "curiosity, responsiveness, openness of mind, so that educators may say that adults are growing in childlikeness" (p. 50).

References

Allen, J. P. (2002, Fall). A community college partnership with an electrical contractor and union. *New Directions for Community Colleges, 119,* 31-36.

Beard, M. (1927). *A short history of the American labor movement.* New York: MacMillan.

Bureau of Labor Statistics. (2004, December). *Current labor statistics, December 2004.* Retrieved December 31, 2007 from http://www.bls.gov/opub/mlr/2004/12/cls0412.pdf

Bureau of Labor Statistics (2007). Union members summary: Union members in 2006.. *News Bureau of Labor Statistics.* Retrieved December 31, 2007 from http://www.bls.gov/news.release/union2.nr0.htm

Bureau of National Affairs. (1995). *Collective bargaining negotiations and contracts, basic patterns in union contracts* (14th ed.), pp. 13-22. Washington, D.C.: Bureau of National Affairs, Inc.

The Business Roundtable (1988). *Government limitations on training innovations: A construction industry cost effectiveness project report* (Report D-2). Washington, DC: U.S. Government Printing Office.

The Business Roundtable (1997). *Confronting the Skilled Construction Work Force Shortage.* Construction Cost Effectiveness Task Force. Washington, DC: U.S. Government Printing Office.

Byrd, B., & Weinstein, M. (2005, March). *Construction apprenticeship in Oregon: An analysis of data on union and open-shop apprenticeship programs.* Oregon: Labor Education and Research Center University of Oregon.

Crosby, O. (2002). Apprenticeship. *Occupational Outlook Quarterly, 202,* 2-13.

Dewey, J. (1916). *Democracy and education: An introduction to the philosophy of education.* New York: MacMillan.

Division of Workforce Development. (2005, September 22). *Division of Workforce Development: Apprenticeship and Training.* Retrieved December 31, 2007 from http://www.dllr.state.md.us/labor/appr.html

Eck, A. (1993). Job-related education and training: their impact on earnings. *Monthly Labor Report, October 1993,* 21-38.

HRSDC. (2001, October). General and Specific Human Capital. In *The impact of unionisation of the incidence and financing of training in Canada* (2.1). Retrieved December 31, 2007, from Government of Canada Web Site: http://www11.hrsdc.gc.ca

Knowles, M. S. (1968). *The modern practice of adult education: From pedagogy to andragogy.* New York: Association Press.

Livingstone, D. W., & Raykov, M. (2005). Union influence on worker education and training in Canada in tough times. *Just Labour, 5,* 50-64.

Londrigan, W. J., & Wise, J. B. (1997). *Apprentice training in Kentucky: A comparison of union and non-union programs in the building trades.* Washington, DC: U.S. Government Printing Office.

McKernan, J. R. (1994). *Making the grade: How a new youth apprenticeship system can change our schools and save American jobs.* New York: Little, Brown and Company.

Merriam, S. B., & Brockett, R. G. (1997). *The profession and practice of adult education.* San Francisco: Jossey-Bass.

National Labor-Management Cooperation Committee. (2003, December 31). *How do electrical workers learn, maintain, and upgrade their skills?* Retrieved September 1, 2007, from NLMCC Web Site: http://thequalityconnection.org

Union Apprenticeship & Training Programs. (2007). Benefits of union apprenticeship programs. Retrieved December 31, 2007 from http://www.unions.org/home/apprenticeshiptrainingprograms.php

US Department of Labor. (1984, April 30). Office of the Secretary of Labor: Labor Standards for the Registration of Apprenticeship Programs. In *Labor* (29). Retrieved December 31, 2007 from Department of Labor Web Site: http://www.dol.gov

US Department of Labor. (1987). *Apprenticeship: Past and present.* Employment and Training Administration, Bureau of Apprenticeship and Training. Retrieved December 31, 2007 from http://www.eric.ed.gov/ERICDocs/data/ericdocs2sql/content_storage_01/000 0019b/80/22/6d/c6.pdf

US Department of Labor Bureau of Apprenticeship and Training (2000). *National guideline apprenticeship and training standards for electrical joint apprenticeship and training committees representing the NECA and the IBEW.* Washington, DC: U.S. Government Printing Office.

US Department of Labor Employment and Training Administration. (2005). Program Standards. In *Program Standards* (Title 29, Part 29.5). Retrieved December 31, 2007 from US Department of Labor Web Site: http://www.doleta.gov

Zack, A. (1964). *Labor training in developing countries: A challenge in responsible democracy.* New York: Frederick A. Praeger Publishers.